THE ROUNDEL

ART ON THE
UNDERGROUND

THE ROUNDEL

100 Artists Remake a London Icon

Edited by Tamsin Dillon

With an introduction by Jonathan Glancey
and contributions by Claire Dobbin and Sally Shaw

ART/BOOKS

PREFACE

Tamsin Dillon

In 2008, Art on the Underground commissioned one hundred new works of art to mark what was a significant anniversary for London Underground: the centenary of its world-famous logo, the Roundel. We invited one hundred international artists at various stages of their careers, from recent graduates to individuals with worldwide reputations, to make a new art work inspired by the symbol and one of the world's most recognized brands. Their responses – imaginative and playful, bold and irreverent – reinterpret, reinvent and celebrate an iconic emblem of the city of London. The resulting contributions present a contemporary vision of the Tube, while building on the long tradition and legacy of artists who have worked under the patronage of London Underground.

An important purpose of the project was to put a spotlight on the Roundel in its centenary year, and on the Art on the Underground programme as a whole, raising its profile among Tube travellers and the workforce alike. An exhibition of the original contributions was held in an east London gallery, and an auction was staged to sell one of a limited edition of two prints of each work. The other prints remain as a collection and a resource that continues to be reproduced for special posters all over the Underground.

Now, on the eve of another important birthday – 150 years of the Tube network – we bring those art works together in this publication. New commentaries by the artists give further insight to the works, while three illuminating essays offer perspectives from the broader history of transport design, branding and public art. Jonathan Glancey's introductory text sets the scene, taking us back to a key moment for London Underground and London itself when Frank Pick, then publicity officer for the Underground Electric Railways Company of London, as the Underground was known at the time, began the process of unifying the brand through the development of the logo. Glancey's fascinating account traces the beginnings of the Roundel's design from the Roman Empire through Renaissance Italy to contemporary London, where London Underground and its logo play an inseparable role in the urban landscape. Claire Dobbin's text considers the history of the Roundel through the eyes of artists and designers down the years, exploring the precedents for the contemporary Art on the Underground programme. Sally Shaw, the curator of the Roundel project, takes a personal view, investigating the themes that emerged in the commissions through a selection of individual pieces.

This book is an opportunity to pay tribute to all those who have played a key role in ensuring the project came to fruition, and on behalf of Transport for London it gives me great pleasure to do so. The task of planning and delivering the original commissions was an enormous challenge in itself, achieved with passion and skill by a dedicated team. The work involved in bringing together the art works and texts for this publication has been similarly intense, and the Art on the Underground team deserve huge recognition for their work on both phases of the project. Many organizations and individuals worked with us to ensure the success of the project and I would like to extend a huge thank you to all of them. They include colleagues at London Underground, Transport for London and the office of the Mayor of London, as well as many external partners and stakeholders. The advisory panel for Art on the Underground remains an essential part of running the programme and was key in advocating for this project. I would also like to acknowledge the vital support of our colleagues at the London Transport Museum, which has been important in helping us to deliver many aspects of it. I would especially like to thank Jonathan Glancey, Claire Dobbin and Sally Shaw for their illuminating texts in this book, and Andrew Brown, our publisher, who has played a central role in realizing this exciting publication. We also acknowledge with great thanks the support of the Arts Council England through the lottery-funded Grants for the Arts, without which we would not have been able to commission these important art works.

Most of all, we are indebted to the artists who responded to the commission with a serious, professional and personal approach. It is they who deserve the biggest thanks and congratulations. As individual images, the works they produced have unique presence and force; together they make a unified whole that is much, much more than the sum of its parts. *The Roundel* publication responds to some extent to the idea that it is a basic human right to experience culture as an integral part of daily life, not as an optional extra. Without those who dedicate themselves to the creation of art, that would be impossible. Long may they continue to do so, especially if the results can be as rich, varied and dynamic as those you will find in this book.

THE ORDERED AND HUMANE ROUNDEL

Jonathan Glancey

In June 1913, the renowned calligrapher Edward Johnston went to see Frank Pick, commercial manager of the Underground Electric Railways Company of London, at his office in Westminster. It would have been fascinating to be a fly on the wall, because that meeting proved to be one of the most important in the history of twentieth-century lettering, typography, design and urban identity. The influence that Johnston and Pick were to have on these disciplines continues to inspire, effect and underpin our very conception not just of London, but of the global city in general, a hundred years on from what would have been a polite, if earnest conversation between two quietly brilliant men, both born in the 1870s.

What that meeting led to was Johnston being commissioned by Pick to design a new display alphabet for the Underground network.

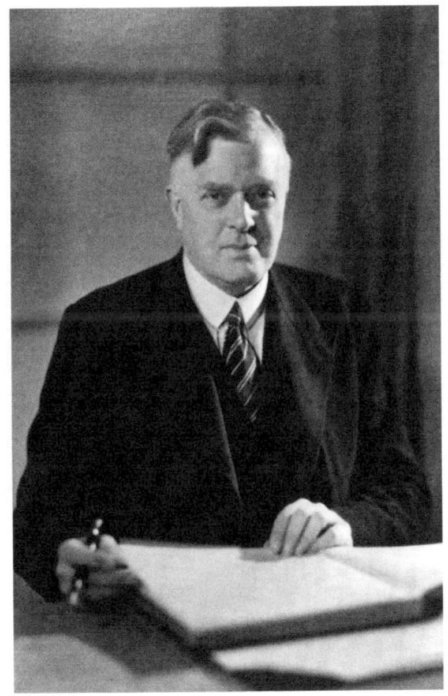

Frank Pick, c. 1939

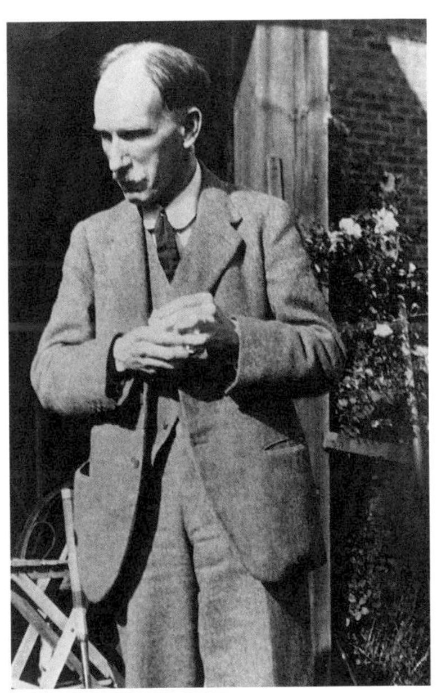

Edward Johnston in his garden, 1930s

Pick wanted this to have 'the bold simplicity of the authentic lettering of the finest periods [of history] and yet belong unmistakably to the 20th century'. The aim was a form of highly legible lettering that would stand out loud and clear – although in a distinctly civilized manner – from the crowd of muddled alphabets that, mostly in the guise of cluttered and hectic Victorian-style advertising, gave Underground stations an unfairly messy and even chaotic appearance.

ABCDEFGHIJ
KLMNOPQRS
TUVWXYZ
abcdefghijk
lmnopqrstuv
wxyz
£1234567890
&,.;:''""?!-*()

Proof sheet of Johnston Sans medium typeface, printed in 1992 from surviving wood blocks used at the Baynard Press

The project hung fire for a couple of years, with Johnston working diligently on the alphabet that was to take his name in the back bedroom of his home in Ditchling, Sussex, during the winter of 1915–16. The result was not just a masterpiece: it was a world revolution in typeface design. This was all the more remarkable given that Johnston was an Arts & Crafts man to his nimble finger-tips. 'The only thing of mine for mass production', he wrote, in

1937, in a letter to the wood engraver John Farleigh, 'is the Block Letter Alphabet which I designed for the Underground Railways.' He goes on to say, 'I might add that this particular design appears to have become of considerable importance (in the world of Alphabets). It is in fact the foundation model of *all modern*, respectable Block letters – including those painted on the Roads and Signs for Motorists and Eric Gill's very popular sans-serif type. It seems also to have made a great impression in parts of Central Europe.'

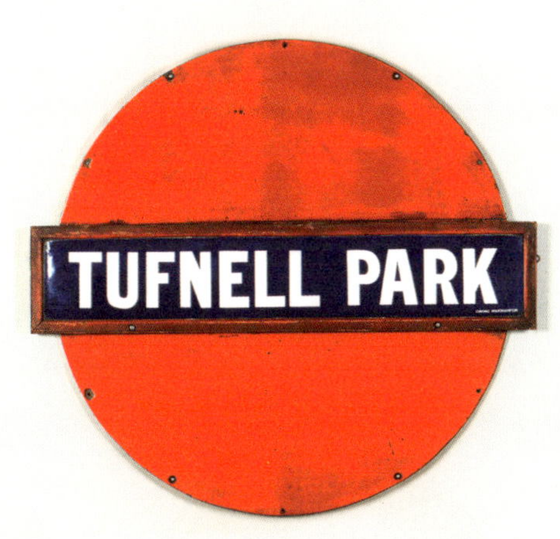

A 'solid disc' station name Roundel, c. 1908

Seems to have made a great impression? The Johnston alphabet spawned, or inspired, pretty much every twentieth-century sans-serif letter, including all those precisely elegant, machine-like typefaces from Germany and Switzerland that did so much to define the look of a self-consciously styled modern world. Ingeniously, though, Johnston had modelled his magisterial and beautifully clear alphabet on the classical capital letters devised by the ancient Romans and perfected at the time Trajan's Column was completed in AD 113. In his 1937 entry for *Who's Who*, Johnston wrote, 'designed block letter based on capital Roman proportions (for London Electric Railways)'. What he had done was to connect the ancient and the modern worlds, to produce an alphabet that was, in effect, timeless while speaking across the millennia – and lettering that was legible, as it soon proved, to hundreds of millions of people around the world.

Then came Johnston's redesign, again for Pick, of the
Underground's motif, known at first as the 'Bullseye' and later as
the Roundel. Now, Johnston's peerless alphabet was to be wedded
with a symbol that defines and characterizes the entire Transport
for London network today. It also serves as a logo for London
and as brilliant visual shorthand for the very nature of the modern
city. Today, the Roundel can be found the length and breadth of
the metropolis, a token – or promise – that a comprehensive and
all-reaching transport network is there to serve the public and,
ideally, in highly organized and civilized manner. There is always
something comforting, especially on cold and sodden winter
evenings, in catching sight of an illuminated red, white and blue
Roundel announcing the presence of an Underground station at the
end of a busy, rain-lashed street; or in emerging from an unfamiliar
maze of roads in some far-flung suburb and coming across a London
Transport bus stop and knowing that you are never that far –
in spirit and design at least – from Charing Cross or St Paul's.

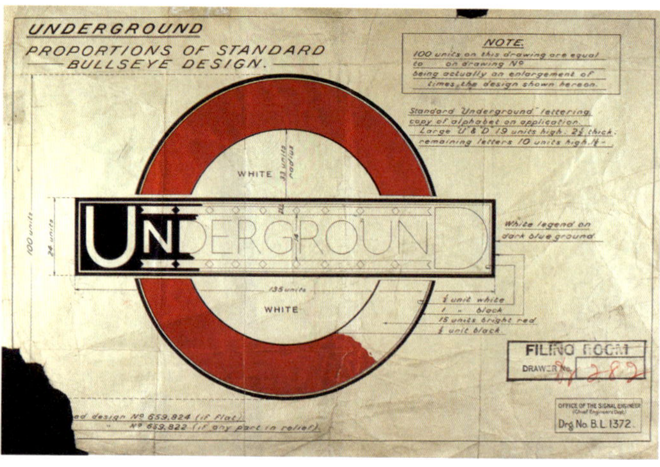

Edward Johnston's design guidelines for the
Underground Roundel, 1925

Again, what Pick had wanted was a sign – initially a station name
board – that would stand out from the rush of platform advertising
and other visual clutter. The Underground had been using a rather
awkward and clumsy version of the Roundel – a blue crossbar through
a solid red disc since 1908. But, from the early 1920s, Underground

stations were adorned with Johnston's striking and harmonious design with the blue crossbar bisecting a red circle with white space between the two. With station names set in Johnston's new alphabet, the Underground leaped ahead in terms of design. Here was what to be one of the most successful, enduring and best loved of all corporate logos. Soon enough, the symbol became universal across the Underground, used for signs and in advertising, and increasingly over the decades as a typeface for posters, timetables and other printed material.

London Passenger Transport Board advertising rates booklet with new logo designed by Cecil Bacon, 1933

The Roundel has been altered over the decades — by Hans Schleger in 1935; by Misha Black and his Design Research Unit in the 1960s; by Henrion, Ludlow and Schmidt in 1984; and again by Wolff Olins in 1987 — but is unlikely ever to be replaced. When, in 1933, the London Passenger Transport Board (LPTB) was formed — the giant, all-embracing public corporation directed and run so very successfully by Lord Ashfield as chairman and Frank Pick

as vice-chairman and chief executive — a new logo, designed by
Cecil Bacon, a young artist and illustrator, lasted just a matter of
months. When Transport for London was formed in 2000, there
was no question that the Roundel was to serve as its logo and that
Johnston's alphabet, although modified, would stay to accompany
it into the new century.

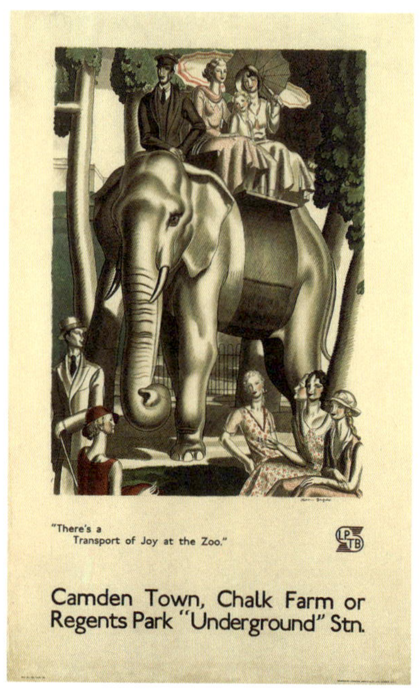

'There's a transport of joy at the zoo',
by Jean Dupas, 1933, with LPTB logo

Johnston's work, over twenty years, with Pick, the Underground
and London Transport (the 'trading' name of LPTB) led to LT's
first corporate Design Manual, published in 1938. This was one
of the first of its kind, explaining and insisting upon a consistency
of design throughout the enterprise, although artists and illustrators
were given licence to play creatively with the Bullseye, using
it — in posters — as heads for passengers, for example, or even
transforming it into a planet, as Man Ray did in 1938, circling Saturn,
that — seen side on — happens to resemble a giant outer-space
Roundel (see page 127). By this time, LPTB had become world famous
for its efficiency, intelligence and exemplary standard of design in

all forms. Justifiably, it had great confidence in its design values; not surprisingly, these were adopted in one form or another in cities elsewhere in the world.

In the Roundel, Edward Johnston and his careful successors had perfected a symbol that spoke eloquently both of London Transport and the very nature of the modern city, while – quietly and thoughtfully – connecting London and twentieth-century urban values to the best of ancient Rome and all that this great (if messy) city implied in the minds of men like Frank Pick, in terms of civilization and the very highest standards of architecture, design, signs, lettering and urbanity itself.

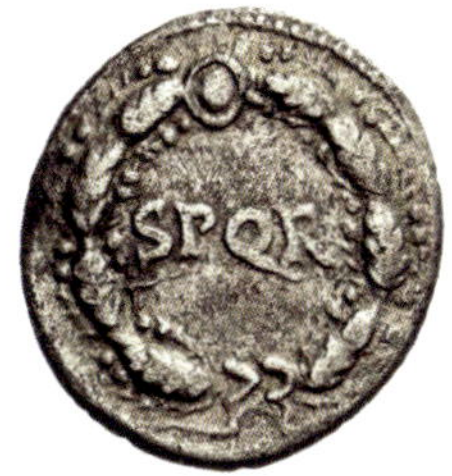

Roman coin stamped with 'SPQR'

The first line of letters around the base of Trajan's Column – so admired by both Johnston and Pick – read Senatus Populusque Romanus (The Senate and People of Rome), and by the time the column was built the initials SPQR were already long established as a symbol of the great city. Today, they form the oldest acronym in everyday use. In fact, there is barely a street in central Rome without these four letters commanding attention from the sides of buildings, drainpipes and even manhole covers. Interestingly, Mussolini ordered SPQR to be stamped into public design at the very same time that Pick was gently, if insistently, imposing his own form of democratic order on the streets of London, a city that he, and many others, liked to see as the true twentieth-century successor, in an ideal way, to ancient Rome.

A lawyer by training with a deep fascination for the origins of Roman law, Pick also believed that business corporations themselves should be imbued with a classical spirit even while pursuing twentieth-century goals in terms of technology and technique. In a speech he gave to the British Association at

Cambridge in September 1938, he was at pains to stress that
'No one has yet done for commerce and industry what the Greek
thinkers did for politics and ethics, or what the Roman lawyers did for
jurisprudence.… Is it not strange to find that in a commercial nation
like ours no serious attempt should yet have been made to turn its
knowledge and experience into something transcending its pedestrian
everyday pursuits?' It is no coincidence that one of the first designers
to play with the Roundel as a form, Alfred France, did so in a poster
featuring classical gods standing for the Underground's corporate
values (see page 124).

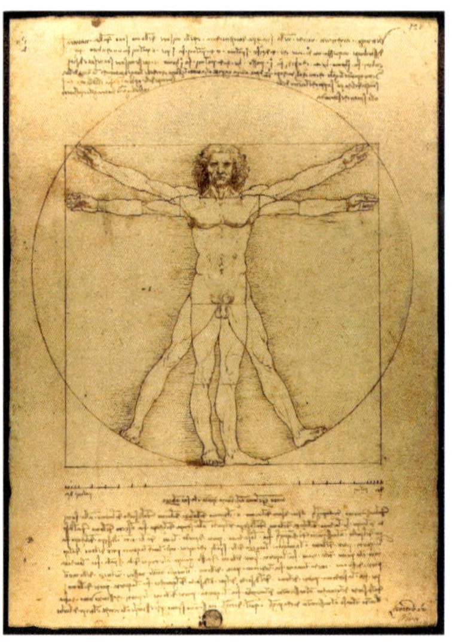

Leonardo da Vinci, *Vitruvian Man*, c. 1487

Johnston's alphabet and its marriage to the Roundel were a
symbol of what Pick was trying to achieve, a balance between order
and freedom, between the classical age and modernity, and a major
contribution by twentieth-century industry and commerce to spur
on the 'good life' that should result from these goals. Significantly,
perhaps, in antique times, the letters SPQR were often embraced –
on flags and banners – by a pair of inward-curving laurel branches,
all but forming a circle around them. This image is not that far
removed from Johnston's Bullseye. The Roundel then is at once,
and by pedigree, an ancient and a modern device symbolizing
a great city as well as a specific function and corporation.

But, its symbolism is wider than Trajan's Rome. It also calls to mind the Buddhist Wheel of Life. This is neither as strange, nor as exotic as it might sound. For, here the circle represents the notion of infinity. The Roundel evokes the infinite numbers of journeys that can be made around London or — and here the crossbar comes into play — across it. London itself is an all but infinite city, offering a range and depth of experience that few others can match; founded by the Romans in the first century AD, it has grown to become a world-in-a-city. The Roundel captures this idea graphically.

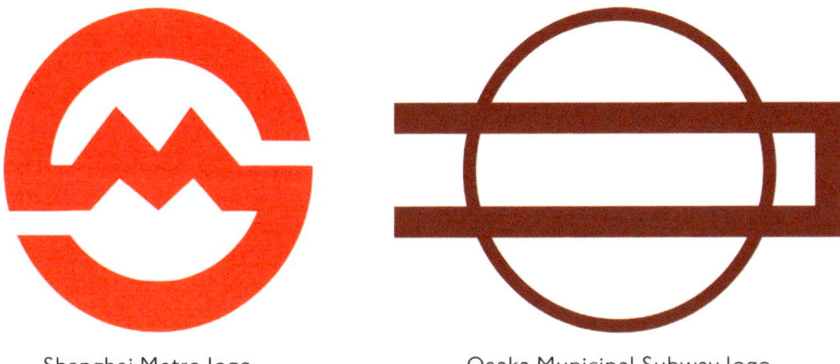

Shanghai Metro logo   Osaka Municipal Subway logo

Equally, the circle is a symbol of the wheel — and today of computer disks — the essential ingredient in free-moving forms of transport. And, when I stand back from the Roundel, I can see echoes, too, of Italian Renaissance images of Vitruvian Man. The most famous of these is a pen-and-ink drawing by Leonardo da Vinci that shows a man with widespread arms fitting these into and across a circle set within a square. The idea here is not simply a demonstration of the humanistic Renaissance idea of man as the measure of all things, but a way of depicting man's (that is, humankind's) connection to both the Earth (the square) and the Cosmos (the circle). Is it too far fetched to compare this to the Roundel? No, because the circle and the crossbar of the Roundel suggest the idea of the city's infinite ways, while the crossbar, evoking roads and railway tracks, makes the connection between the 'cosmos' of the city and its earthly side — the things that make it work, including transport systems, the arteries of a healthy city. So, the Roundel captures the idea that the metropolis is boundless and yet manageable at one and the same time.

All truly great cities are a marriage of order and barely contained chaos, freedom and law, the planned and the spontaneous.

It should be no surprise, then, that, just as Johnston's alphabet went global, so the Roundel forms the basis for symbols of Metro systems and cities around the world. It is fun to try and spot these. I have come across Roundel-like logos for underground and light rail systems in Kuala Lumpur, Salt Lake City, Shanghai and Osaka; doubtless there are more. Most impressive, however, is the fact that no one, no transport undertaking, no city has yet bettered either Johnston's alphabet or the Roundel. The sense implied by both lettering and sign, of creativity and order, was to become extremely significant and important in 2012 when London hosted the Olympic Games. The onus was placed heavily on Transport for London to ensure that the capital's transport coped with the tremendous pressure the event would place on the city and its roads and railways. Significantly, the Olympics chose for its logo a bizarrely fractured and wilfully ugly symbol of pure chaos; the ordered and humane Roundel would be there, it seemed, to ride to its rescue.

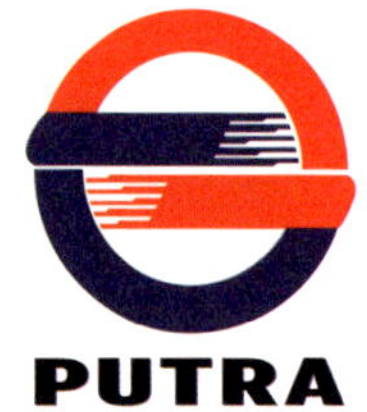

PUTRA

Logo of the Putra LRT,
Kuala Lumpur

Logo of the Utah Transit Authority, Salt Lake City

The difference in these two logos is instructive. Where the latter is an expression of modern 'branding', an exercise in applying a novel image to an event and organization by marketing and advertising agencies, the Roundel emerged as a functional sign that became a corporate symbol – and as we have seen, far more than this alone – and was created by a calligrapher and a transport manager. The London Underground Roundel works well a century on precisely because it is not a gimmick; it is a practical, workaday device that, because of the intelligence and artistry of Pick and Johnston, remains one of the most effective, best-known and most fondly regarded logos in the world.

THE ROUNDELS

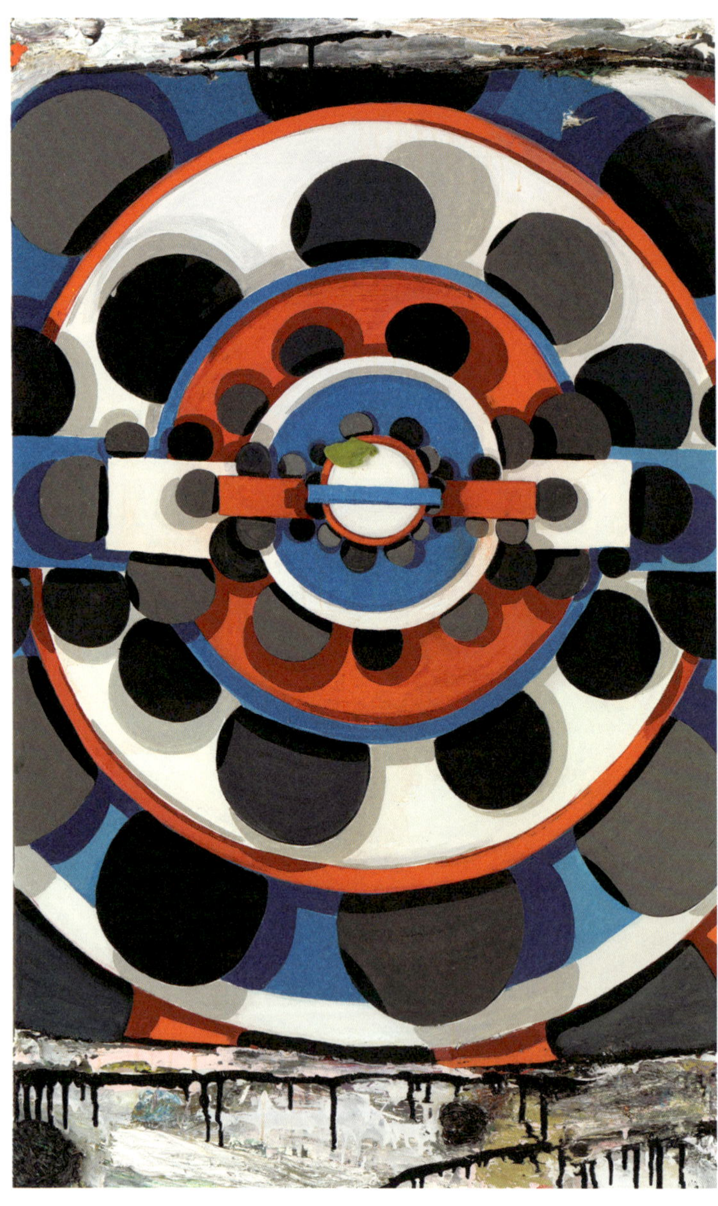

Phillip Allen
Inner Circle Portion

The Roundel instils a nostalgia for the Northern Line, the wooden slats of the escalators, the warmth of the Underground, strap-hanging to Morden. The Roundel remains a constant in London's psyche. It's a historic emblem of London's past, present and future.

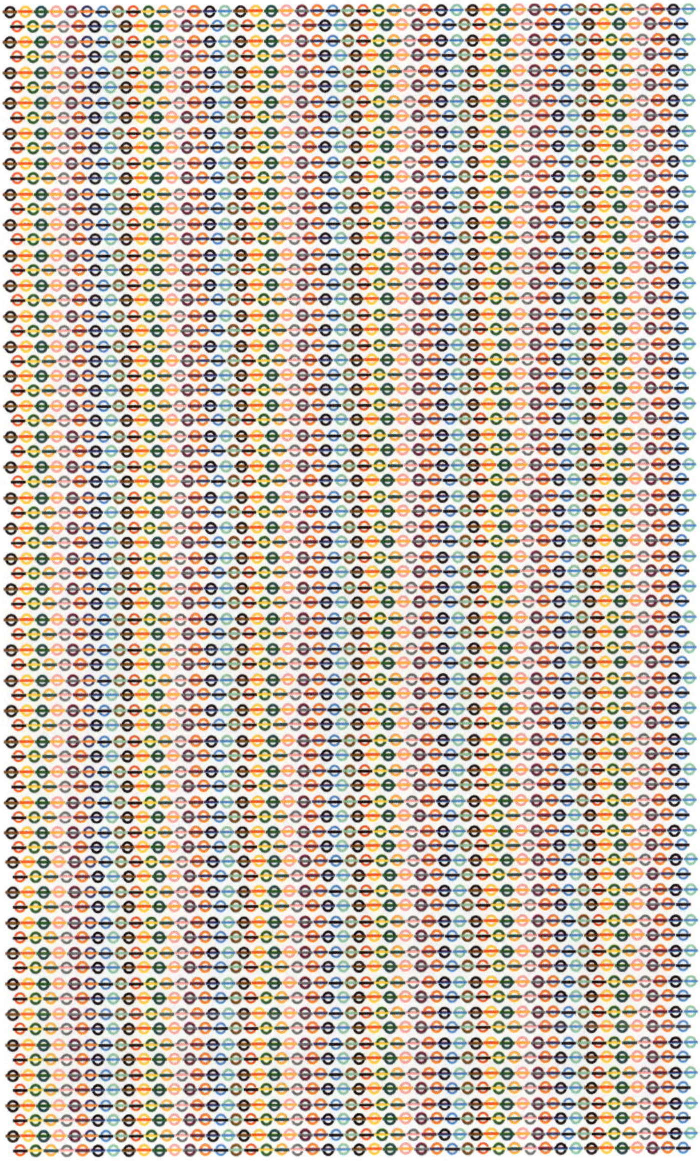

Polly Apfelbaum
Rainbow Roundels

Originally inspired by Andy Warhol's flower images, my Roundels are based on dingbats, ornamental characters used in typesetting. Simple colour-wheel hues animate each character.

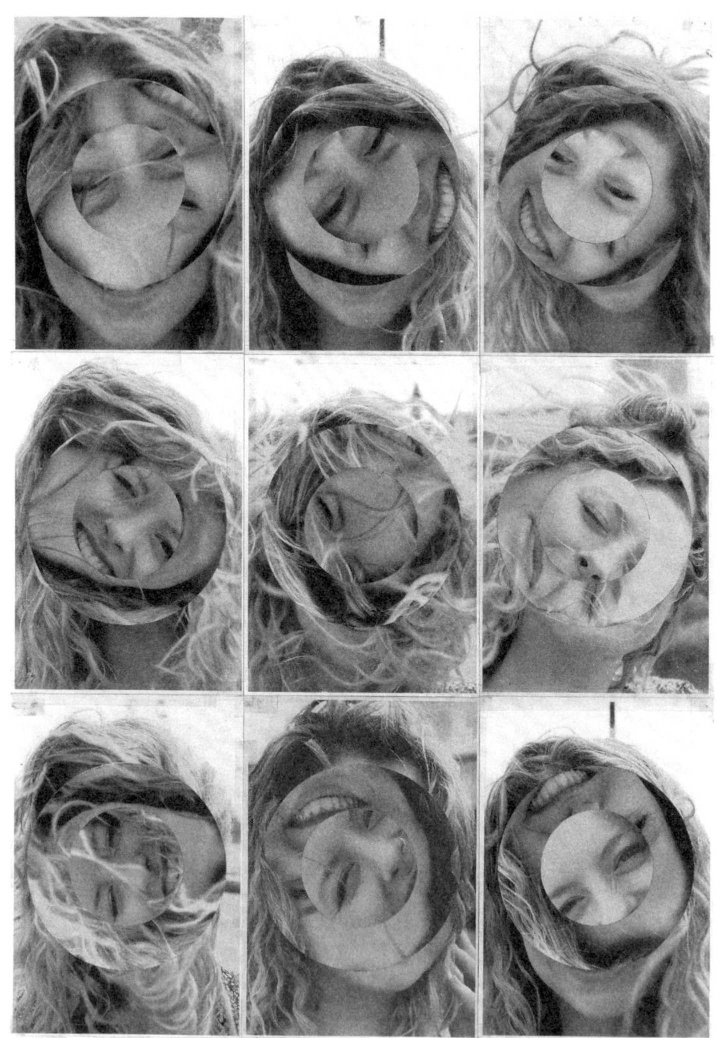

David Austen
London Girl

I photographed my daughter Mia, born and bred in London, on a windy Waterloo Bridge. Everything moving and turning. Riverboats, red buses, trains on bridges, black taxis, bicycles and cars. I used the Johnston typeface. I like the way 'London' has two perfect Os. It gives it wheels.

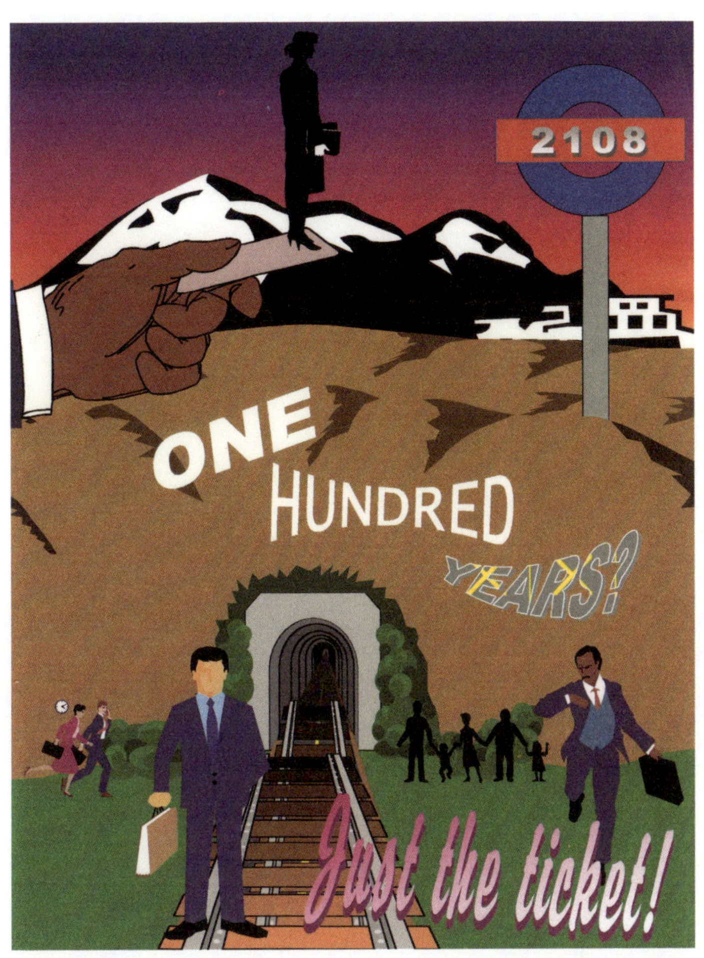

Simon Bedwell
*Untitled
(Artists and Workers!
Another 100 years!
Let us all march
forward as one!)*

I used the ugliest, tackiest way of doing a design, as the opposite of the cuddly nostalgia aesthetic usually referenced in anything to do with the Tube; and the '100 more years' was to indicate a future anniversary, when we'll all be dead.

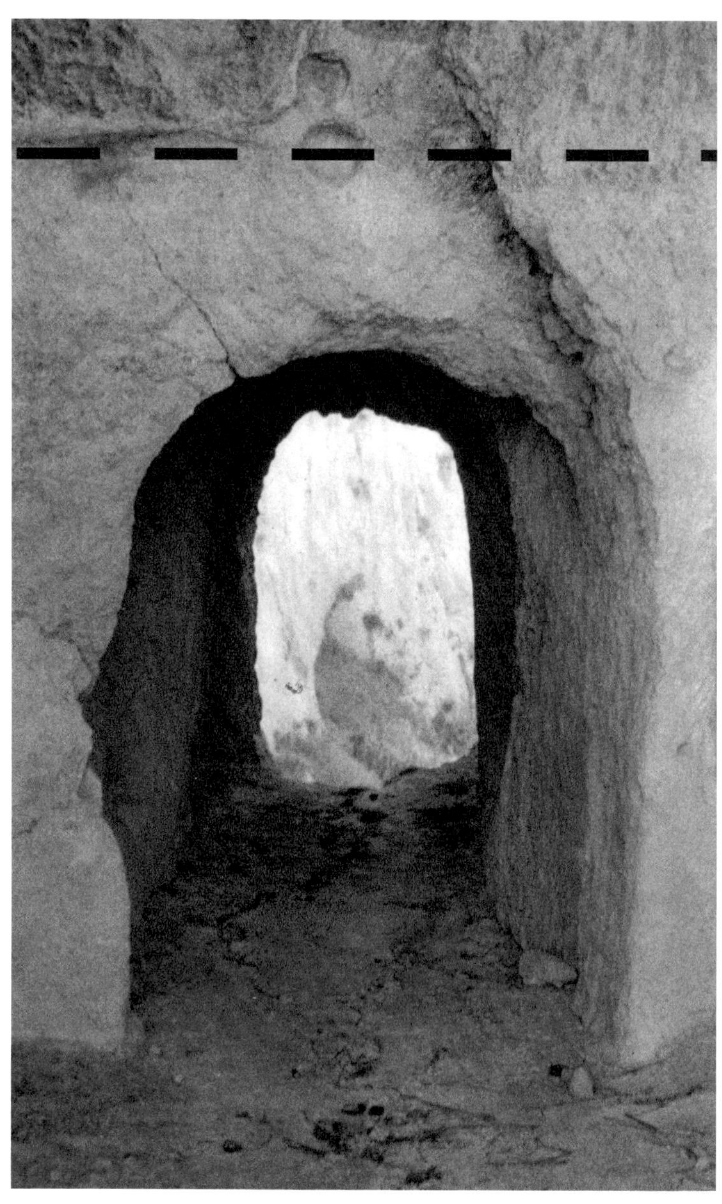

Vanessa Billy
Ways of Getting Around

I was thinking about tunnels and how extraordinary they are, and of how we don't really have a sense of their physicality as we travel through them. I chose an image of an ancient tunnel to convey the enormity of achievement at its most basic. The dotted line bisecting a carved circle on top of the tunnel alludes to the Roundel.

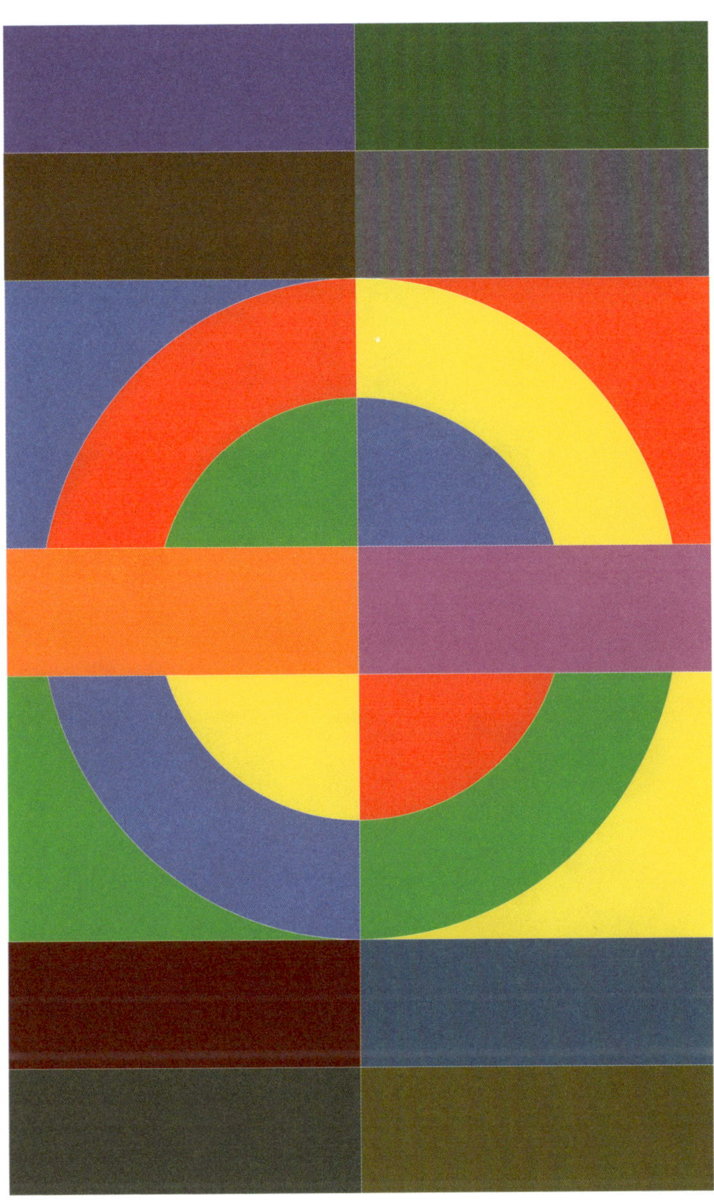

Sir Peter Blake
Untitled

Alphabet of Underground Soul

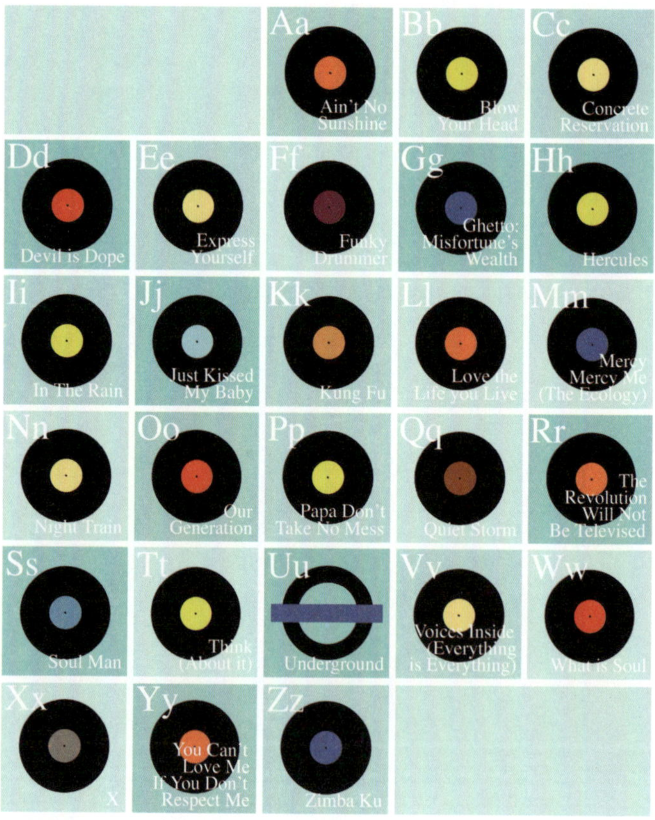

David Blandy
Alphabet of Underground Soul

Underground hip-hop and soul have been a constant soundtrack for my journeys on the Underground. 'Underground' by Curtis Mayfield became a song where, through the unintentional pun, these two worlds of London life and American black creativity came together. *Alphabet of Underground Soul* is a celebration of the richness of musical culture, and how music can transform the way we understand our surroundings.

Rut Blees Luxemburg
Many Rays' (Half Open)

All of our very own higher beings & power

Solitary shadow originates every signal given, component used, message said and place built.

Only, who, what and where might hide, live and operate, from behind, inside and underneath the camouflage, shield and fortress?

Text by Douglas Park

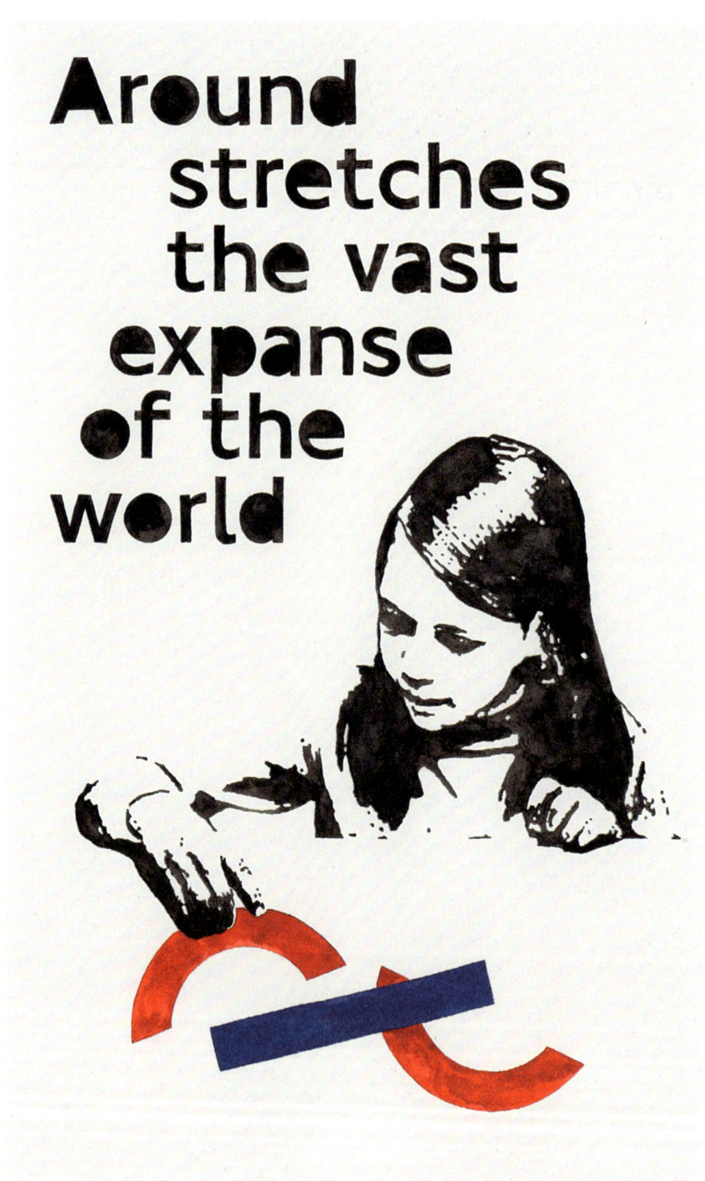

Simon & Tom Bloor
Around stretches the vast expanse of the world

We like the way the Roundel is such an economical piece of design it is still immediately recognizable even before a young girl has assembled it. A quote from London Underground's mid-twentieth-century art champion Frank Pick offers a utopian possibility: escape.

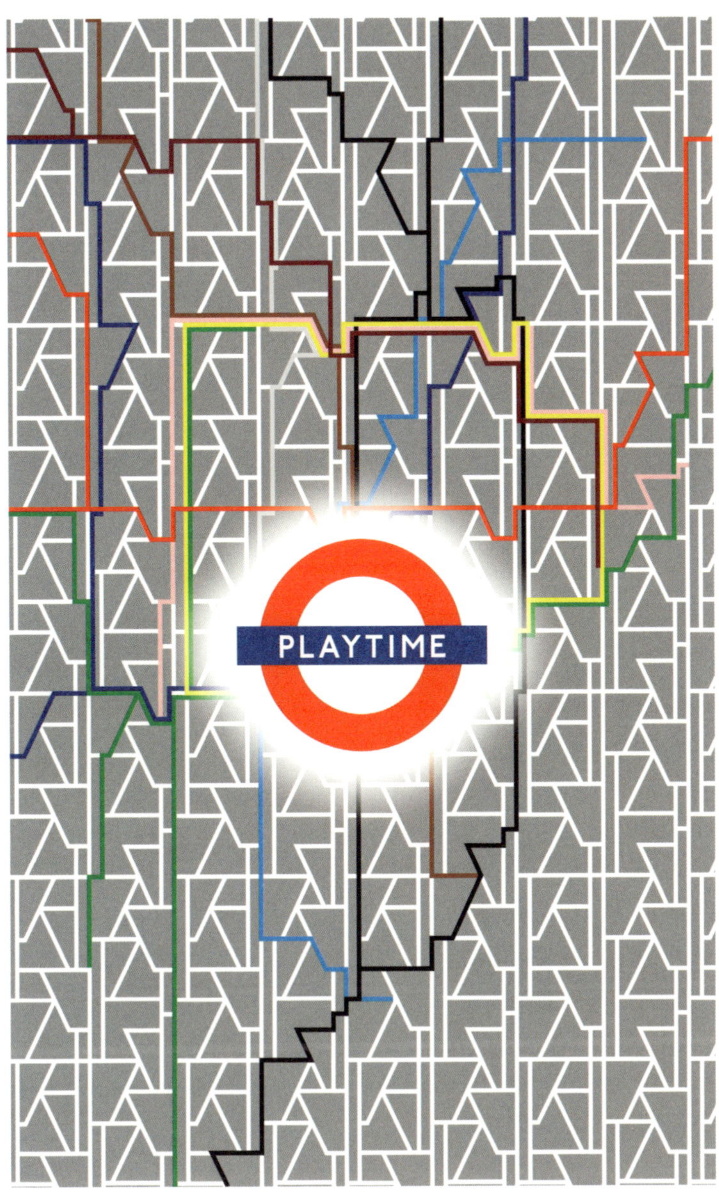

Martin Boyce
Playtime Underground

Cars are like the ticks on the back of any city, crawling and breeding and irritating. The Underground is the blood flowing through its veins: a democratic, no-first-class-carriage portal from here to there. Some days, it's just a means to an end; other days, it's playtime!

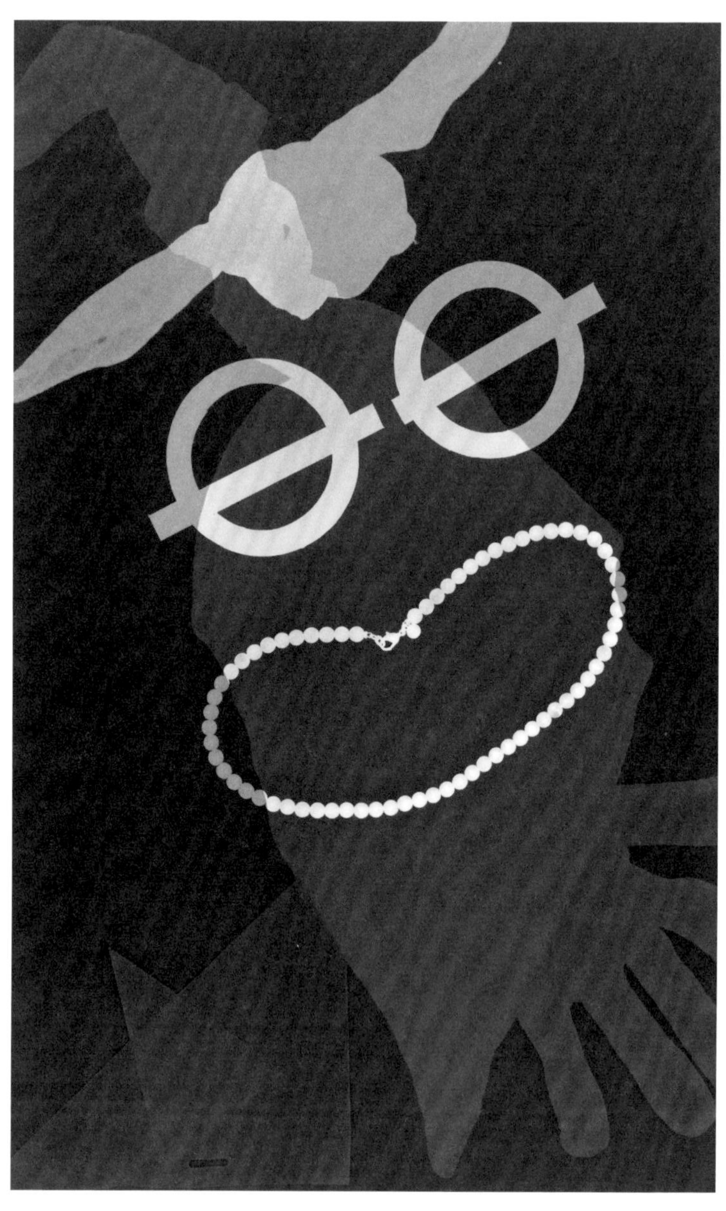

Rachal Bradley
Untitled (Bandage)

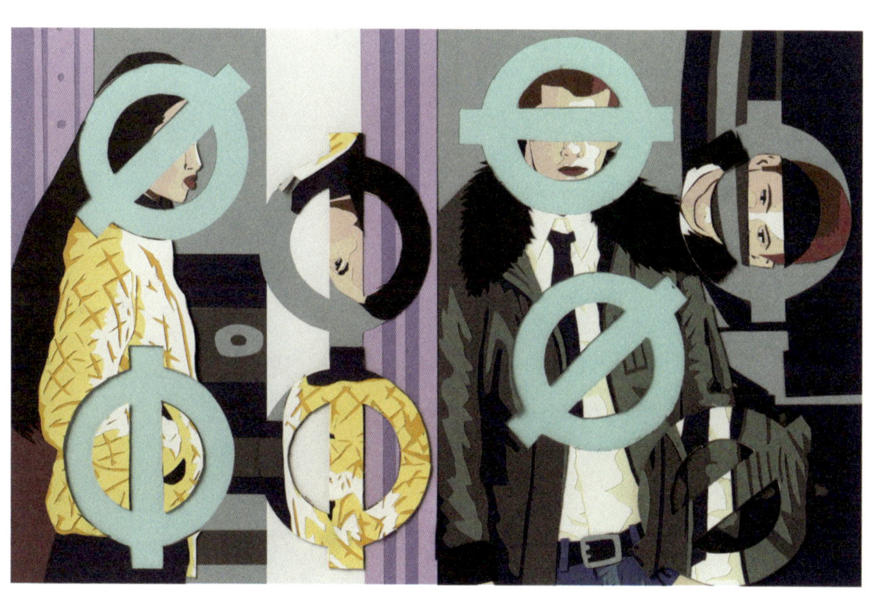

David Burrows
Roundel Cut-Up

A spell to counter the networked individual.

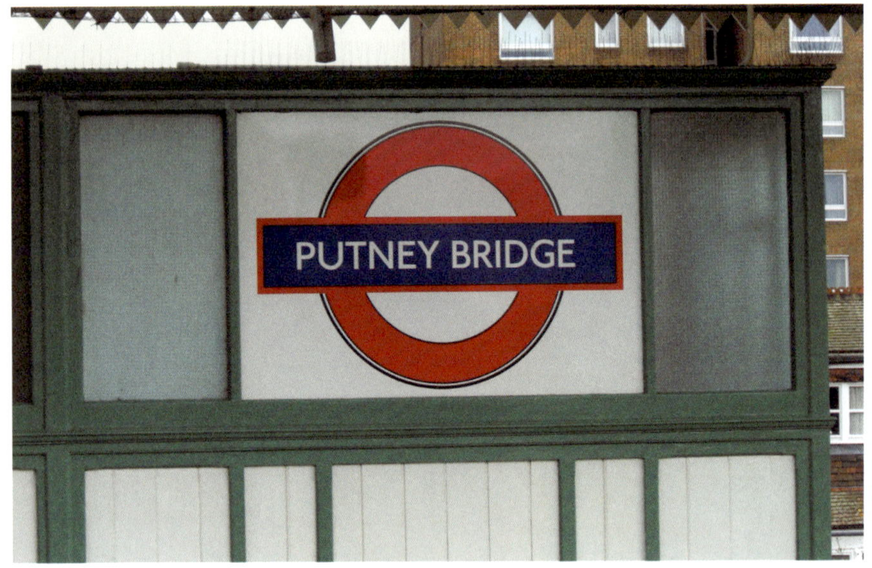

Andrea Büttner
Untitled

The photo was taken by my sister, Marion Büttner, when she visited me.

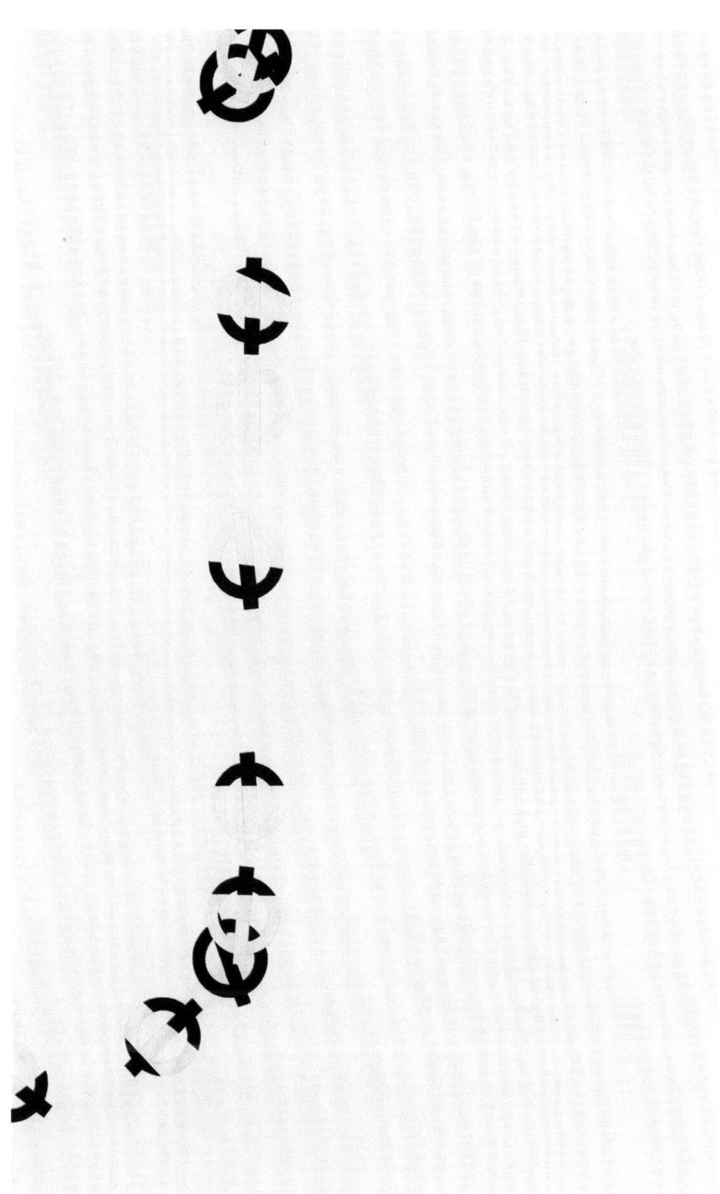

Alice Channer
Untitled (water and gouache
in and on paper)

Declan Clarke
Let's Go Underground

I tried to contrast the radical modernity of the early twentieth century as encapsulated in the Underground system, with the methods that many revolutionary thinkers use to circulate alternative perspectives.

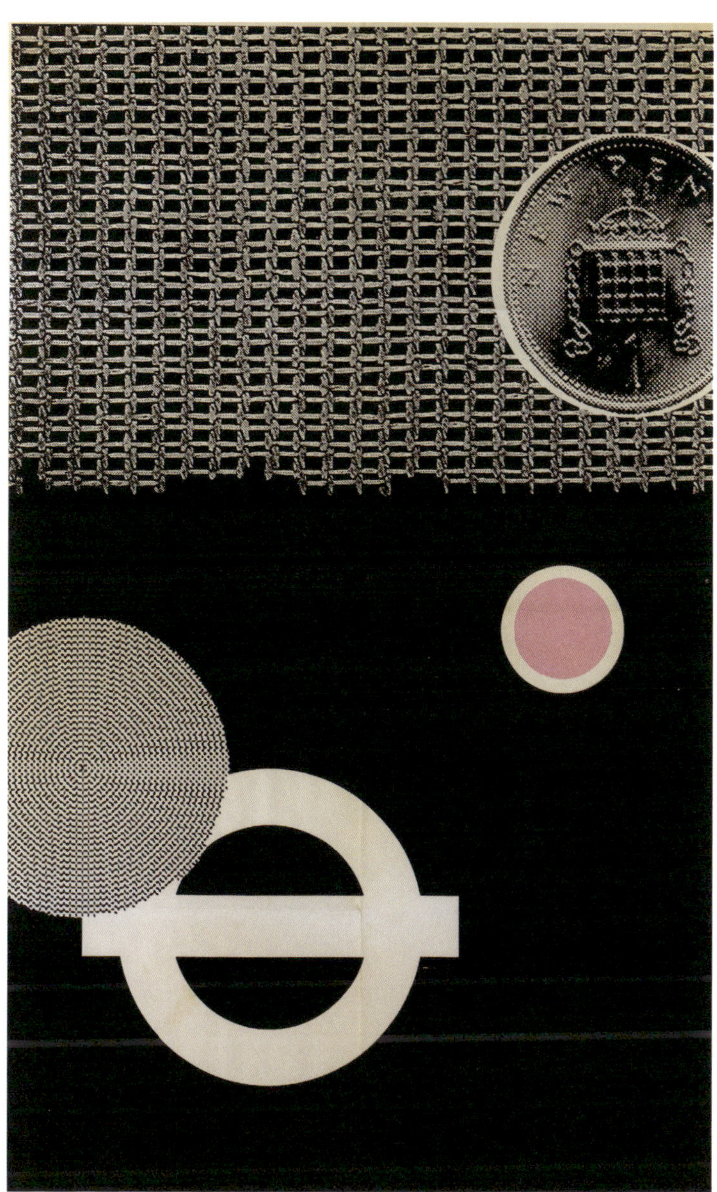

Steven Claydon
UndergrounD

This work is autobiographical in as much as I drew on childhood memories of the Tube. Subterranean gloom, smoking carriages, pubs on the platform, the high-pitched yellow stench of electricity, rubber and grating steel, pink paper tickets, wooden escalators, looming lights emerging from the grime amid the gigantic music of machinery.

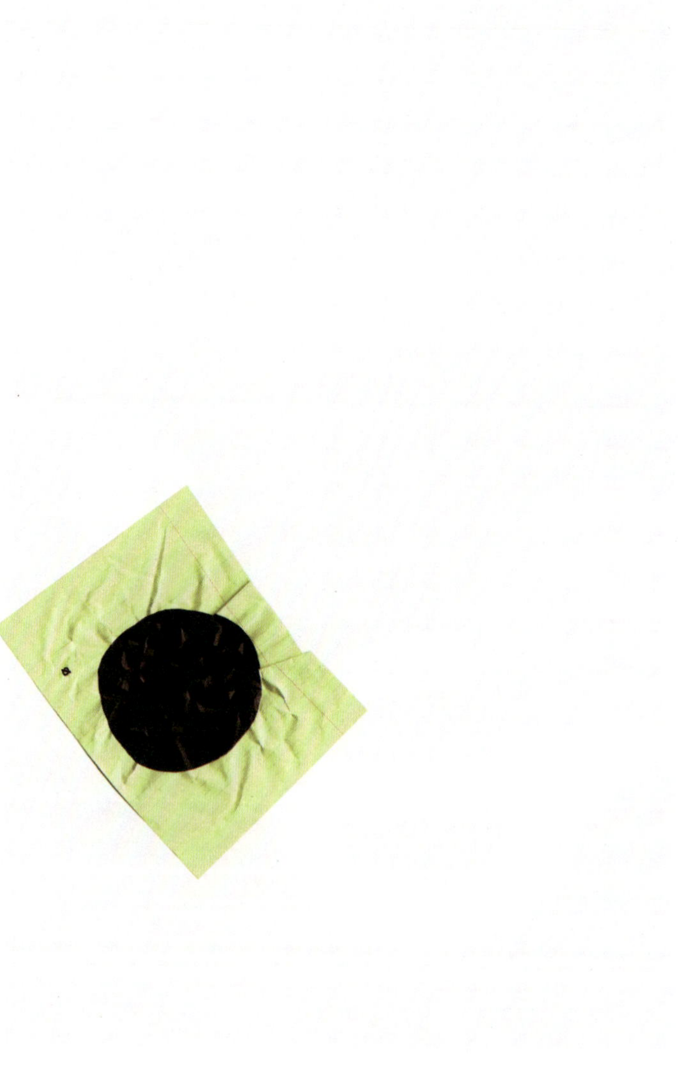

Lucy Clout
Smalltime

For Russell Hoban with love and wonder.

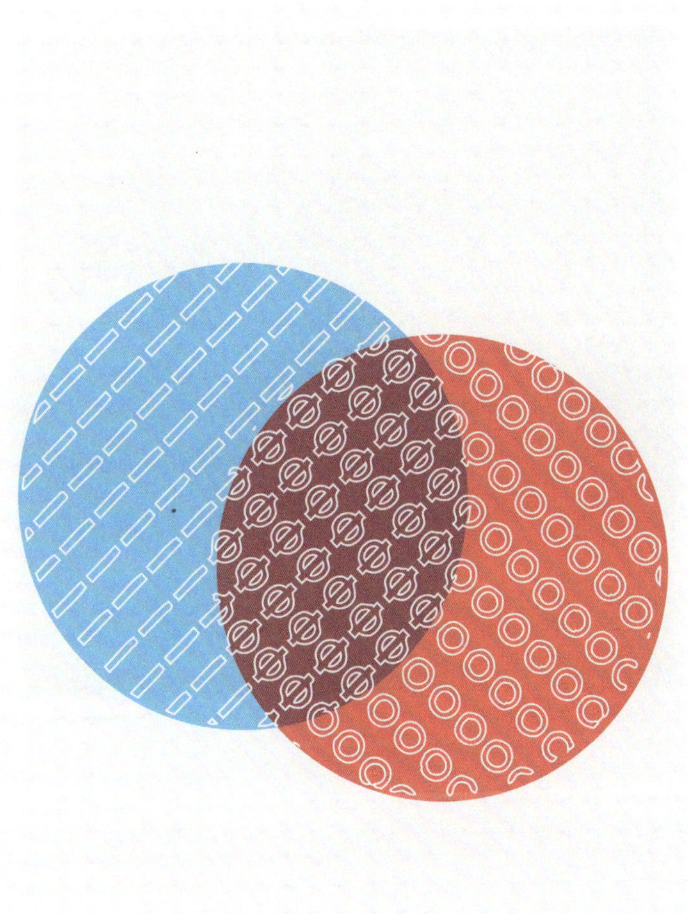

Henry Coleman
Poster Design
(Venn Roundel)

When you think of the Roundel, you think of two things: a ring, and then a bar crossing the ring. Later comes the blue and the red. And when all those points meet you get the Roundel. The poster tries to represent that process visually.

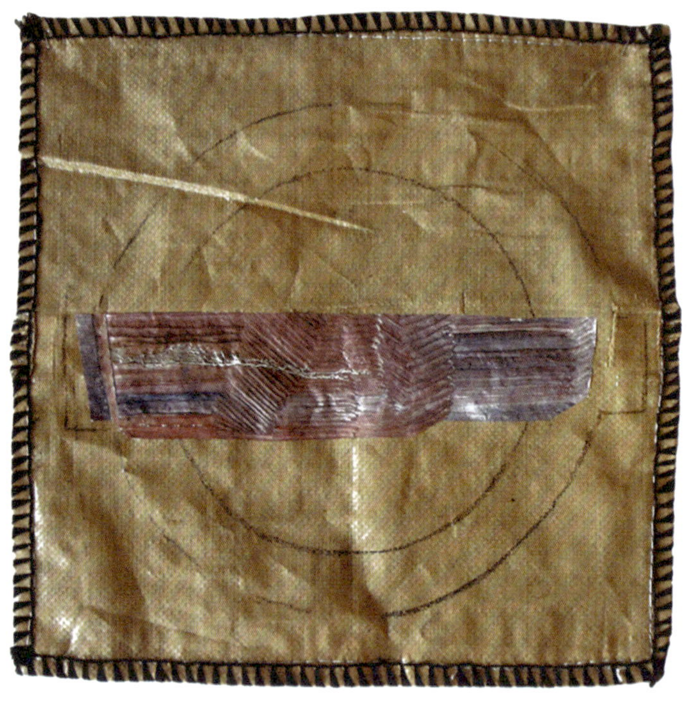

Joel Croxson
Happy Birthday

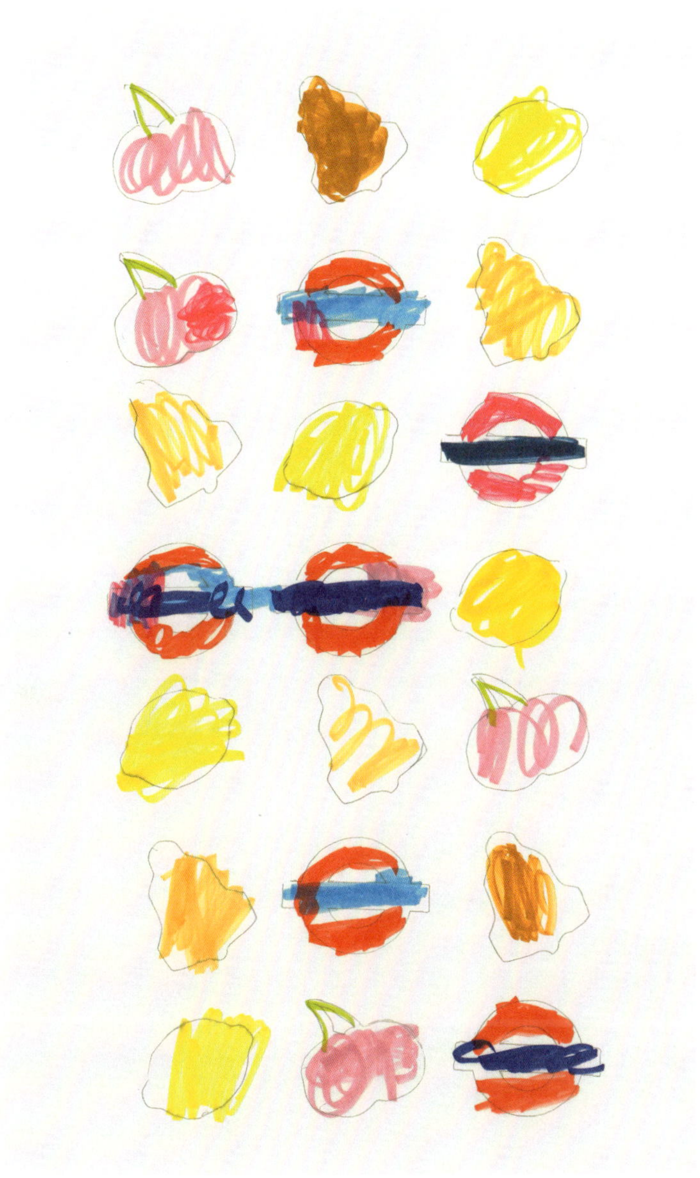

Stuart Cumberland
Fruit Machine

Prior to the commission, I had been drawing fruit-machine graphics such as lemons, bells and cherries. For the Roundel, I simply added the London Underground logo and then enjoyed colouring in. The result: repetition, abandon and a chance of winning!

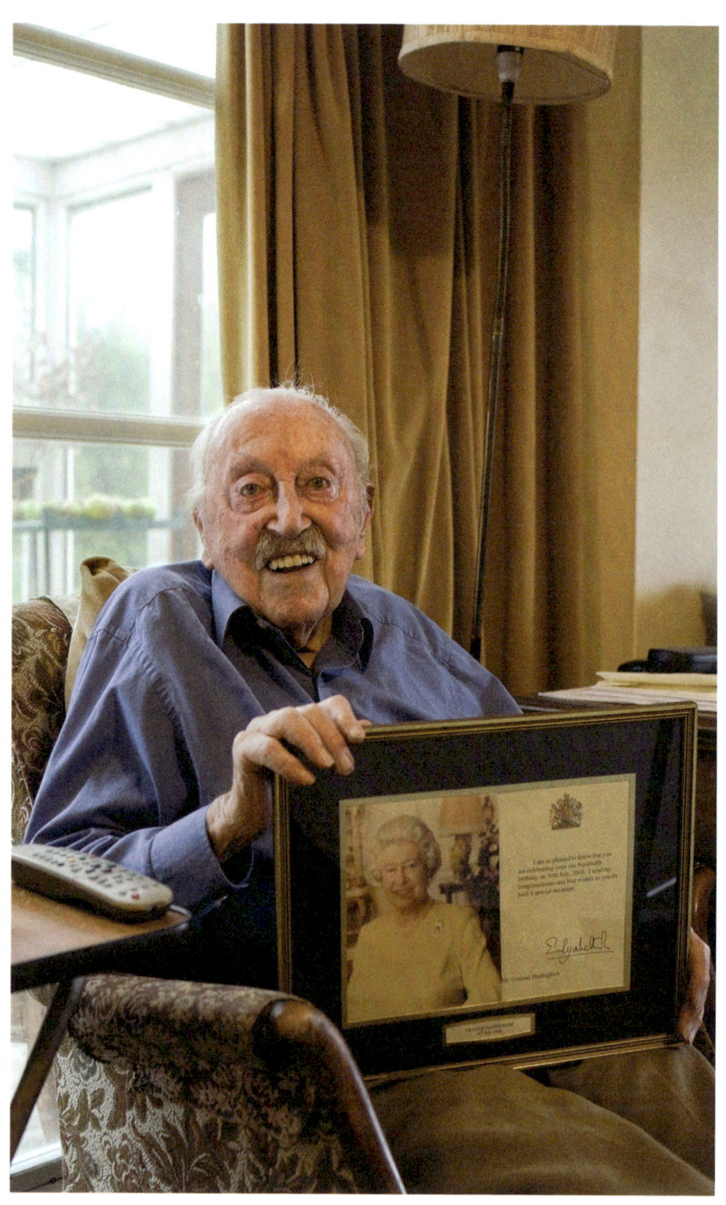

Jeremy Deller
*Graham Hadingham, born
30th July 1908. London
Underground employee –
8th February 1926 until
31st March 1974*

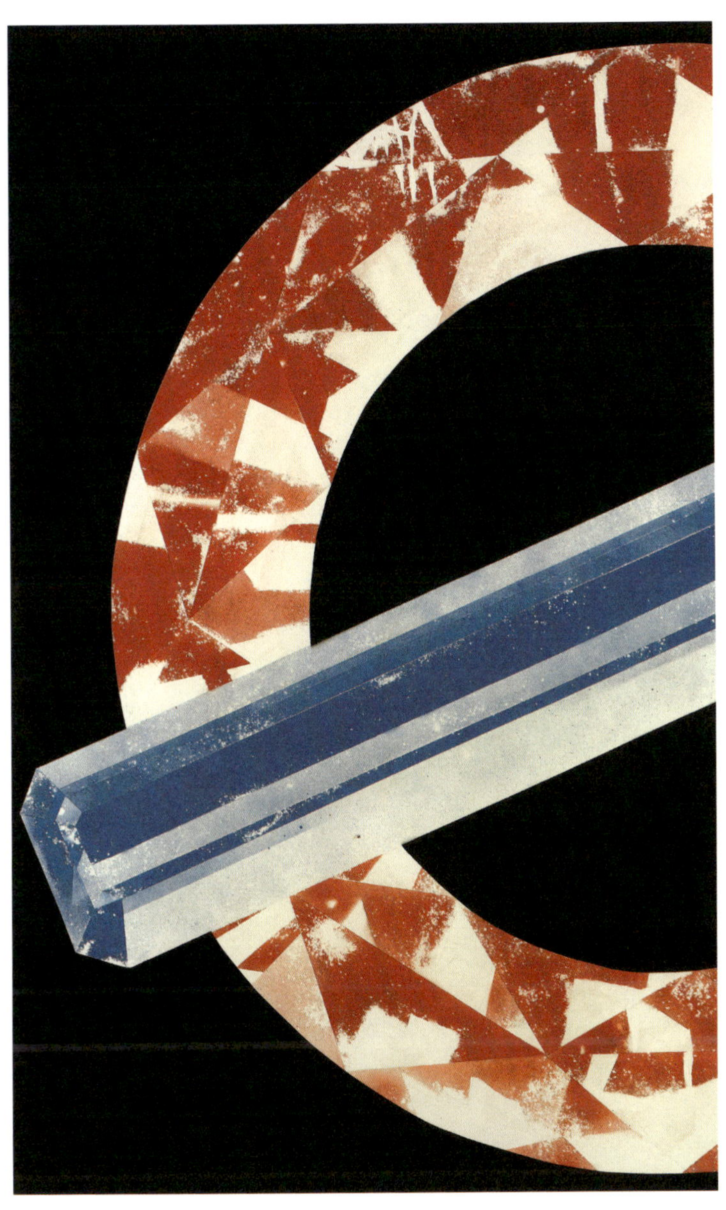

Luke Dowd
Untitled (Roundel)

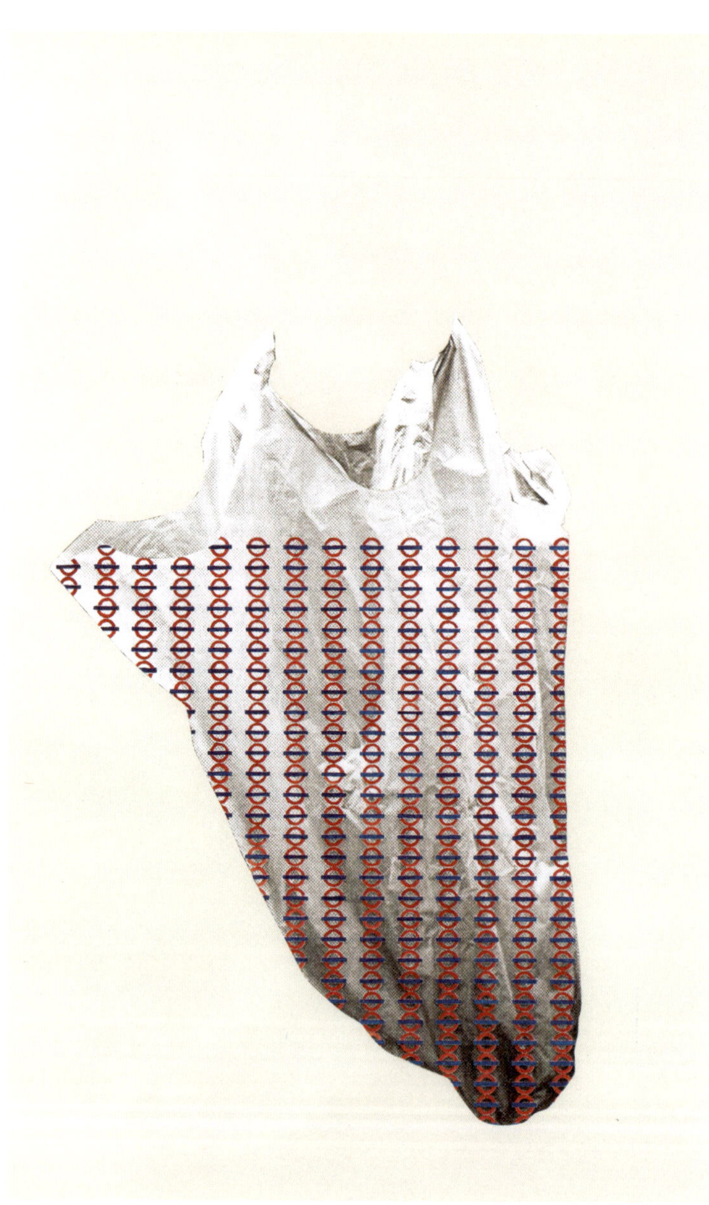

Sean Edwards
No Title

The Roundel as a graphic on the bag indicates potential movement dictated not by the tracks but by the movement of the carrier. A sign of the transporter becoming the transported.

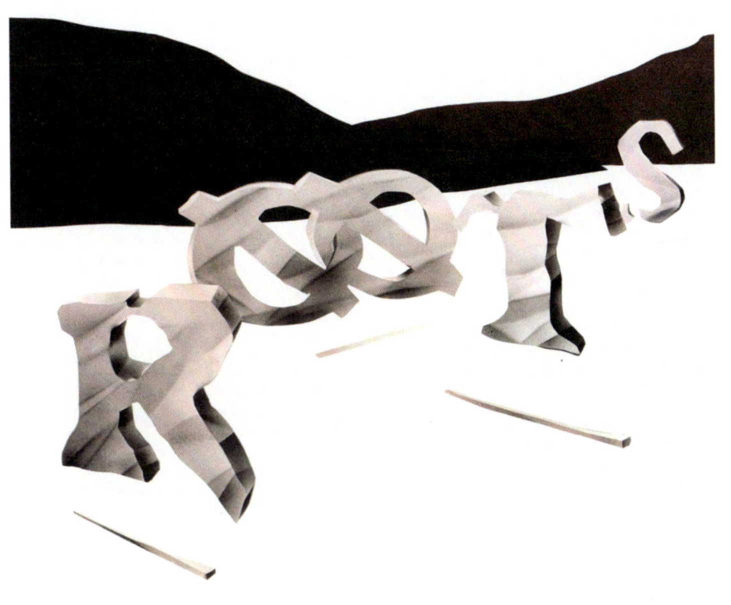

Chris Evans
Roots

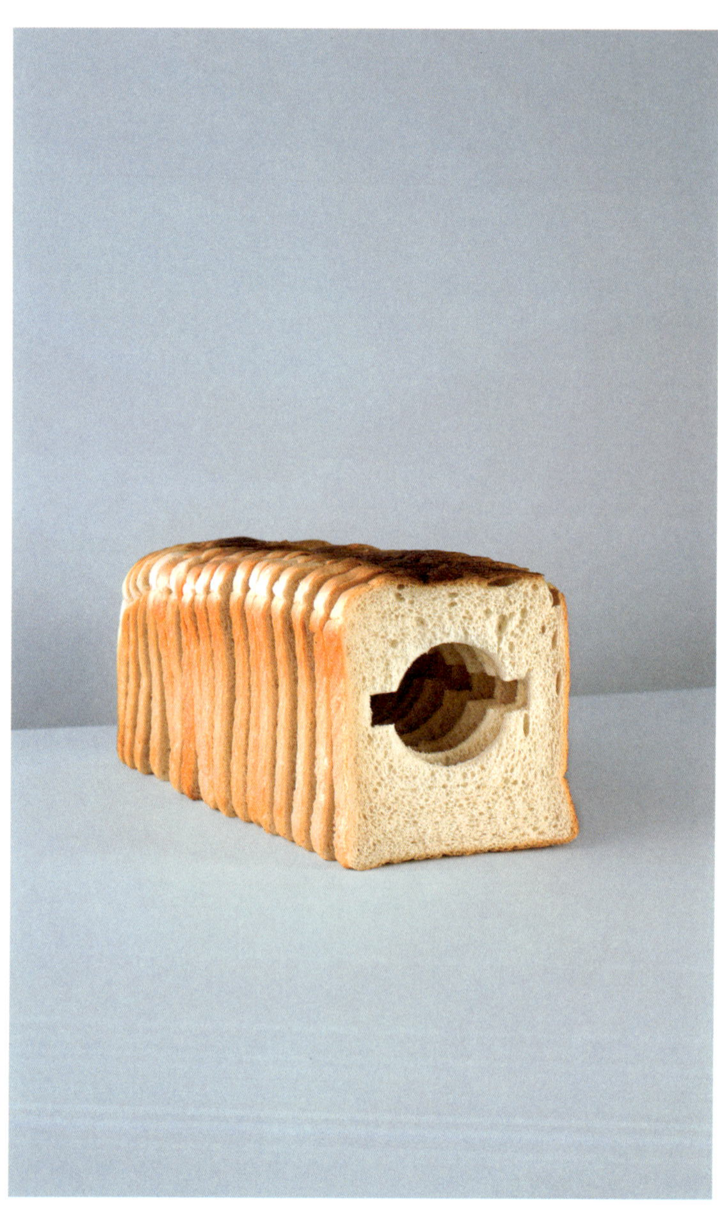

Rose Finn-Kelcey
Untitled

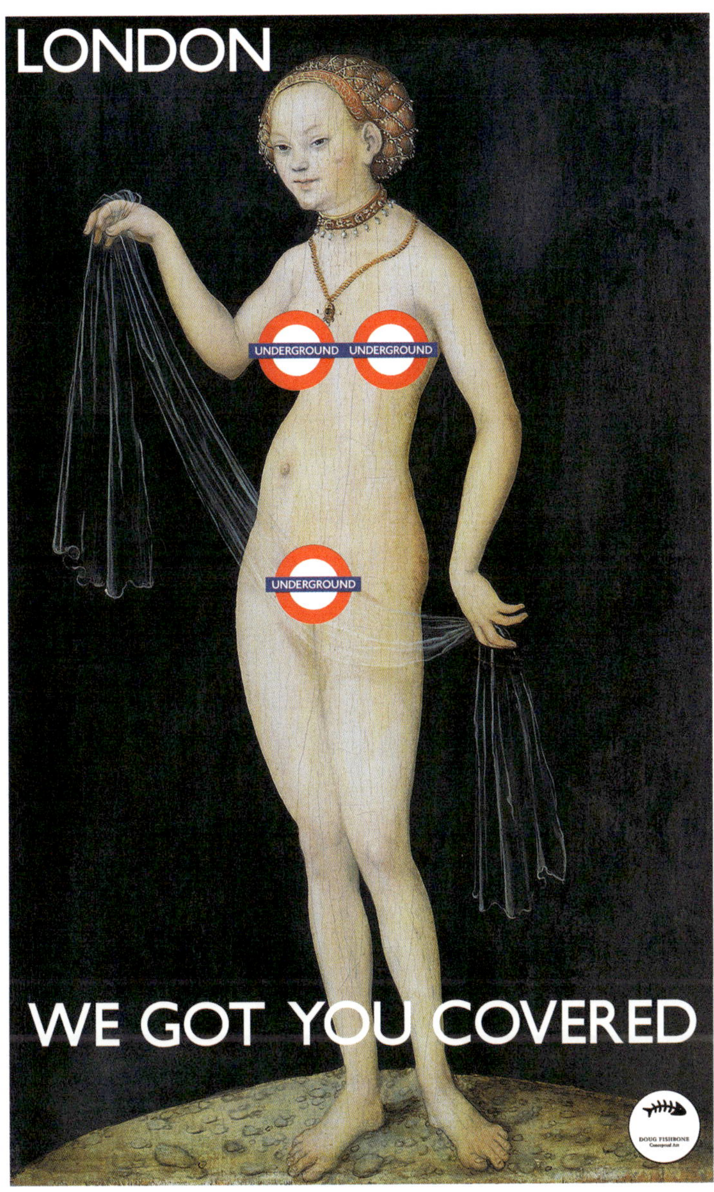

Doug Fishbone
Untitled

In 2008, the advertisement for the Royal Academy's 'Lucas Cranach' exhibition, featuring his depiction of Venus, was deemed too racy and banned from the Underground. Thanks to her Roundel bikini, Venus has cleaned up her act, and was able to return.

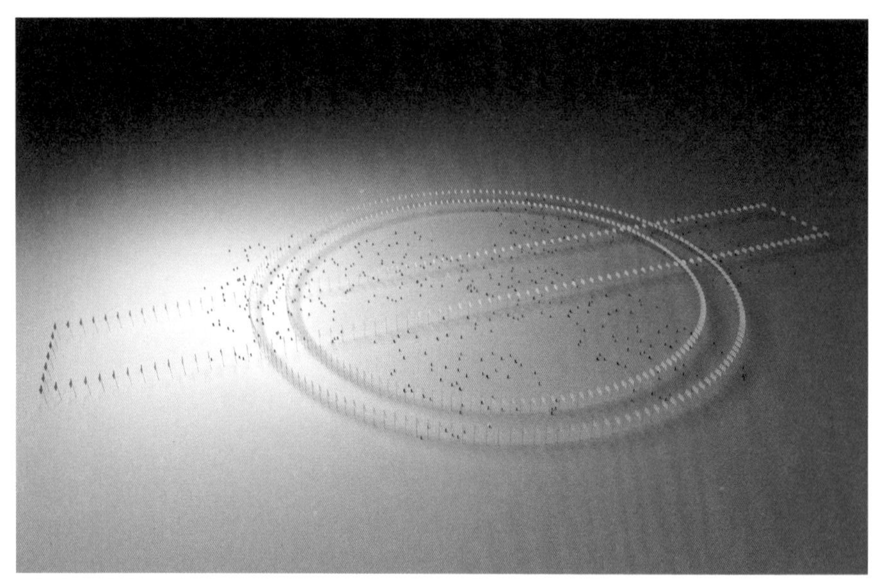

Alicia Framis
560 White Flags

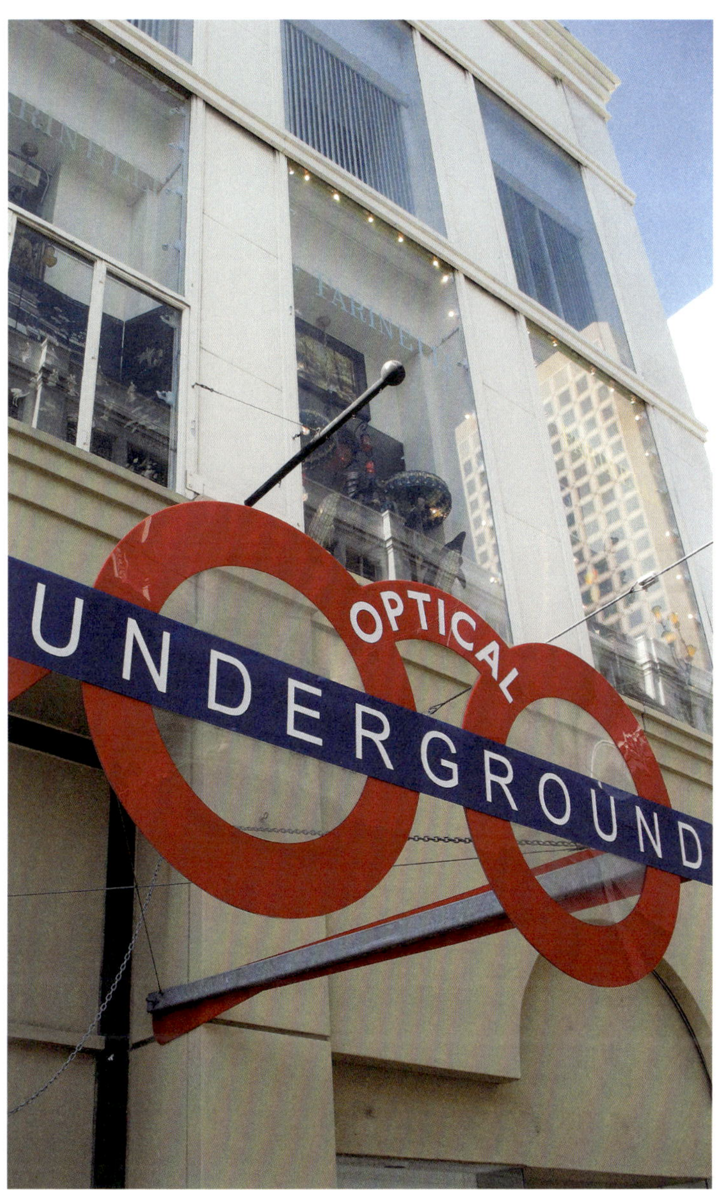

Alex Frost
Optical Underground

The optician's shop-front was photographed by a friend of a friend in San Francisco (Lev Anderson). This was arranged by email. It's a sign I had seen and remembered from a few years ago while I was on holiday. At the time, I didn't have a camera with me.

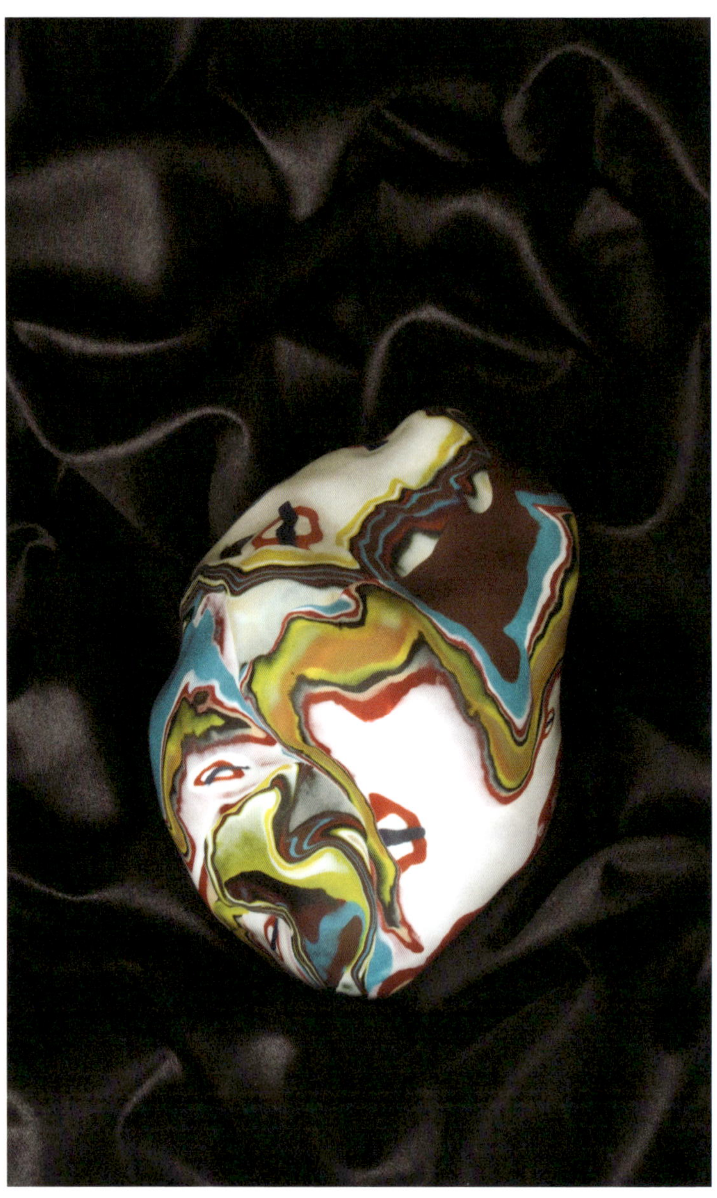

Franziska Furter
Agate

The Roundel logo was found on an agate, like a very precious stone that grew in a gas hole in cold lava under pressure over thousands of years.

Ryan Gander
Seriously Underground
(Edward shifts back his chair,
rises to his feet, moves away
from his desk and exits
stage left)

A section of a partially completed drawing by Edward
Johnston made during the realization of the Roundel as
London Underground logo around 1925, cut and extracted
as if it had literally fallen from one page into another.

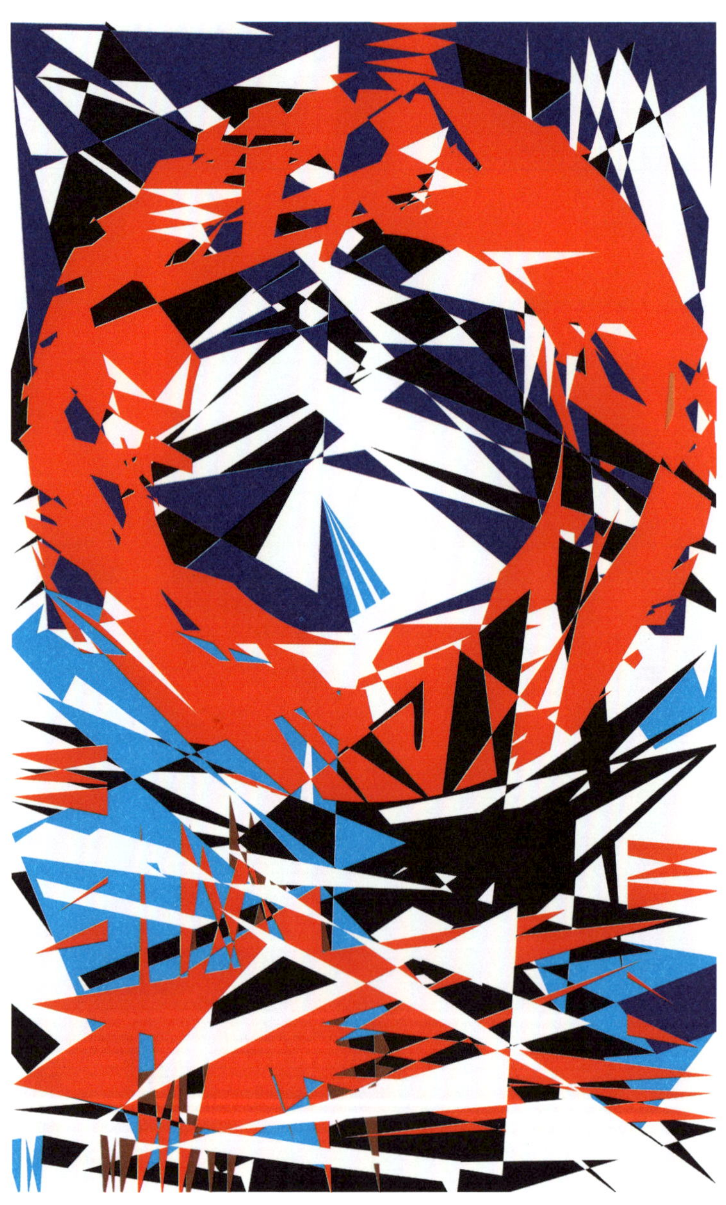

Jaime Gili
A150 Anjos

This is an attempt to fragment as much as possible the perfect
Roundel image, but leaving it recognizable in the context where
it is supposed to be displayed. The final image looks perhaps
right between one of my paintings and the iconic Roundel.

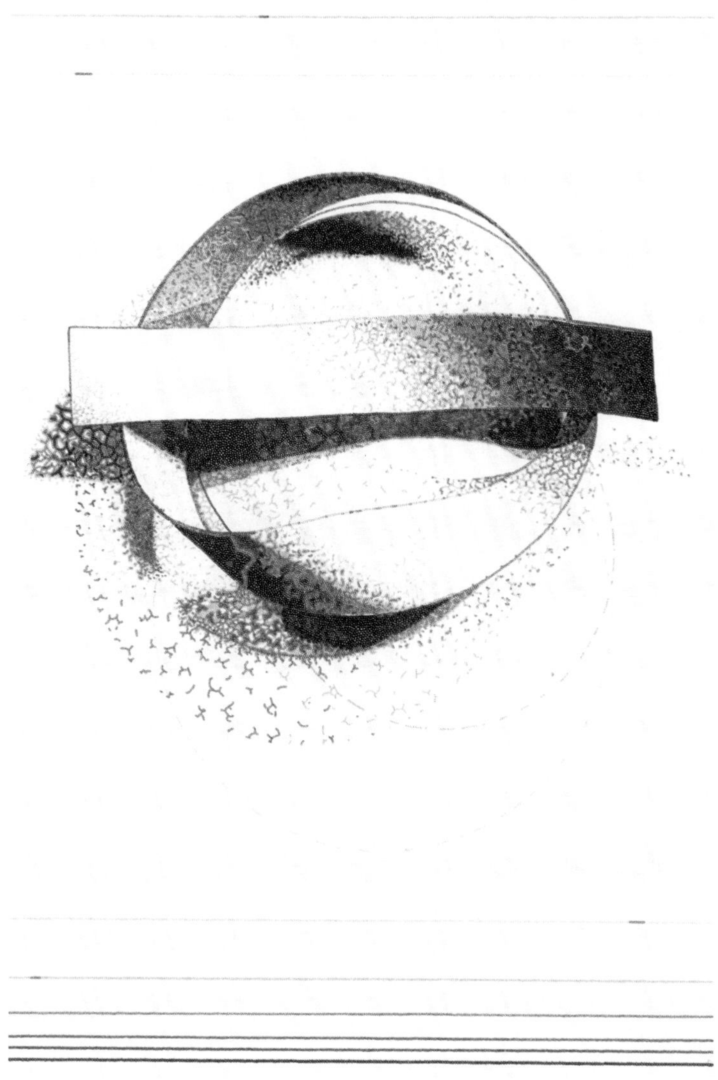

Alison Gill
Untitled

The Roundel signifies something unseen from the ground, a subterranean knot where limits and boundaries are unclear. I made a topological paper sculpture, a möbius strip, a continuous surface and built closed loops (unknots), forming an occult abstraction in space.

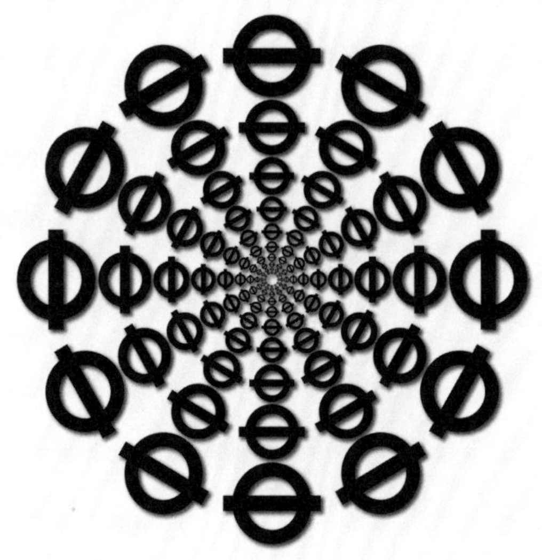

Liam Gillick
onehundredandninetytwofeet

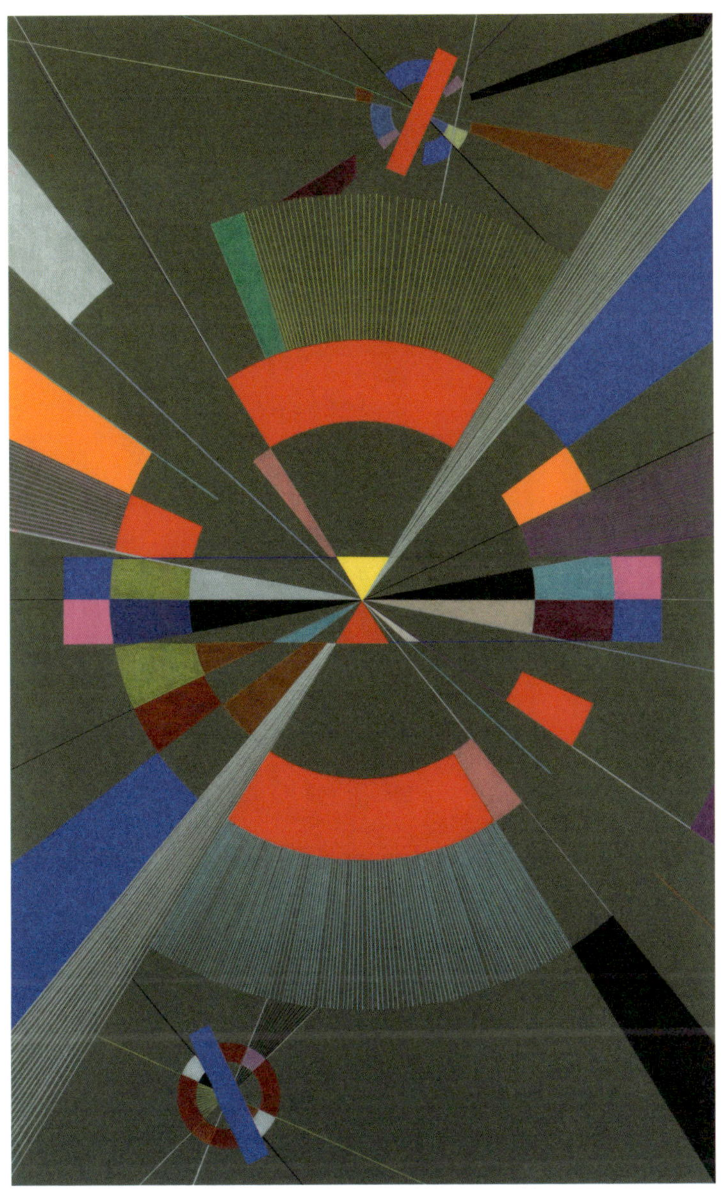

Lothar Götz
Vision of a Roundel

Imagine the Roundel's perfect house, a place to reflect on everything seen on its busy journeys. A retreat at the day's end, out along the Central line, in the quiet dark woodland of Wanstead Park, to awake refreshed to the endless surprises of London.

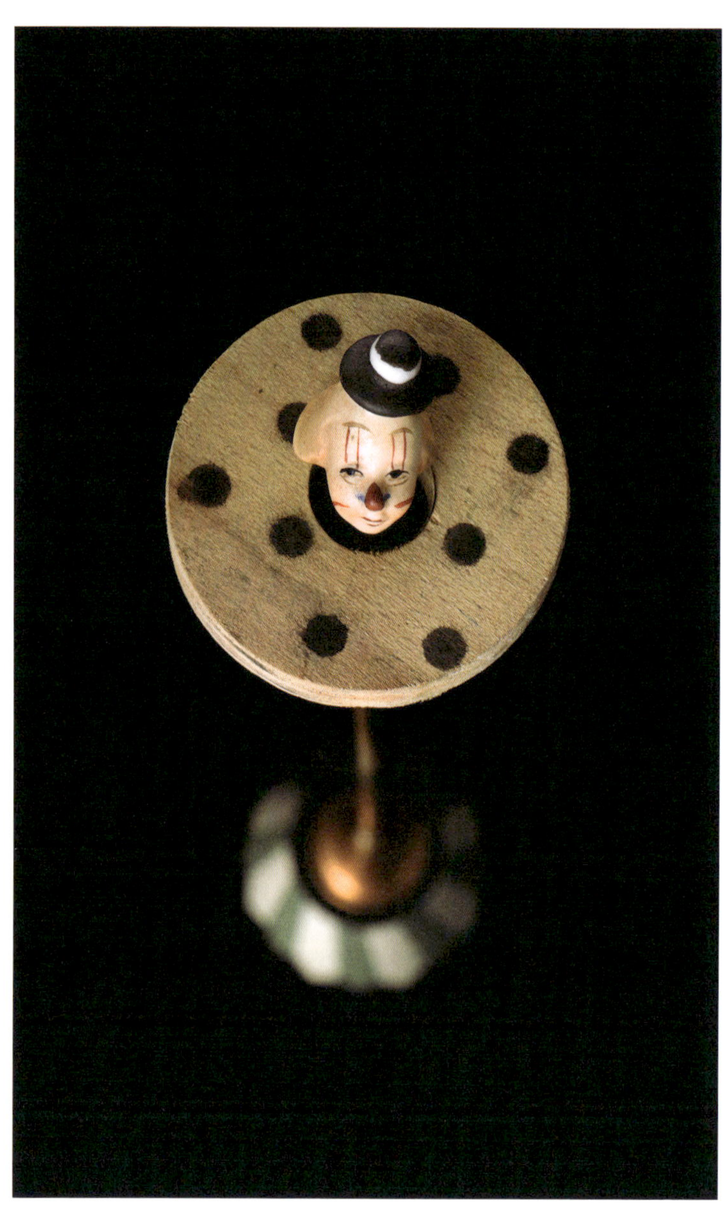

Brian Griffiths
Old Spot

56

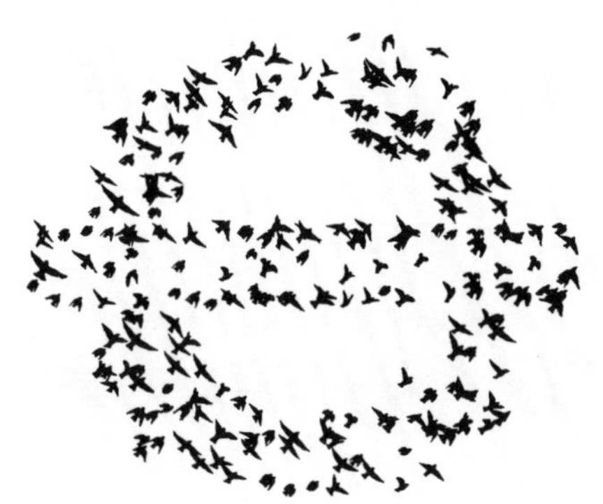

Henrik Håkansson
Untitled (underground)

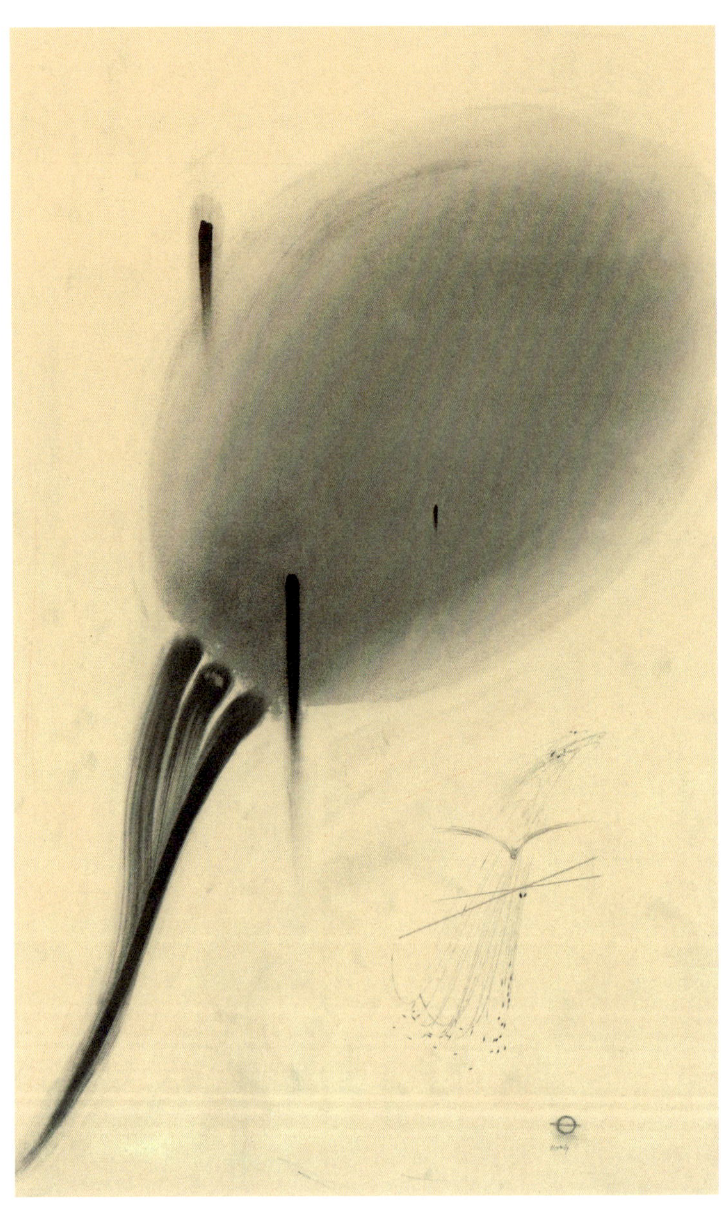

Thomas Helbig
Balloon

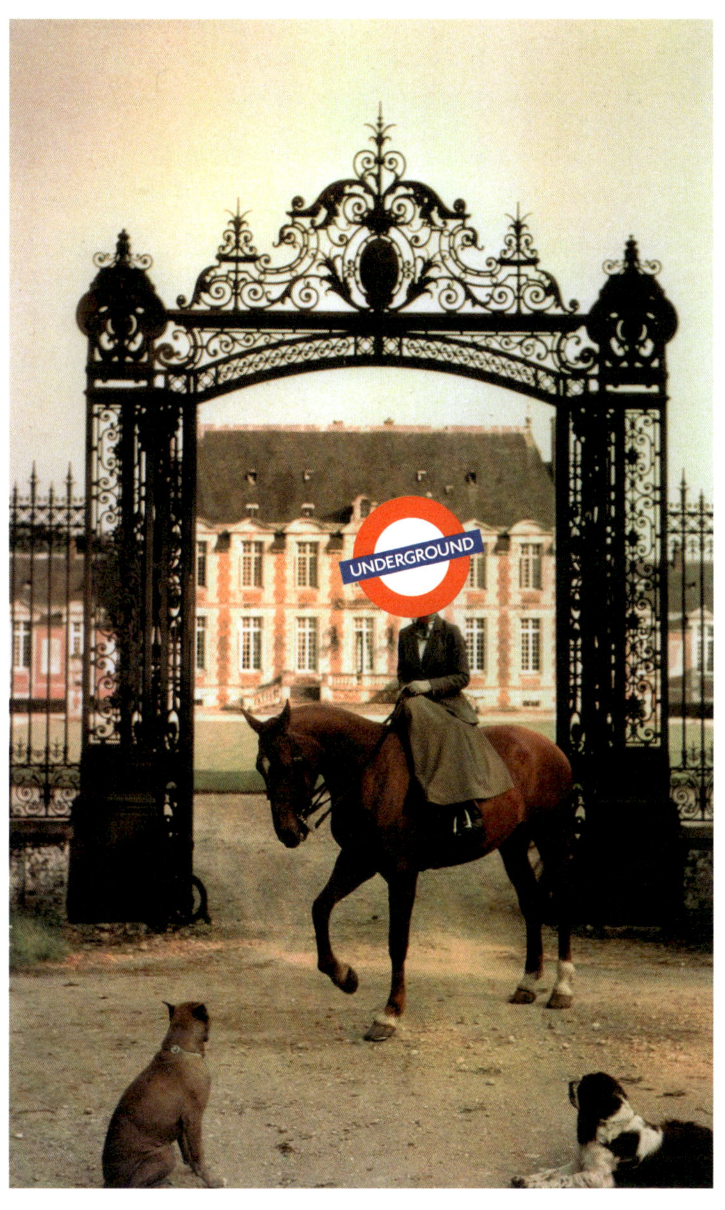

Lothar Hempel
UNDERGROUND

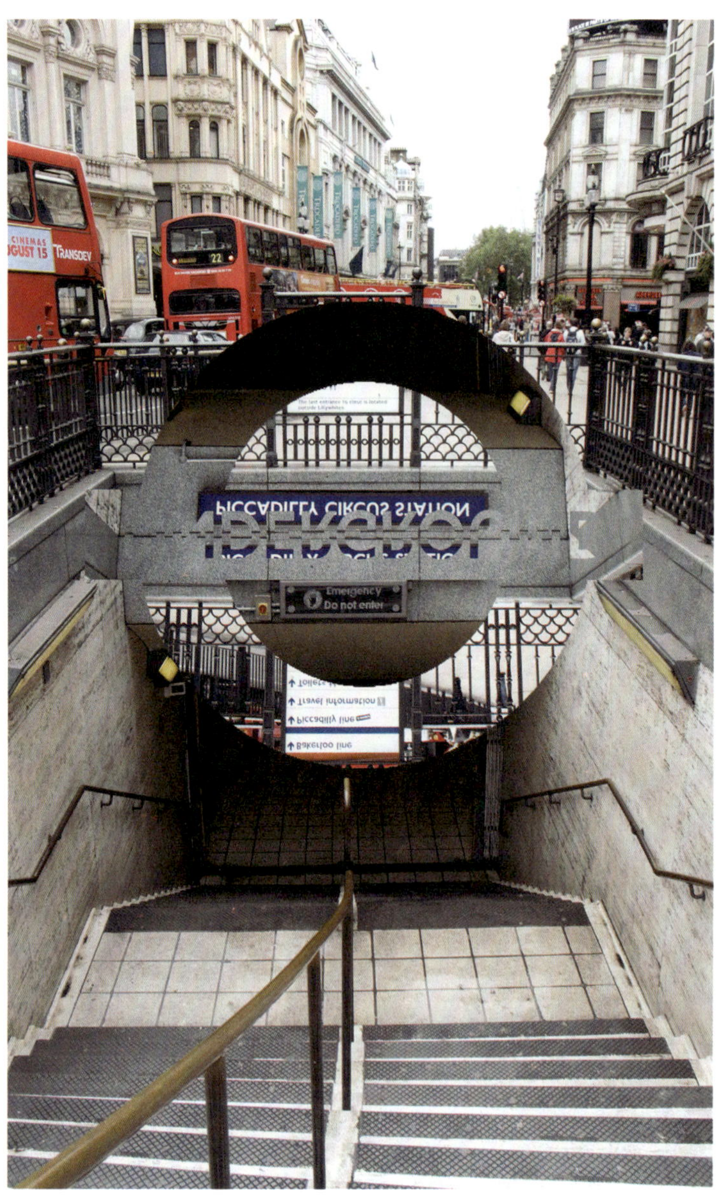

Knut Henrik Henriksen
undergroundoverground

In 2009, I developed two permanent sculptures for King's Cross station. The sculptures were called *Full Circle* and visualized the architecture and materials on site. This image employs the same strategy, using its surroundings to define the logo.

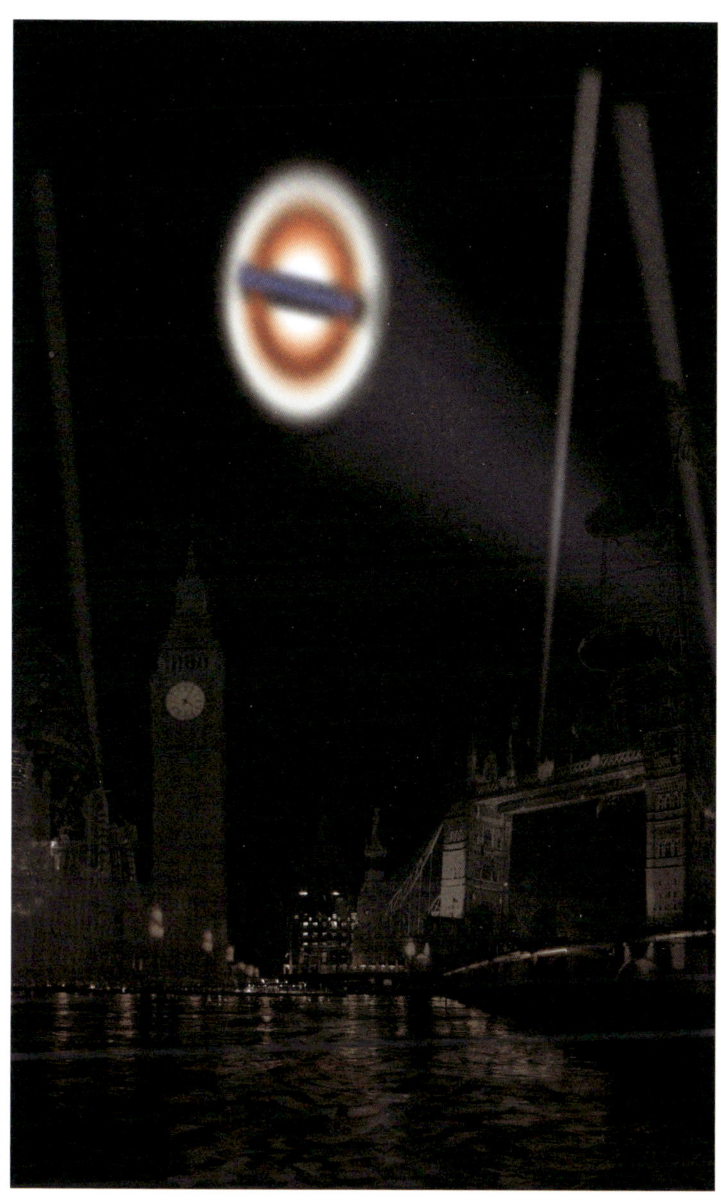

Susan Hiller
Untitled

I was more interested in the Roundel's symbolic or psychological aspects than its design aspects. Projected in a beam of light in the sky over London, like the Batman symbol, it illuminates the darkness and stands for reliability, safety and security.

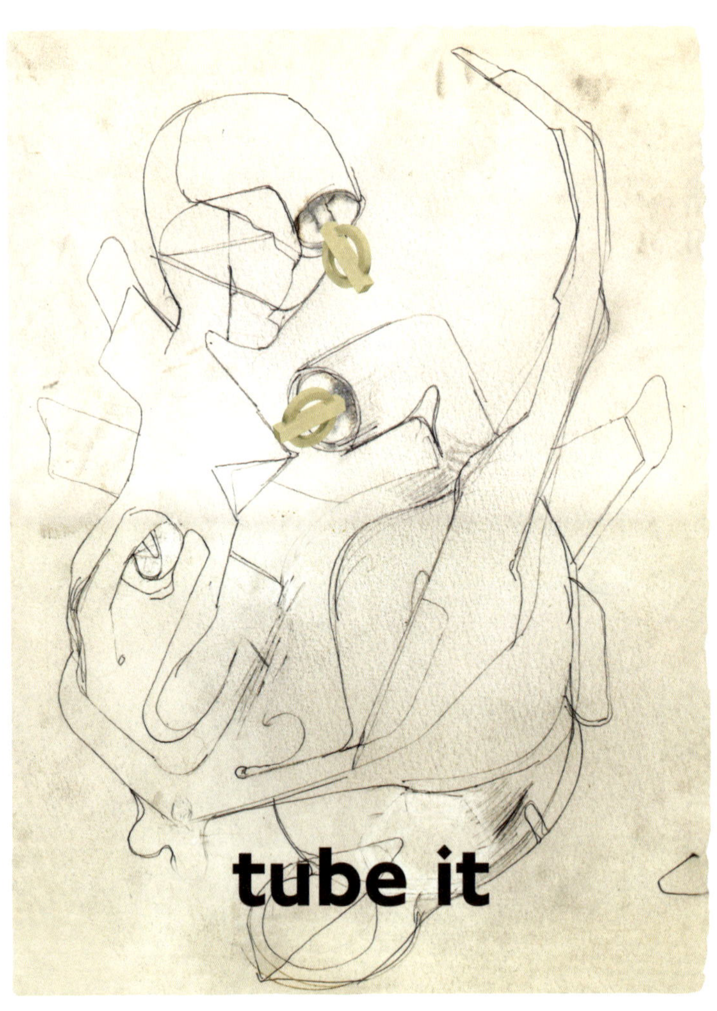

Roger Hiorns
Untitled

62

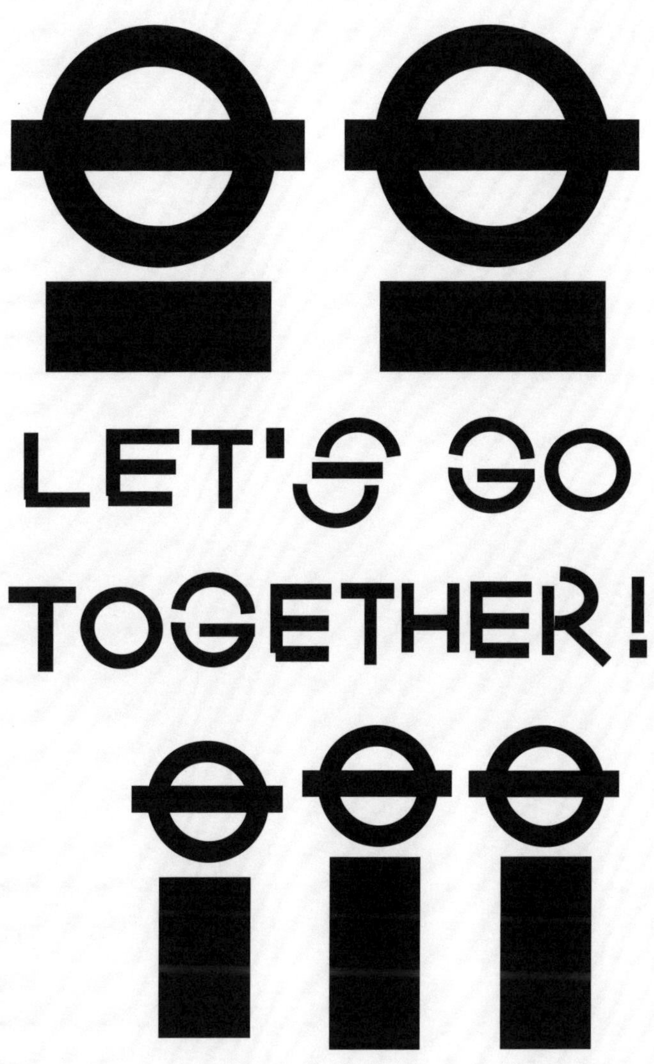

Karl Holmqvist
Let's Go Together

The message of this poster comes from its halfway 'slogan', 'Let's Go Together', deliberately mixing up 'Let's Go' and 'Come Together'. It's spelled out in a DIY font made from fragmented Tube Roundels and is meant to have a humanizing effect, in contrast to the kind of Cool Britannia advertising that is usually surrounding commuters on the Underground. It's tentatively 'selling' the idea that it's nice to ride together — because it is.

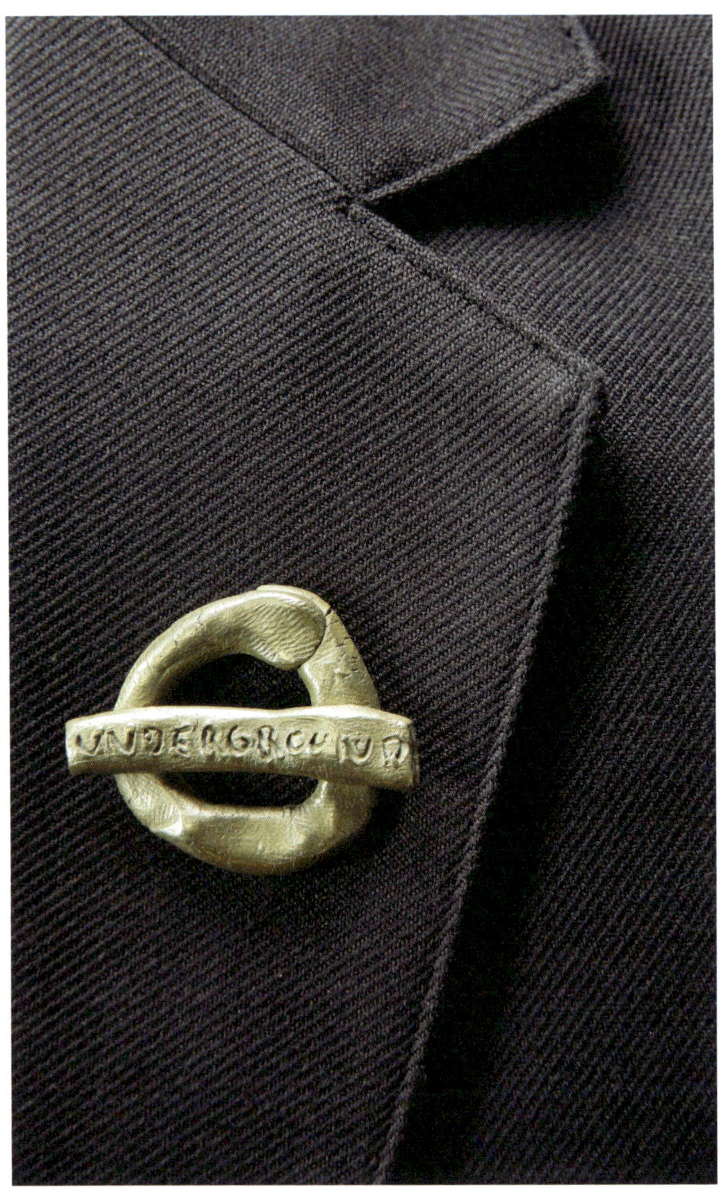

Des Hughes
The Collector

The Roundel is omnipresent throughout London, so I imagined a group of dedicated followers who might fashion homemade images of their idol to decorate their improvised uniforms as a sign of their allegiance.

The Hut Project
100 Years. 100 Artists.
100 Works of Art

We've chosen forty words that explain our inspiration for the Roundel project. They're from the original invitation from Sally Shaw:

'I have identified these artists specifically as I think they will find the project of interest historically, as well as it being, what I hope they will find through the process, an interesting articulation of their work.'

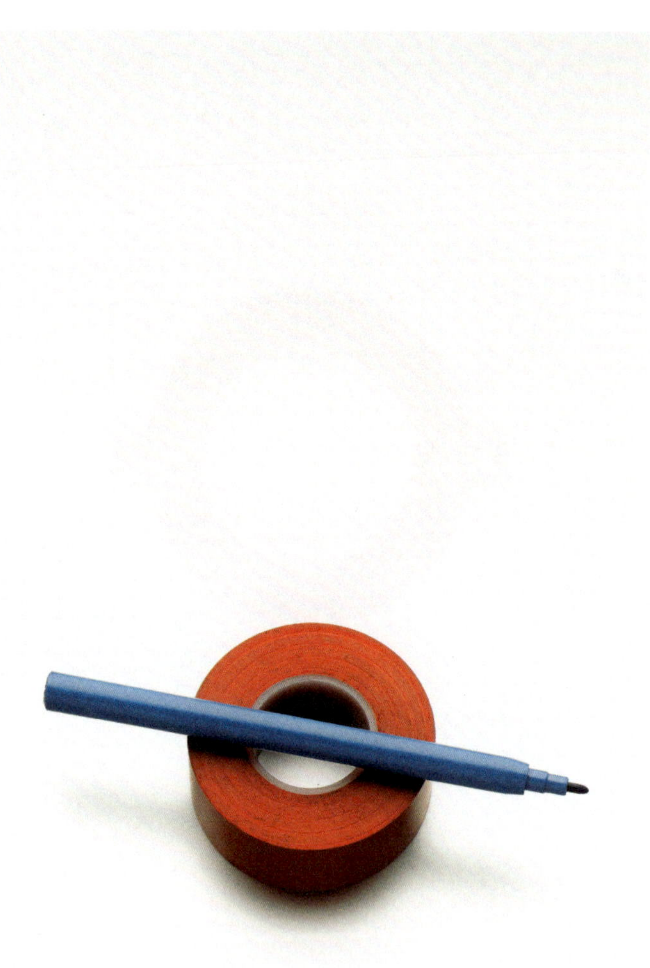

James Ireland
Pen & Tape Roundel

I wanted to make a sculpture. I wanted to make something as simple as the Roundel. So I looked around my studio to see what I could use.

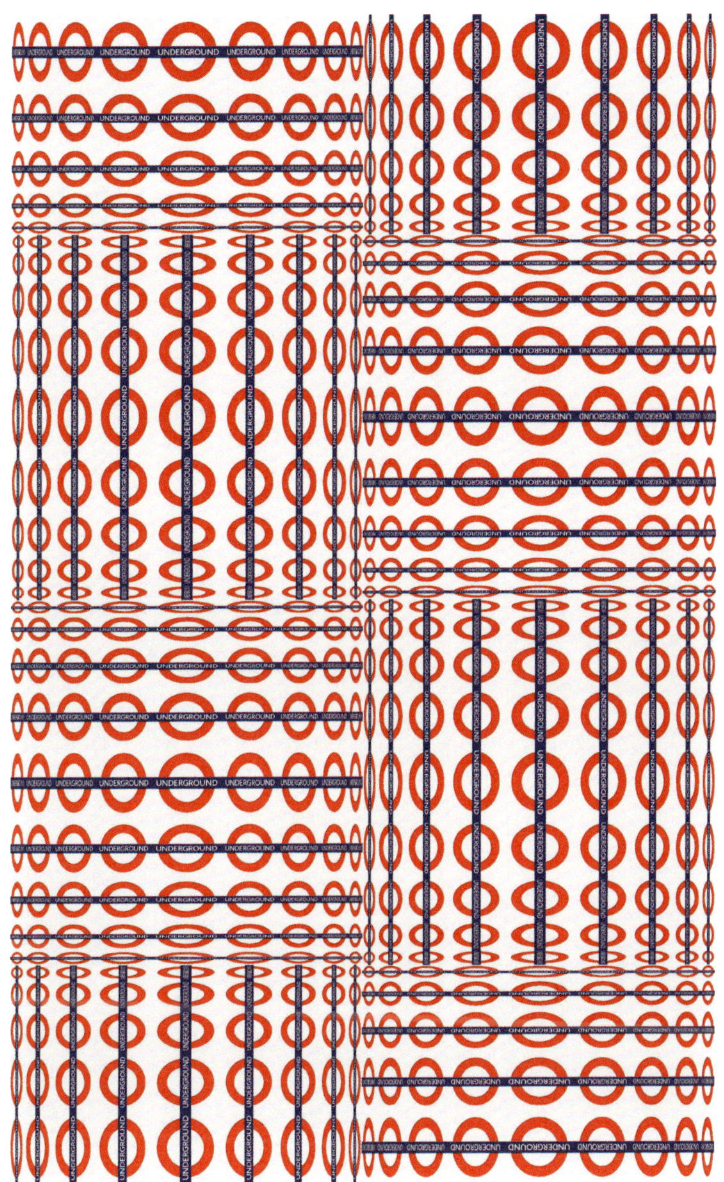

Jim Isermann
Untitled (Underground)

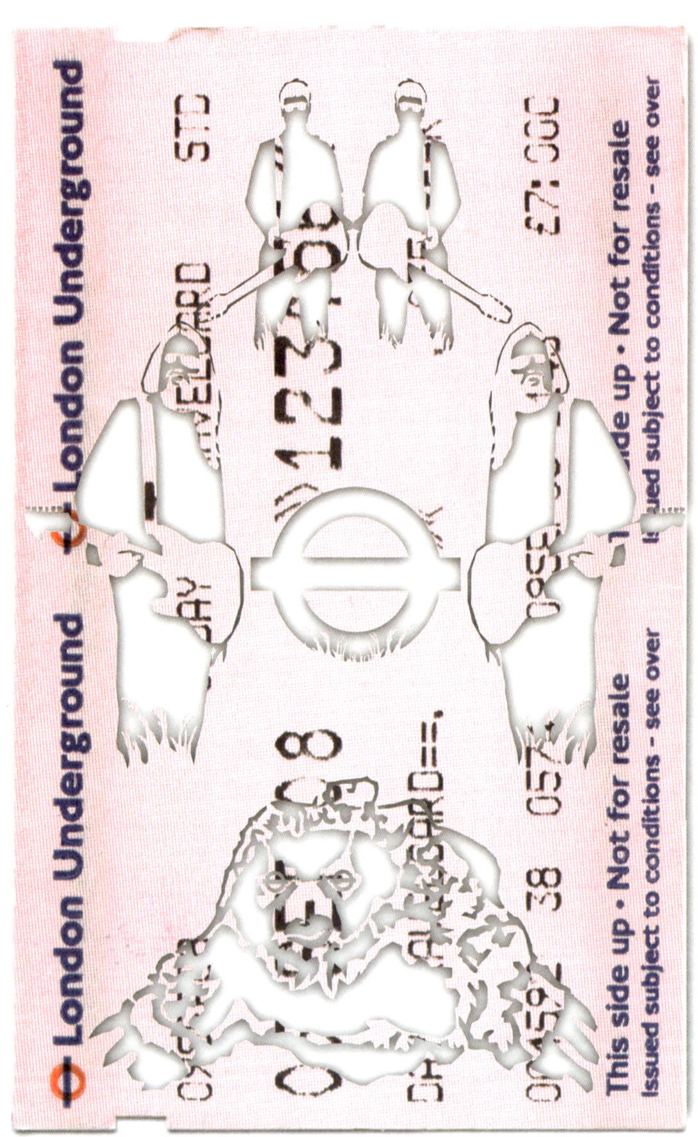

Juneau Projects
*Cockades of the
Revolutionaries*

The Roundel, for us, is a symbol of anticipation and relief,
a silent travelling companion, whether outward or homeward
bound. A travelcard becomes a canvas for daydreaming of
moles and guitars impossibly torn from its surface.

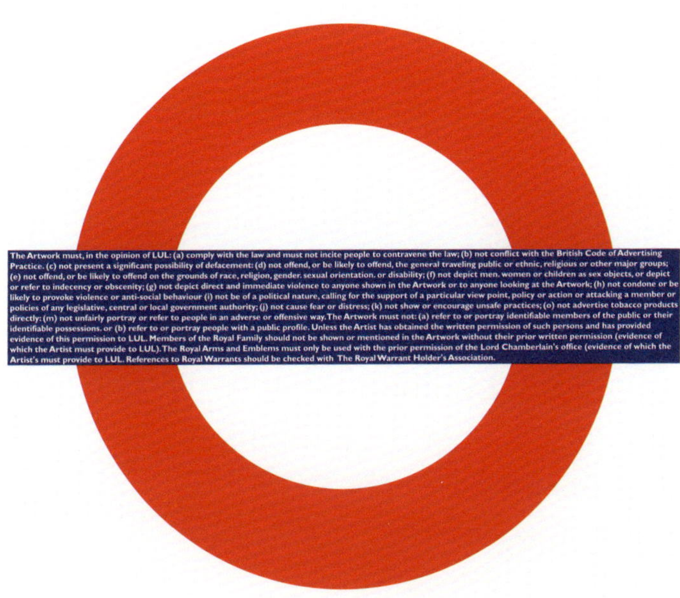

Alan Kane
The artwork must ...

Meanwhile brought
back to the
subterranean action
of   economic facts,
the "old mole"
revolution hollows
out chambers in a
decomposed soil
repugnant to the
delicate   nose of the
utopians.

Ian Kiaer
Old Mole

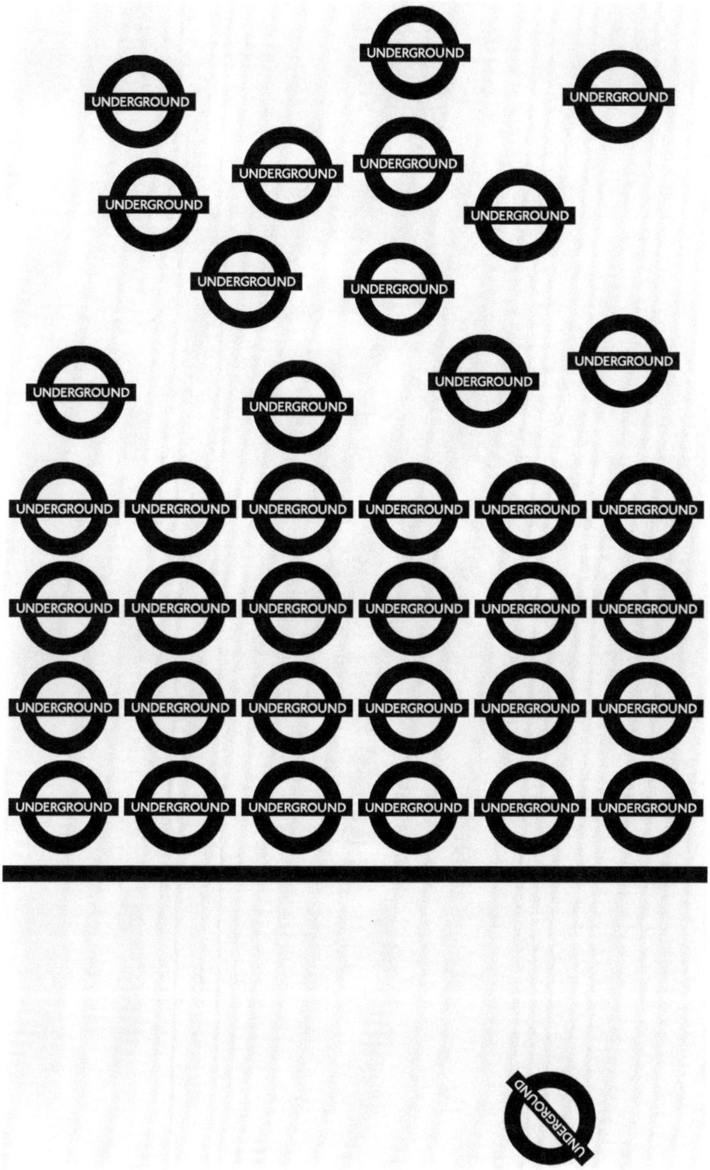

Scott King
Untitled

This is a diagrammatic representation of a 'Tube death' at rush hour. Whether the Roundel jumped, tripped or was pushed is unclear.

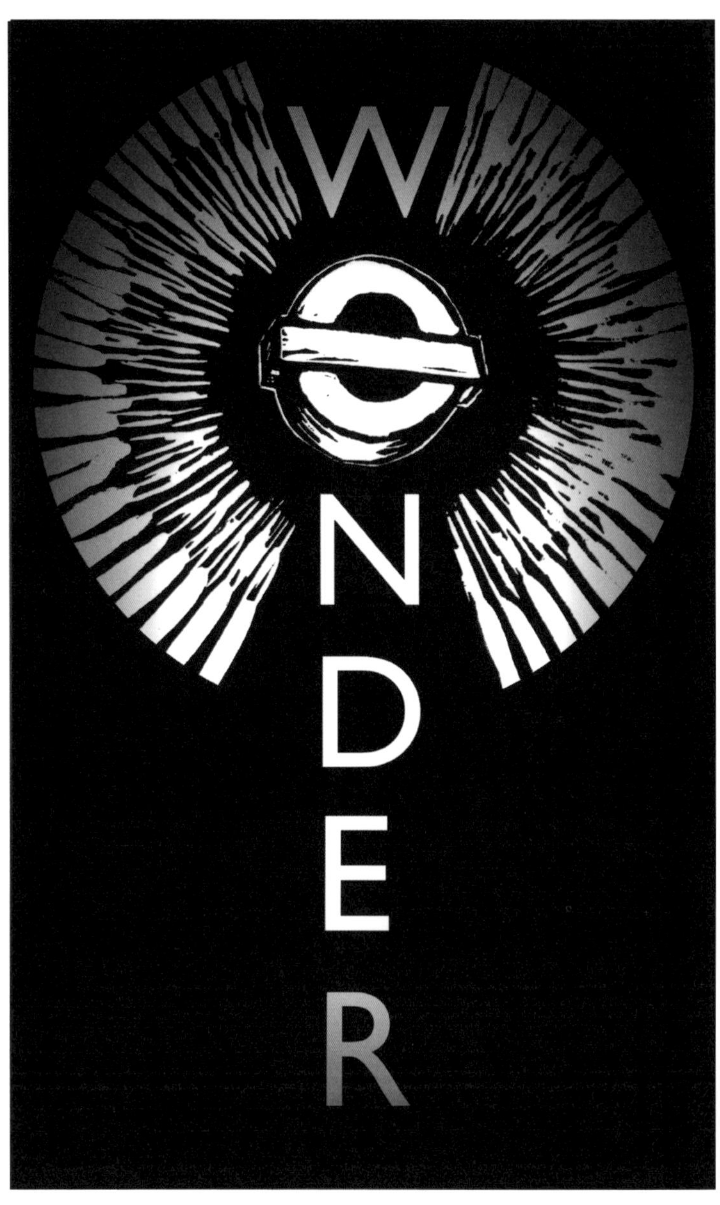

Serena Korda
Wonder

Wonder at the Roundel glowing in the sky.
Wonder at the person sitting by your side.
Wonder at the announcement you just missed.
Wonder at the tunnel curving round and round.
Wonder at the mouse scurrying away.
Wonder at the Underground every single day.

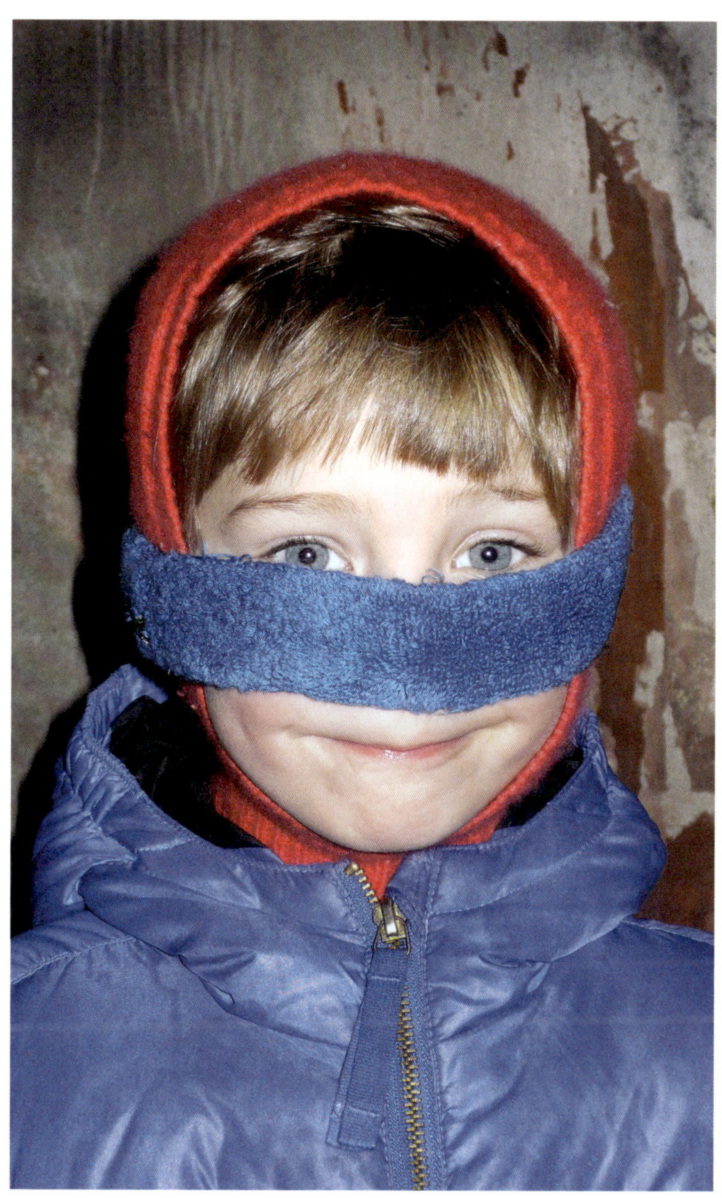

Torsten Lauschmann
Balaclava & Sweatband

The idea came while I was playing with my six-year-old son Hans. We played with a few coloured objects until we were both happy. Hans is very proud to feature on a London Underground poster.

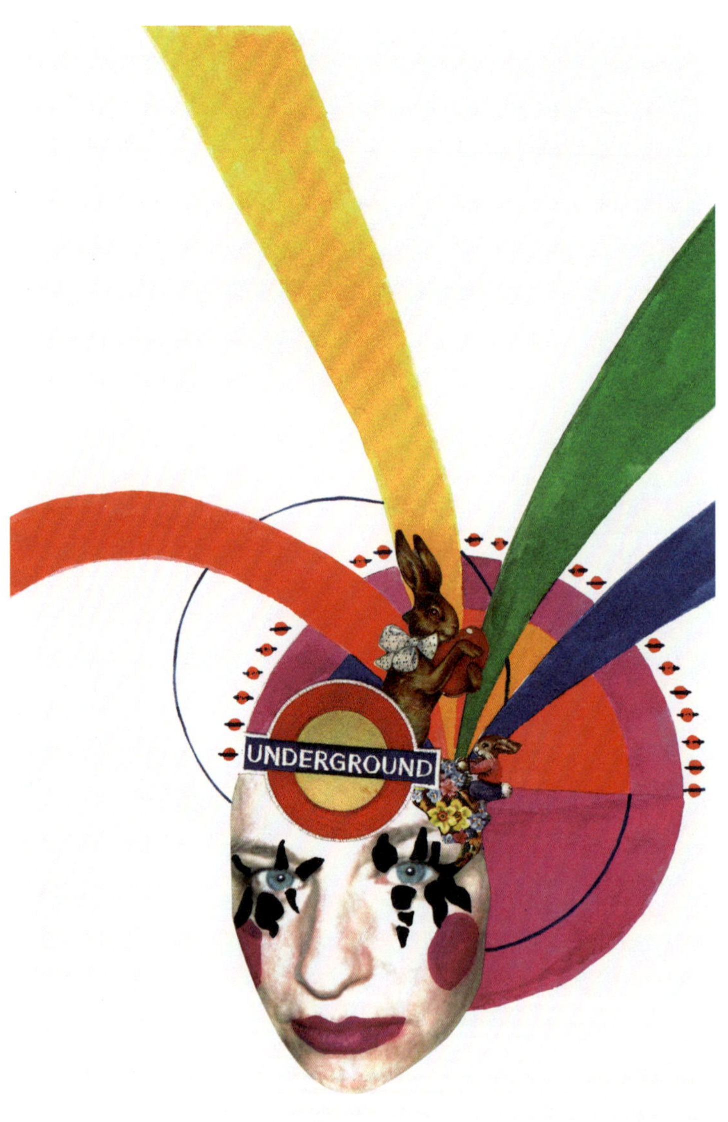

Delaine Le Bas
Metropolitan City

Metropolis: past, present, future experience of different 'worlds'. Going underground like Alice's rabbit, but where will we be going this time? Along 'Tracks' leading us to another place.

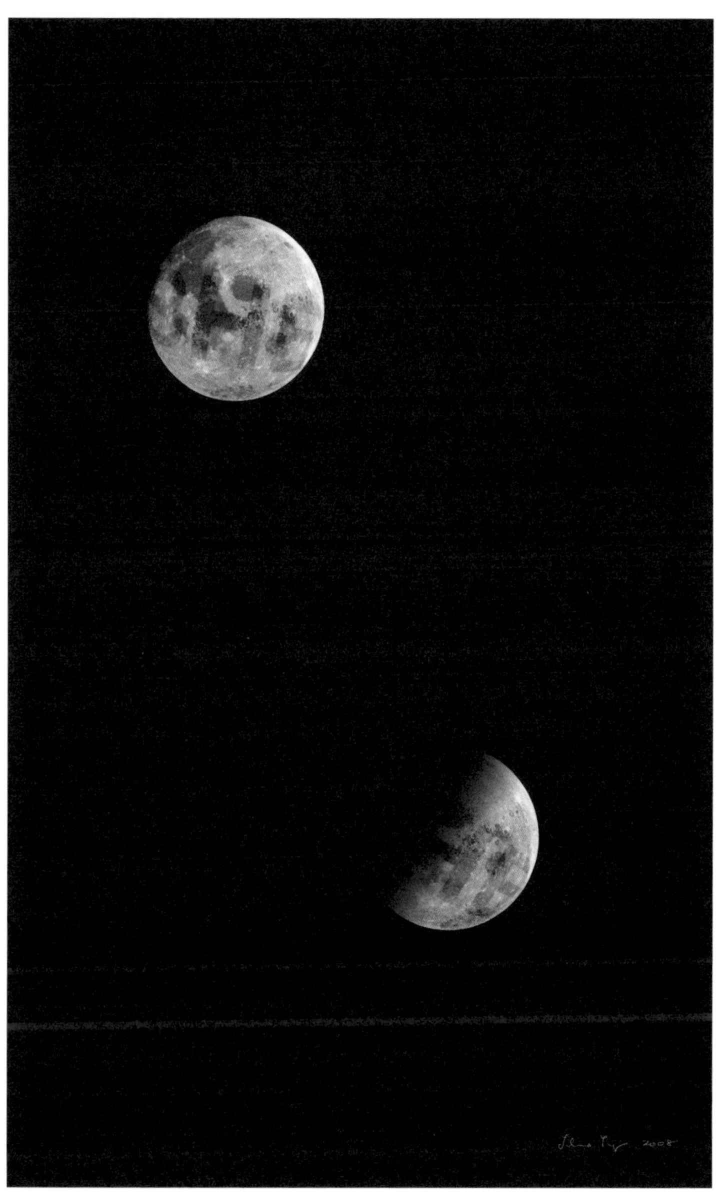

Liliane Lijn
Moonmeme

I have contributed an image of the moon seen as a meme,
its lunation changing the meaning of a word projected on
its surface.

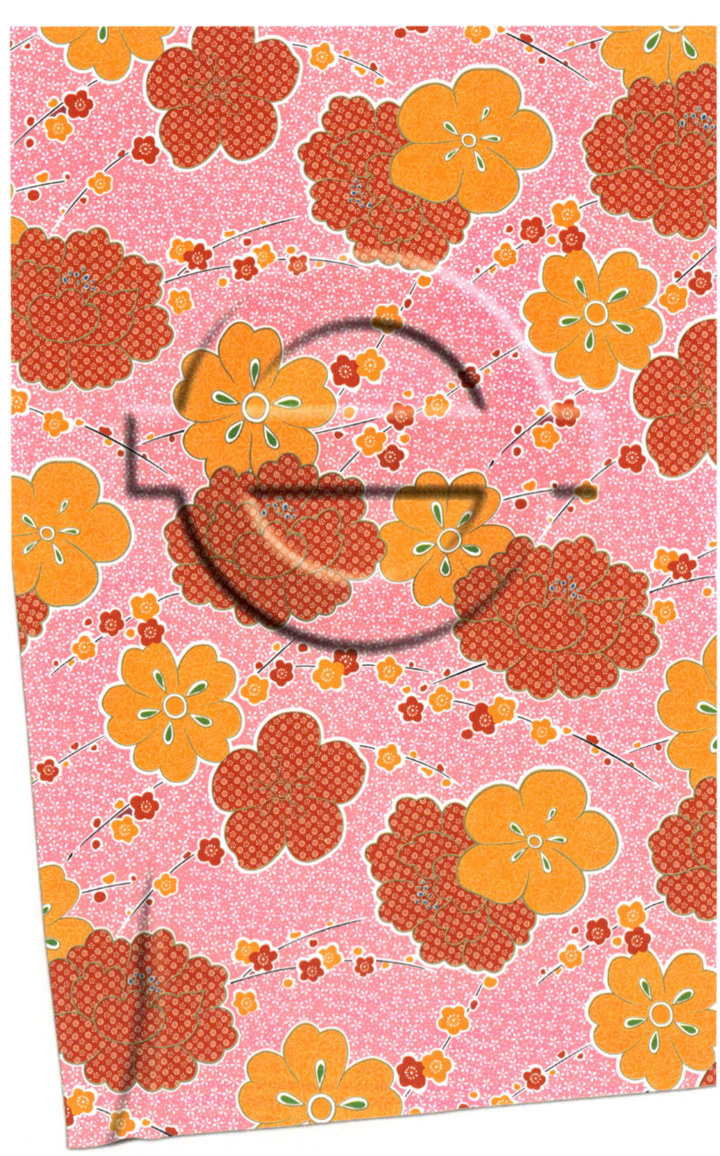

Michael Lin
Untitled

Promise

Tim Machin
Promise

I wanted to take the Roundel back to its origins as a piece
of typography, referencing a past golden age of the London
Underground poster, the promise of Metroland.

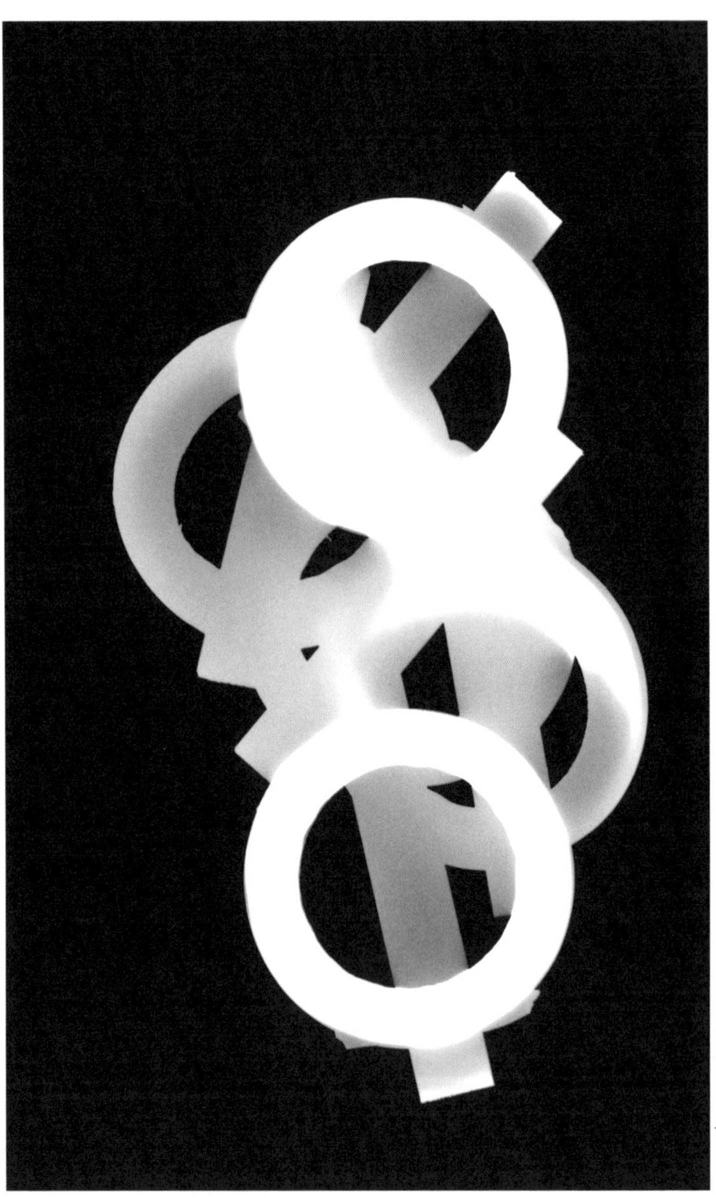

Lorna Macintyre
Untitled

The Roundel became translated into a three-dimensional object in my studio made from a roll of masking tape and some balsa wood. Several of these were thrown at random onto paper in the darkroom and exposed.

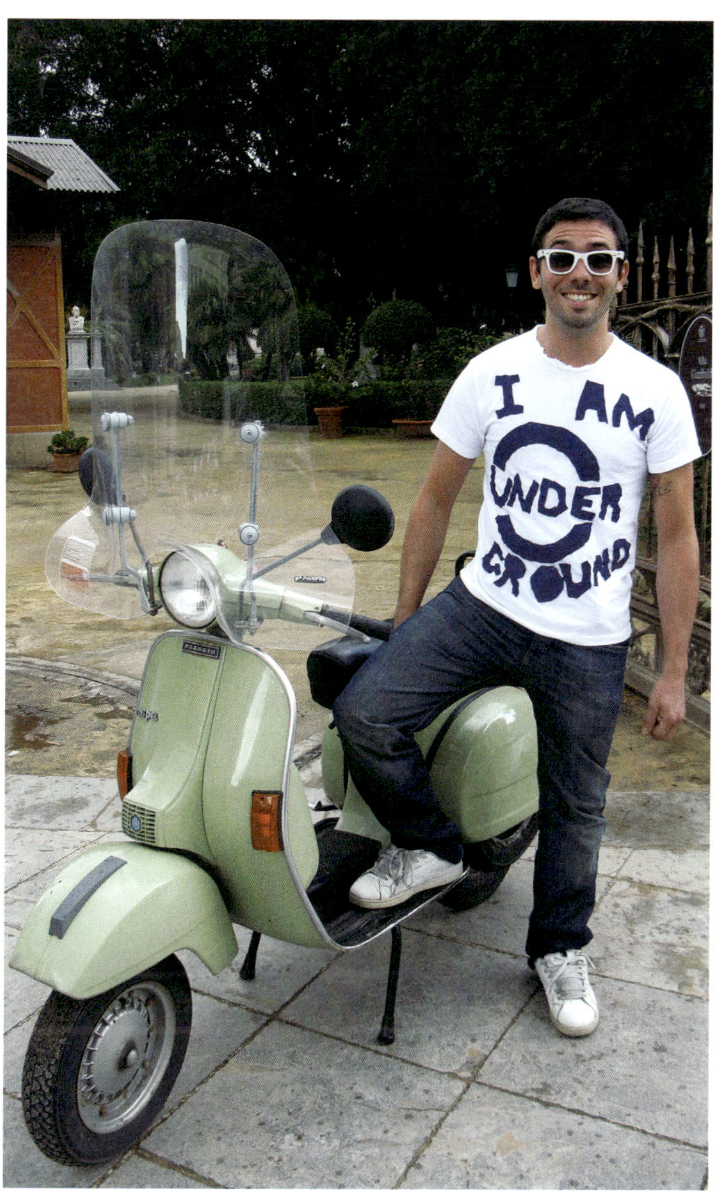

Andrew Mania
Untitled

I have been making T-shirts for myself for some time with
blue appliqué felt and I took the opportunity to make a new
one when I was in Palermo, Sicily, where I made this image.
I have adopted the Roundel and used it as a pun on someone
whois alternative with their interests. After making the T-shirt,
I photographed my friend Renaldo with his moped in the local
park wearing it and his smile.

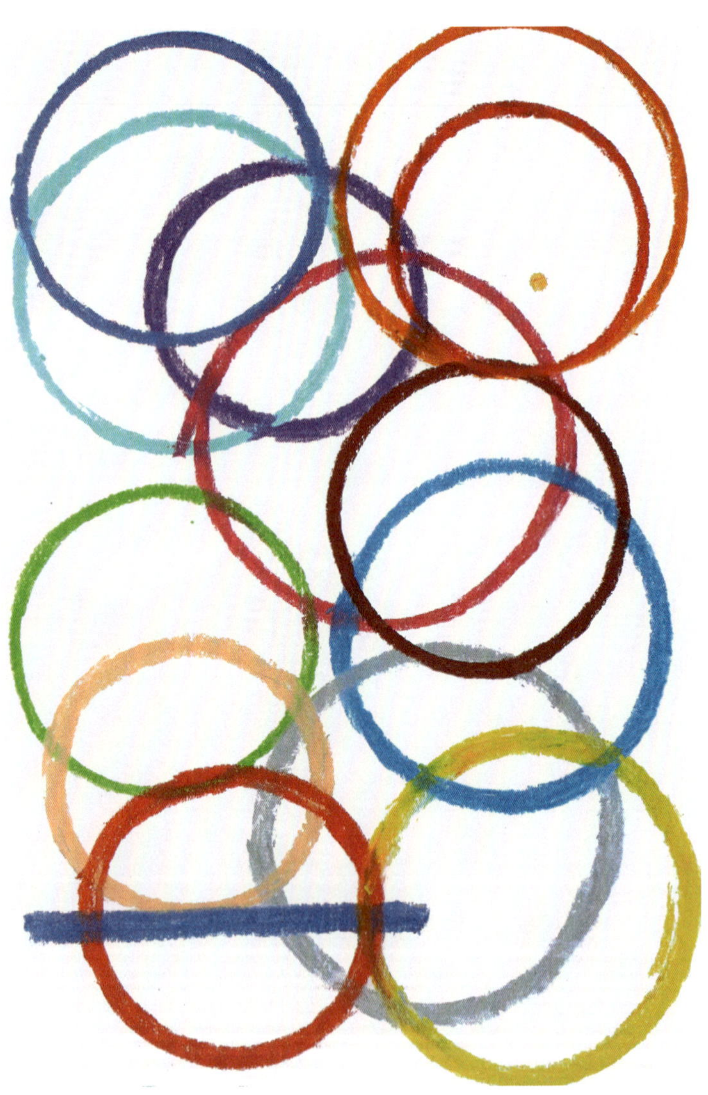

Marta Marcé
Circulating

I was thinking about the Tube as an endless system of circuits that takes you round and round the city. The Roundel took the form of the basic shape of a circle, element of endless movement, which I found beautifully fundamental.

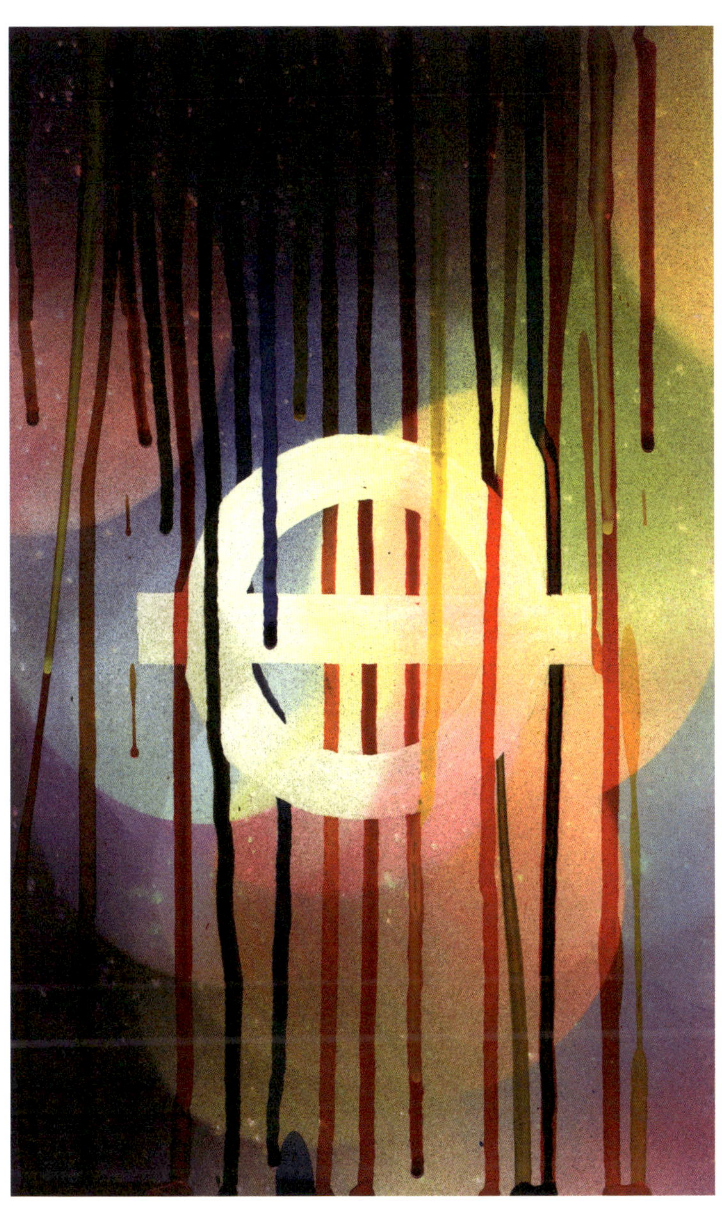

Paul McDevitt
Untitled

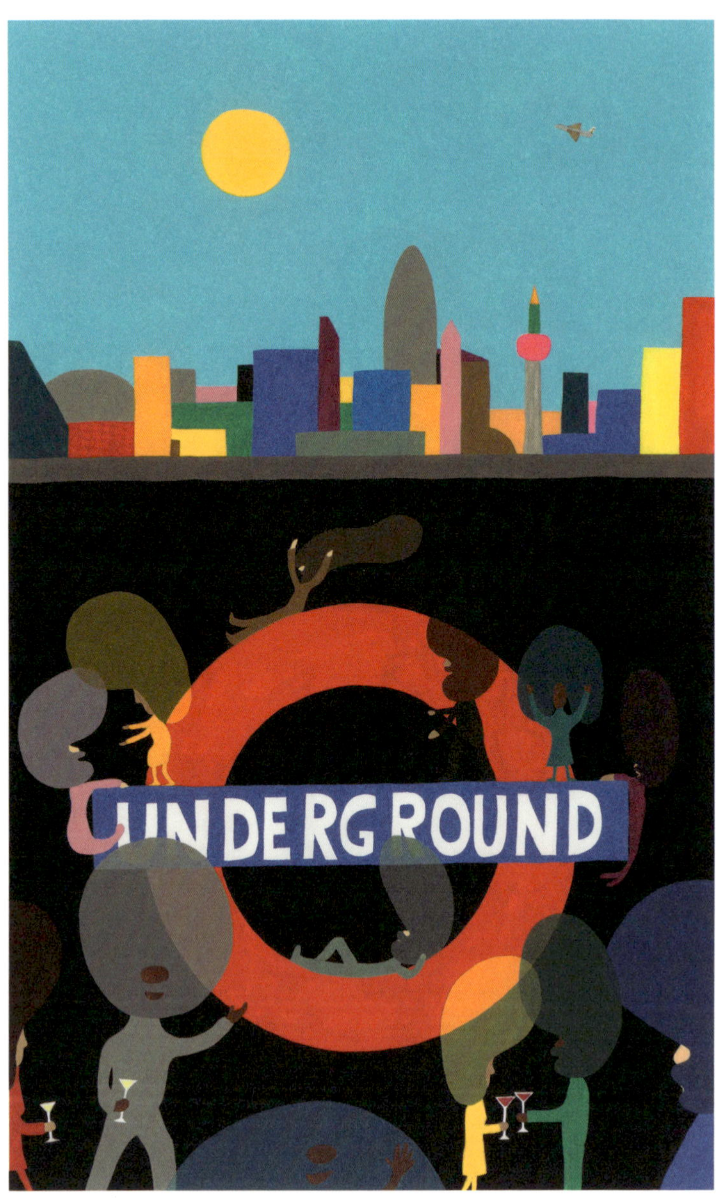

Peter McDonald
London Underground Party

Brown: Bakerloo, Red: Central, Yellow: Circle, Green: District, Orange: East London, Pink: Hammersmith and City, Grey: Jubilee, Deep Magenta: Metropolitan, Black: Northern, Ultramarine Blue: Piccadilly, Cerulean Blue: Victoria, Ash Green: Waterloo and City. And somebody in a blue-green dress.

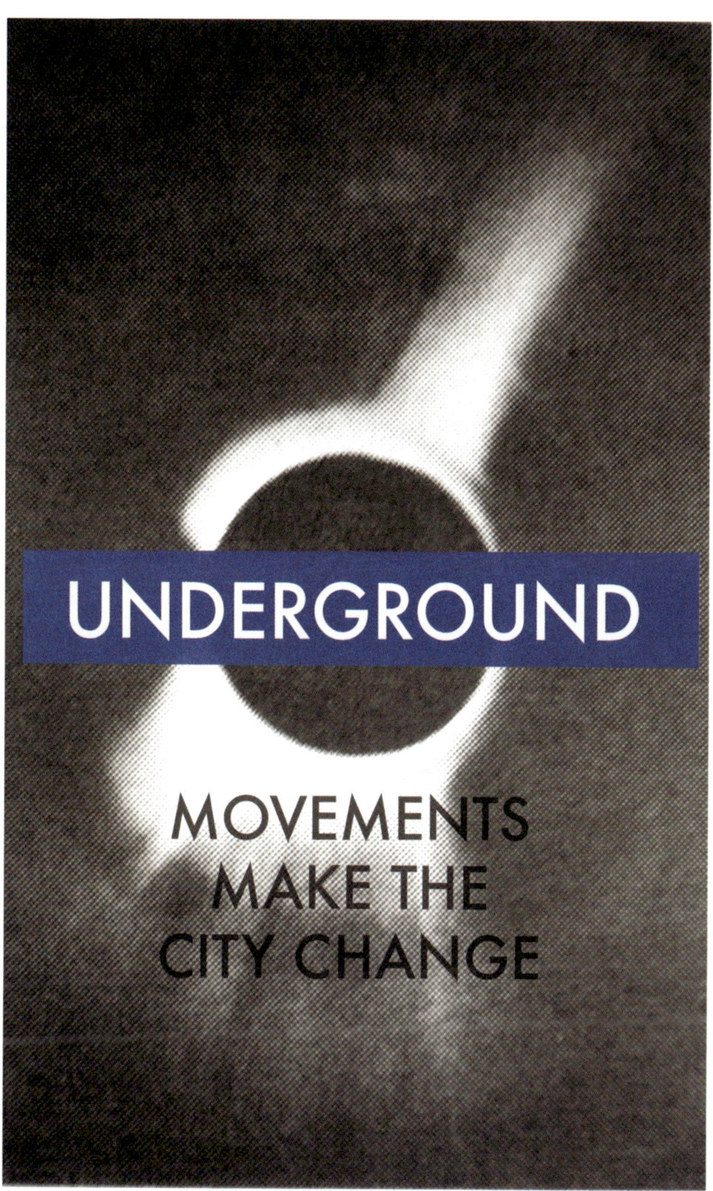

Eline McGeorge
*Movements Make
the City Change*

The Roundel logo can be seen everywhere throughout
the subway system, reminding us of the otherwise invisible
network of underground activity that fundamentally changes
our 'overground' life. Metaphorically and literally, 'Underground
movements make the city change.'

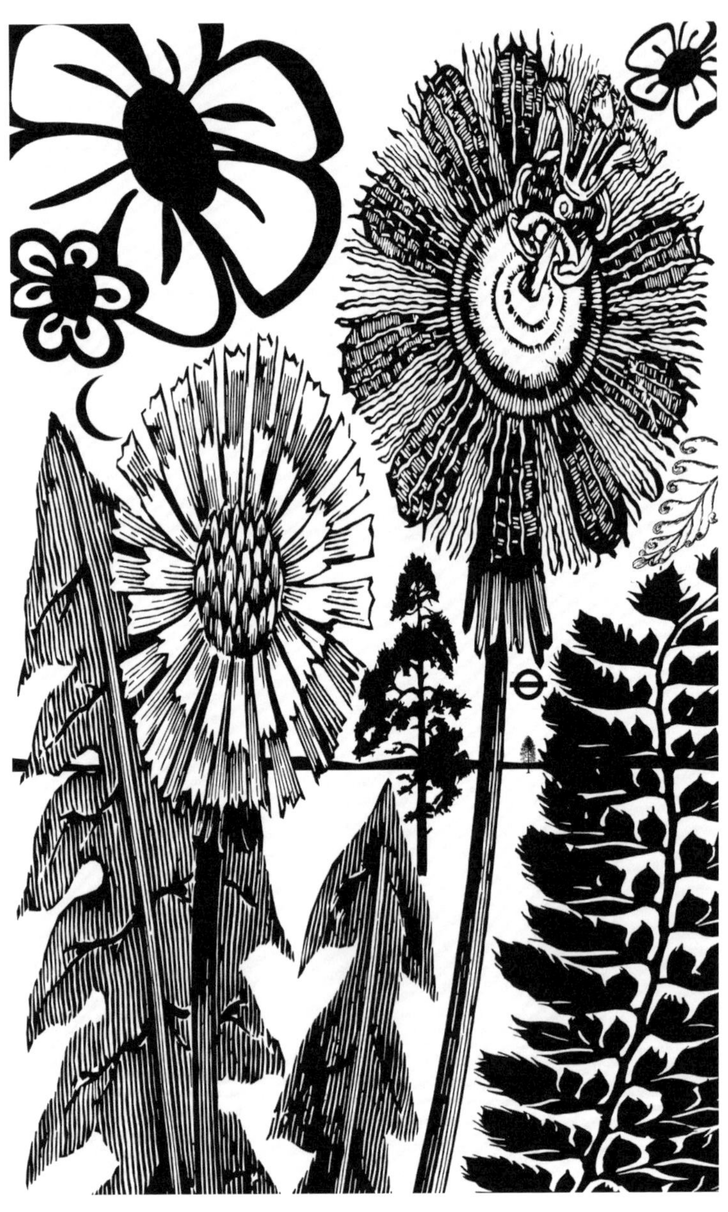

Paul Morrison
Pollonia

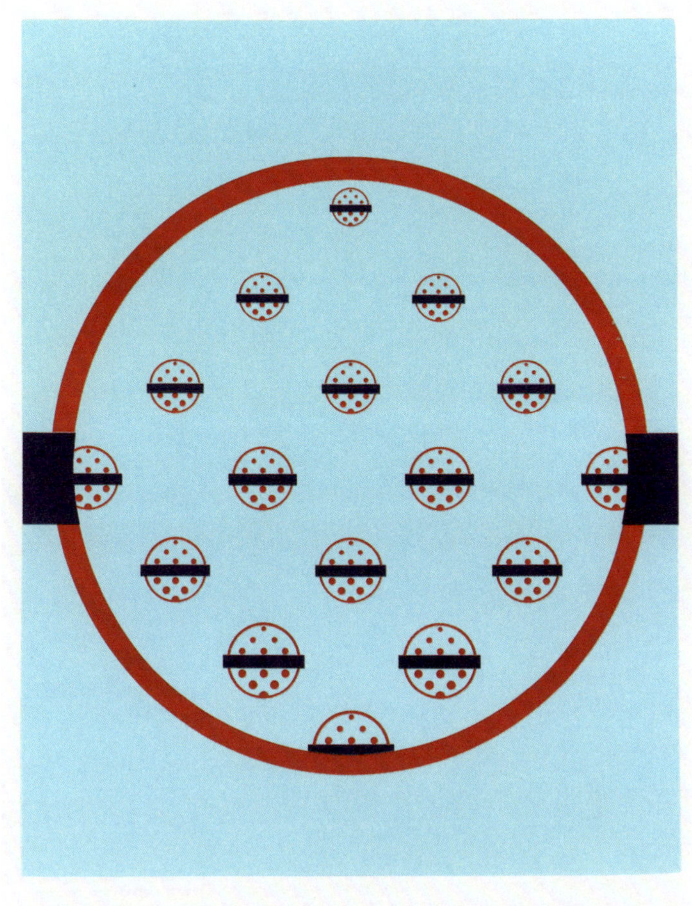

Jack Newling
Plans and Points

This is a three-colour screenprint that crops, shrinks and repeats the Roundel logo to make a poster where the graphic puts the motif in motion.

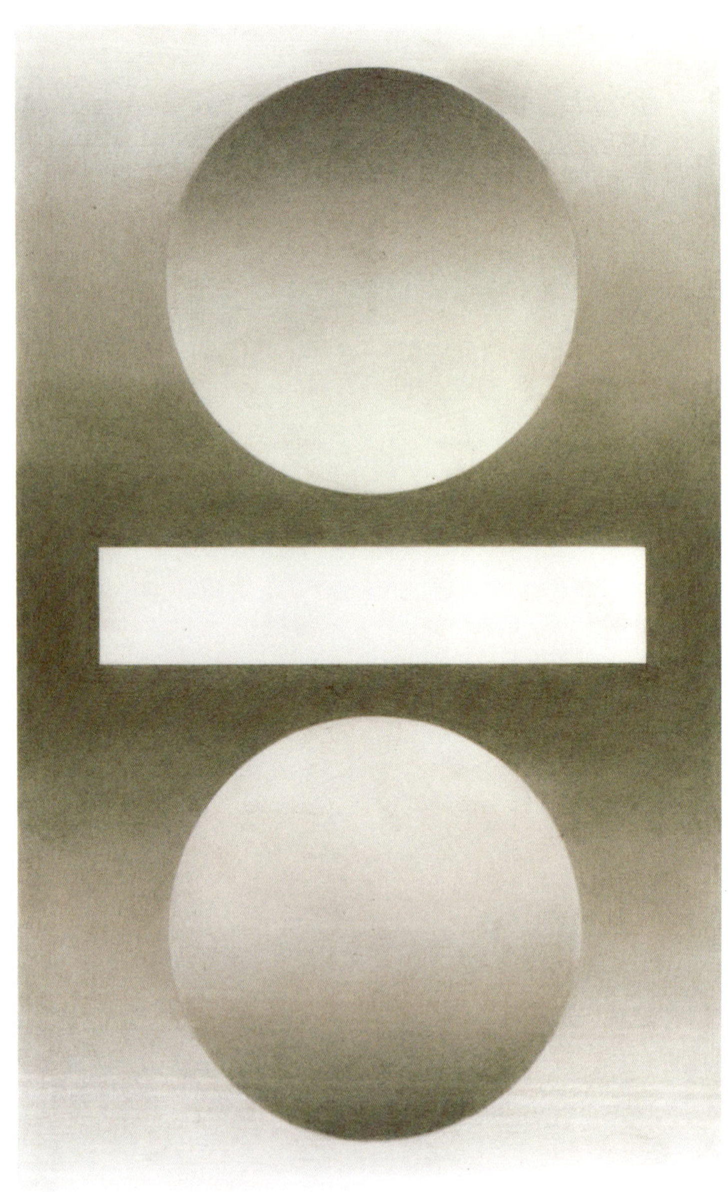

Paul Noble
O I O

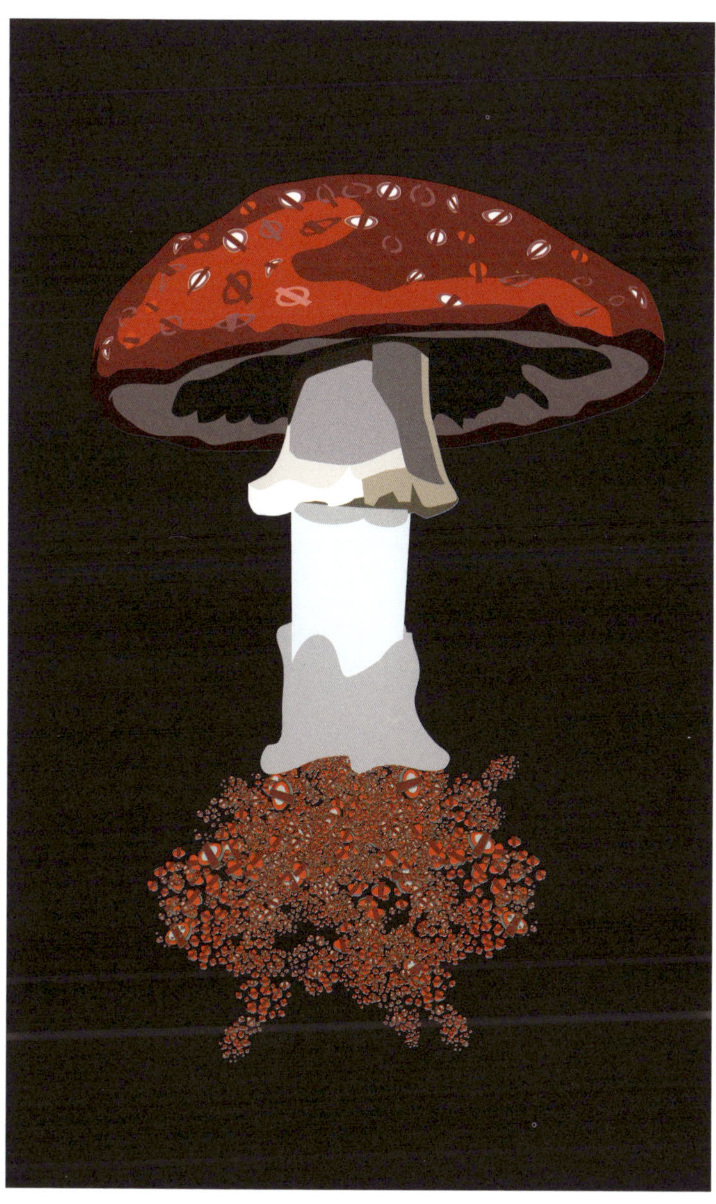

Nils Norman
PPP Mushroom

A Public-Private Partnership (PPP) as a poisonous and psychoactive fungus.

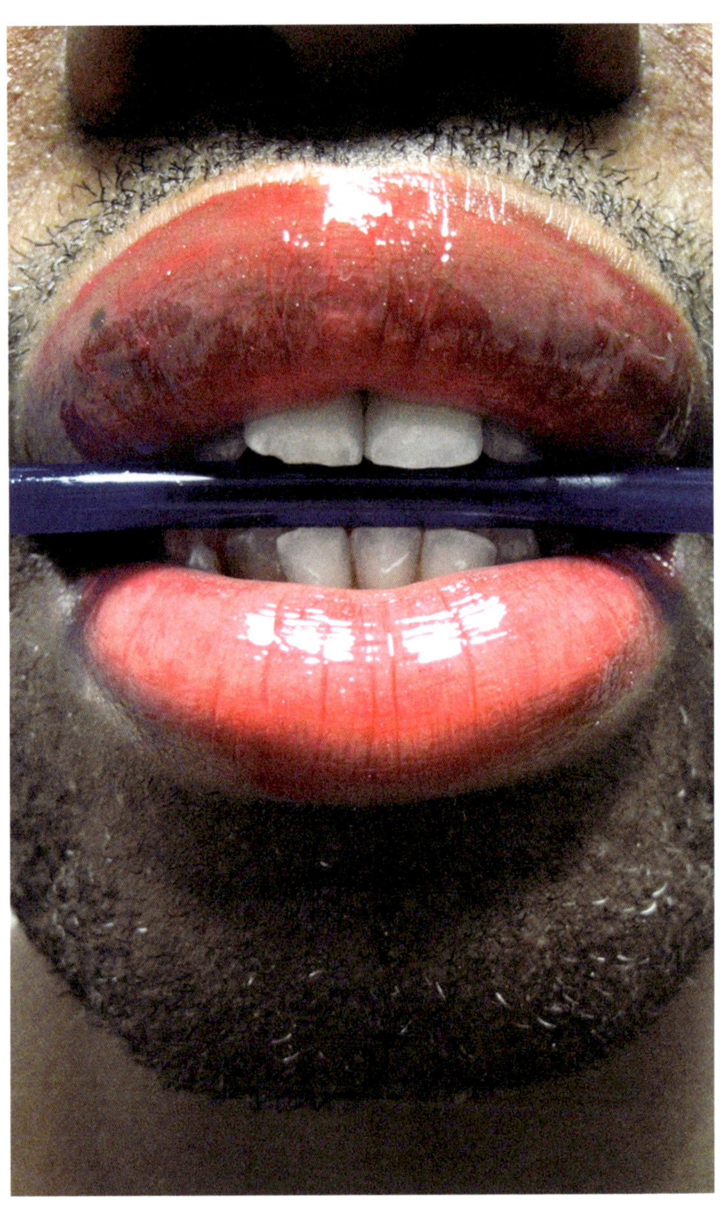

Harold Offeh
Lips & Tube

The Roundel is ever present in my daily life. Its image *is* the London Underground. I often explore ideas through performative actions or gestures and I wanted to see if I could re-create the Roundel by just using my body.

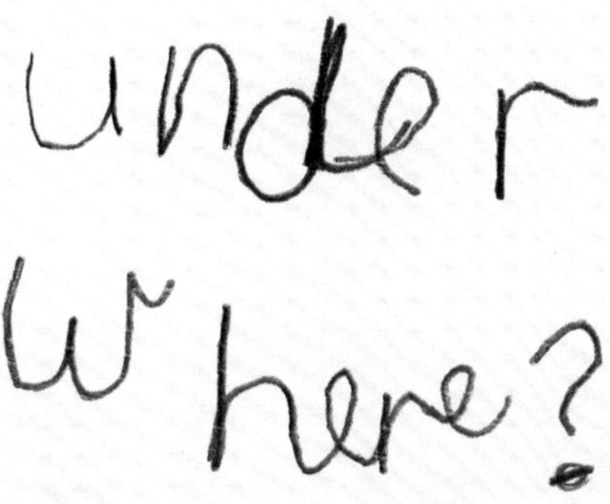

Cornelia Parker
Under Where?

Travelling on the Underground, my young daughter would
ask 'Where are we? What part of London are we under now?'
A question I found hard to answer, the Underground map being
a remix of geography rather than an accurate representation.

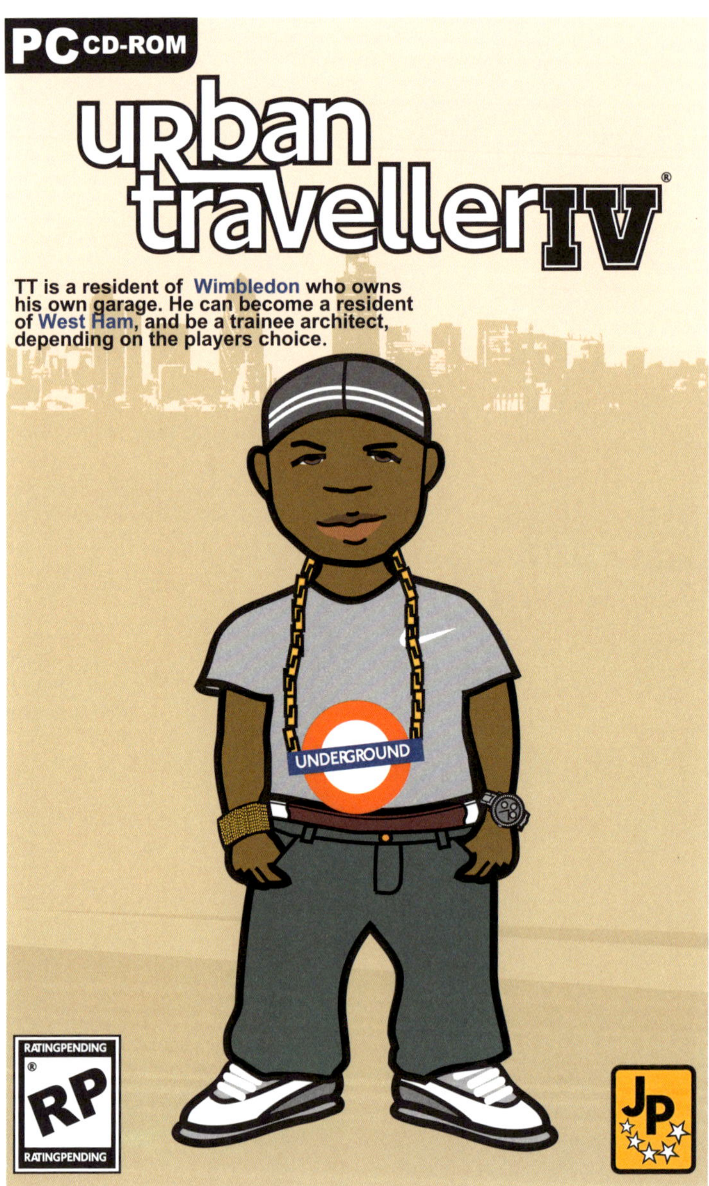

Janette Parris
Urban Traveller

The Roundel inspired me to design a computer-game character called Urban Traveller who wears an oversized Roundel pendant as a desirable bit of bling.

90

Toby Paterson
Pastel Roundel
(Low Visibility)

This work draws on another famous British roundel, that of the RAF, and inverts the Underground symbol's graphic clarity by adopting the low-visibility colour palette first applied to military aircraft in the 1980s, thus rendering its meaning uncertain.

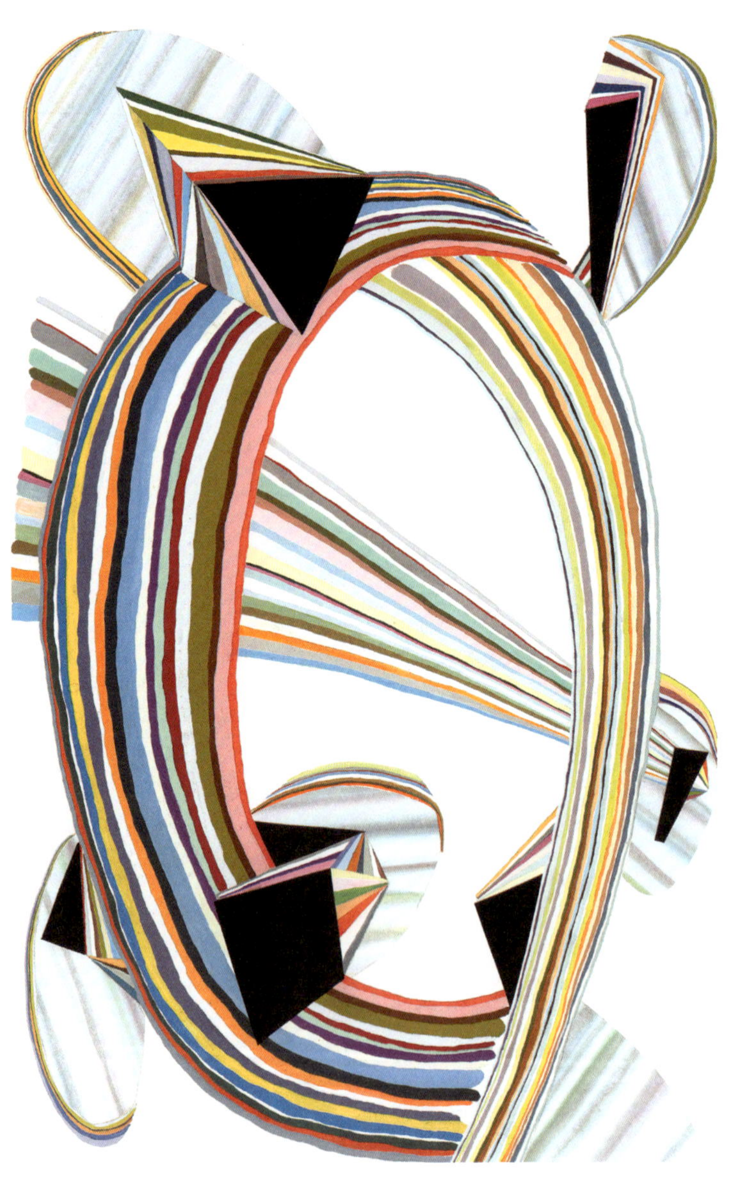

Paul Peden
Untitled

I wanted to make a simple and dynamic image. Something that built upon the Roundel's classic design but contained an inherent complexity and rhythmic energy, perhaps echoing that found within the Tube network itself.

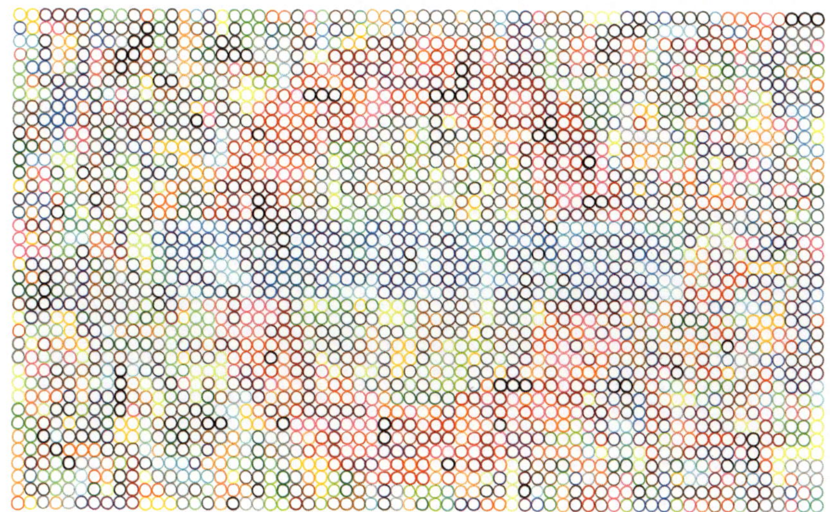

Paola Pivi
Time to Circle

Live life in comfort.

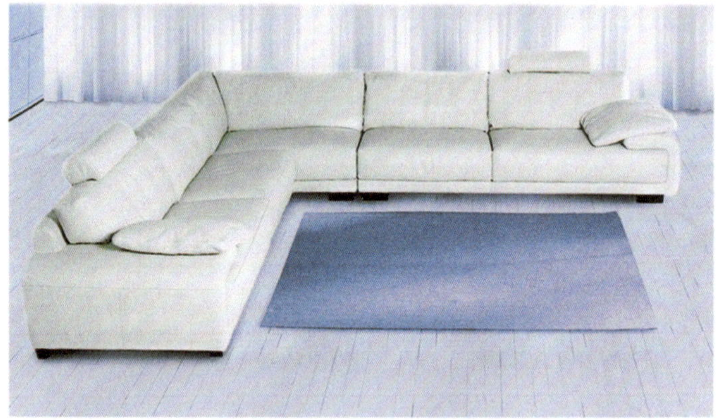

We are working on making your journey more comfortable.
With new advancements in our seat design you might just not
want to get off at your stop...

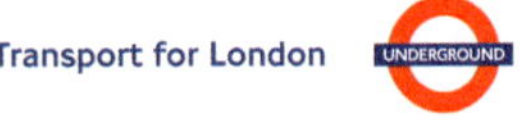

Sam Plagerson
Live Life in Comfort

This is inspired by early Tube posters and British Rail adverts, presenting travel as a utopian enterprise. The Roundel is used in this case as a branding of lifestyle marketing, and what the poster proposes is a complete deception.

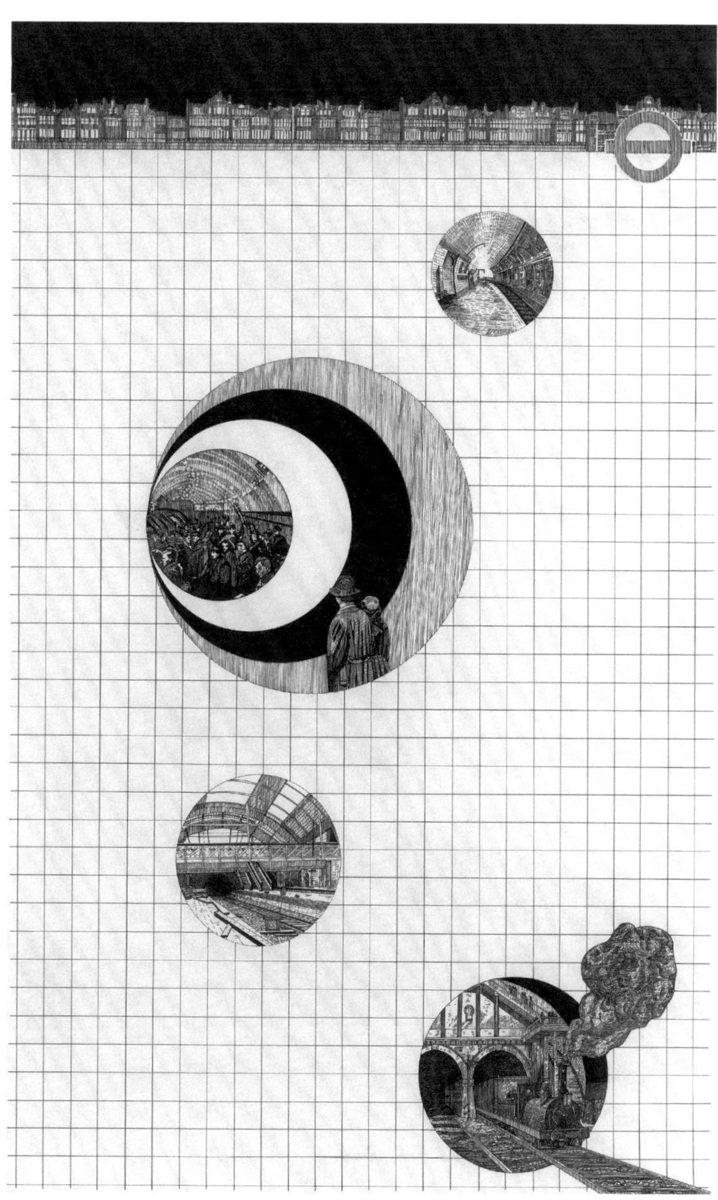

Olivia Plender

*A desire to have the best
of both worlds*

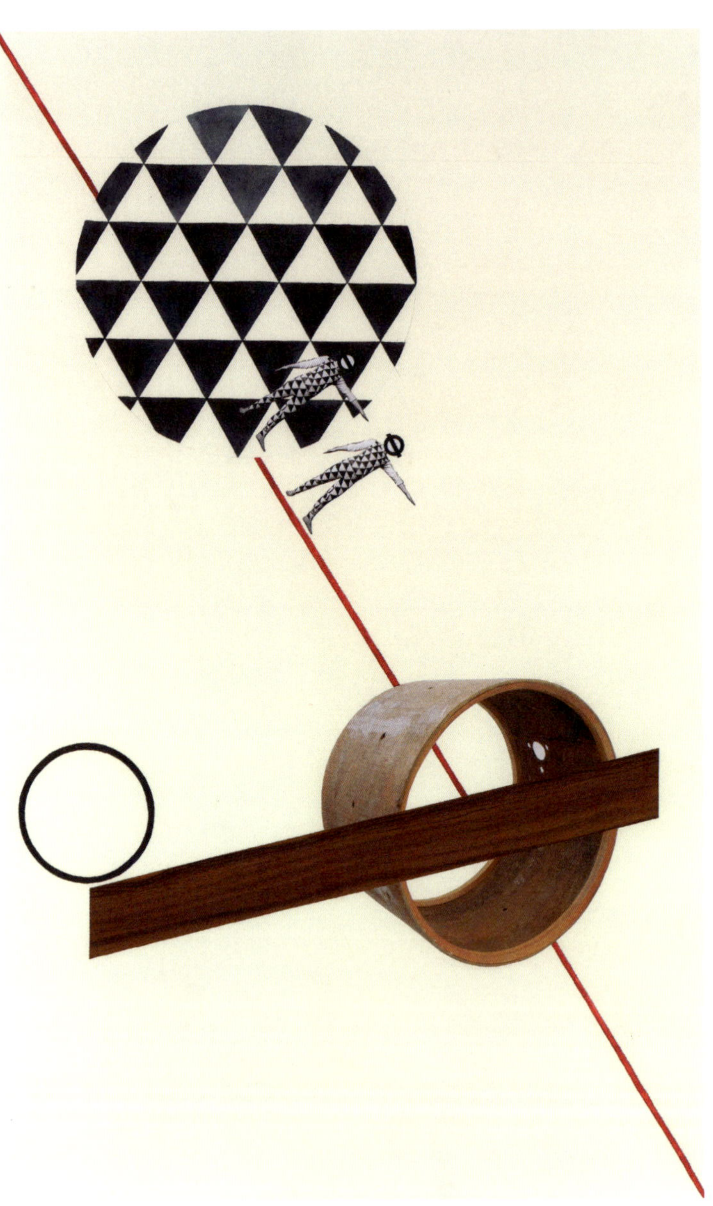

Ruth Proctor
Every One an Island

The Roundel seems like both a tunnel and an island in the midst of the city. Each pointing to another place and time; people walking, gliding, moving in their own worlds, drifting in a sea of others to a destination undisclosed.

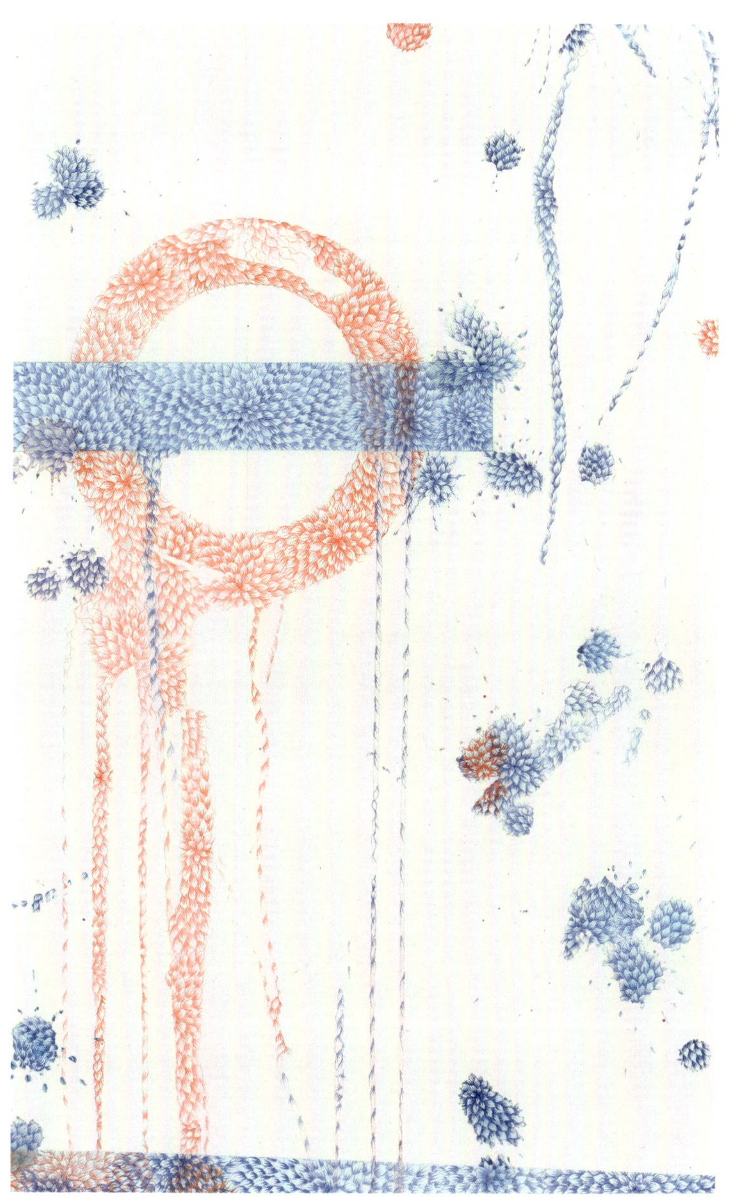

Imran Qureshi
Art on the Platform

I have always been fascinated by the culture of the London Underground. With this work, I have tried to bring nature in the shape of foliate patterns inside Tube stations, where usually there is a complete lack of sunlight or verdant landscapes. These foliate seepages are a testament to both the beauty and resilience of nature.

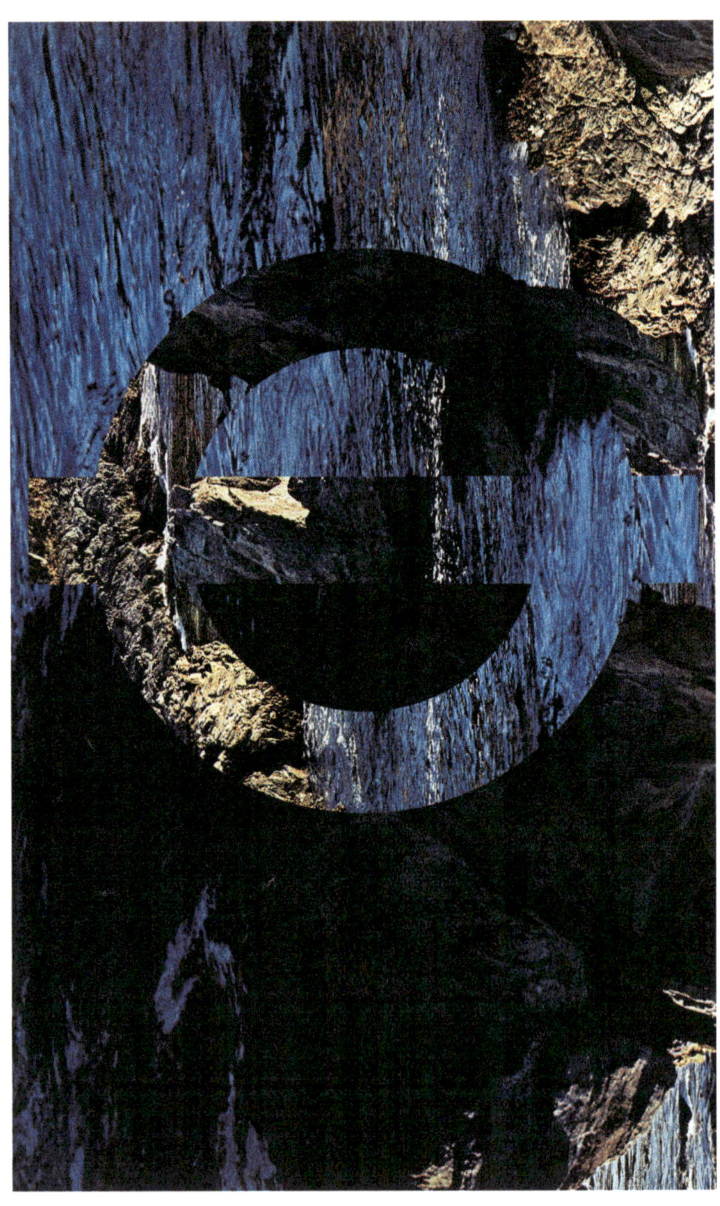

Damien Roach
Variation #6 (Roundel)

A transport system rewires space in a literal and conceptual way, radically transforming perceptions of a city's temporal and geographic characteristics. I hope that this and other ideas are somehow refracted through the poster.

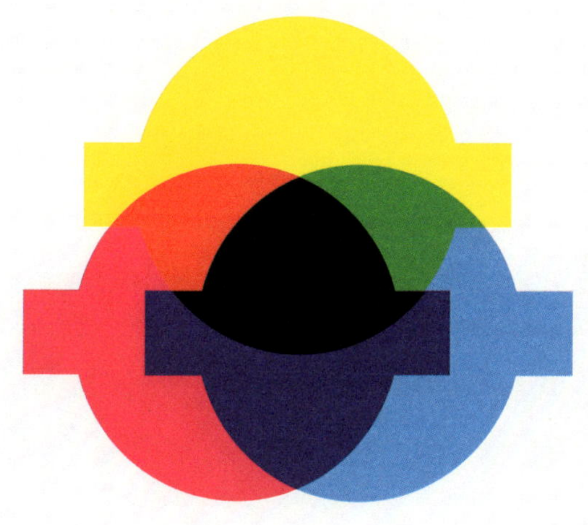

Roland Ross
Untitled

I chose to directly appropriate the Cyan, Magenta, Yellow,
Key (CMYK) colour diagram by removing its corresponding
text and applying its colour usage to that of the similarly
shaped Roundel.

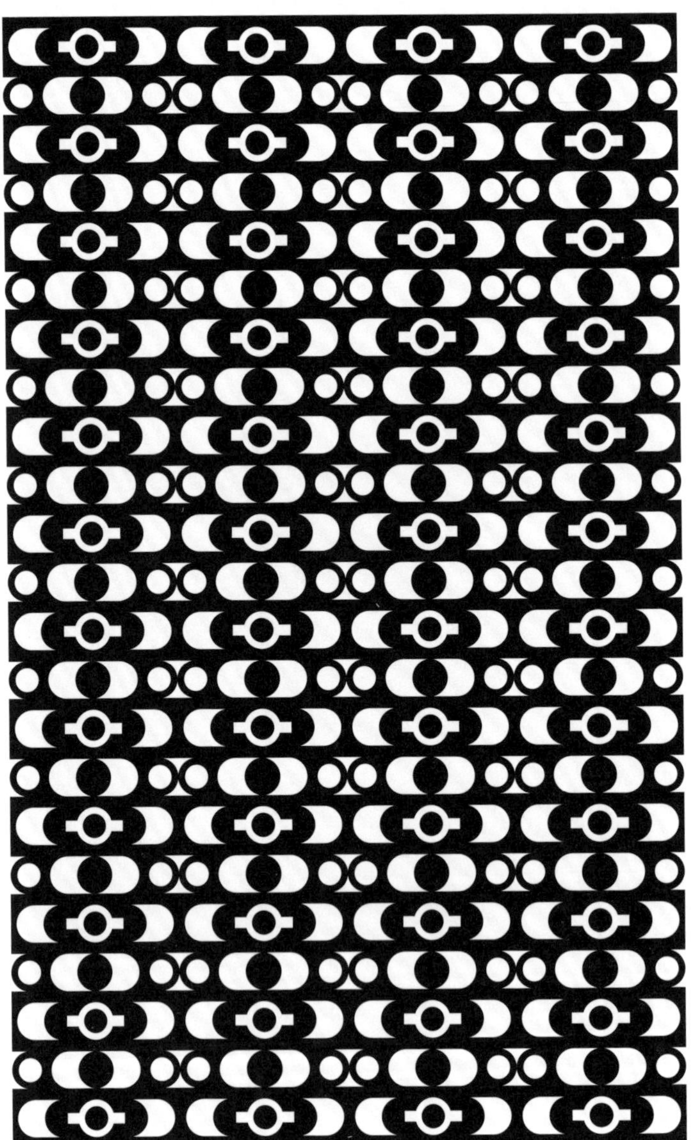

Giles Round
Fabric Design for the
London Underground

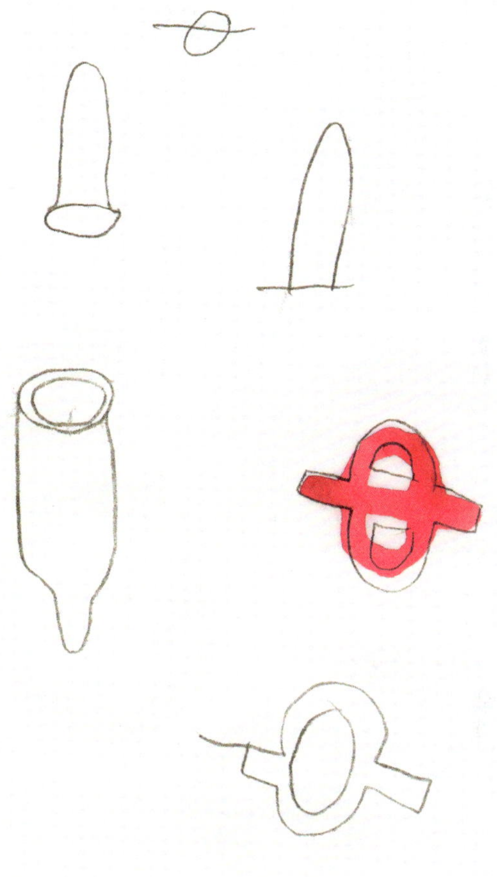

Paul Ryan
Travel Safely

The Roundel commission followed my exhibition 'REBOUND: Two Decades of Notes on HIV', at the Wellcome Collection in London. I imagined a 'Safer Sex' poster, maybe for World AIDS Day, containing a Roundel shape (perhaps inappropriately?) as a condom.

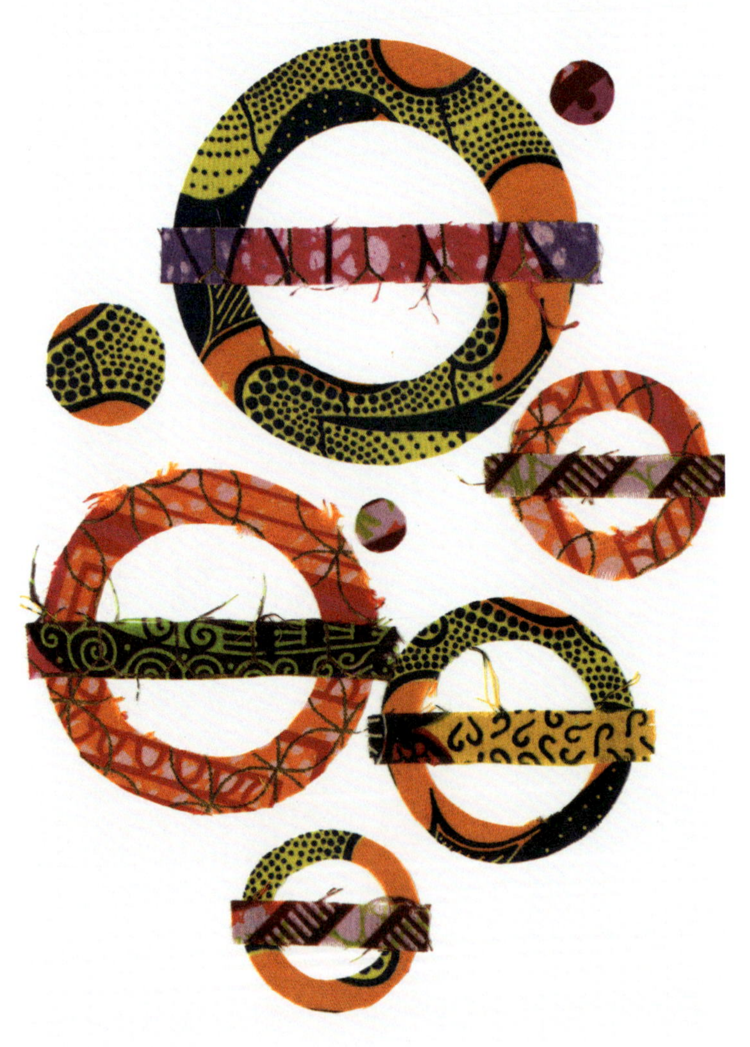

Yinka Shonibare MBE
Untitled

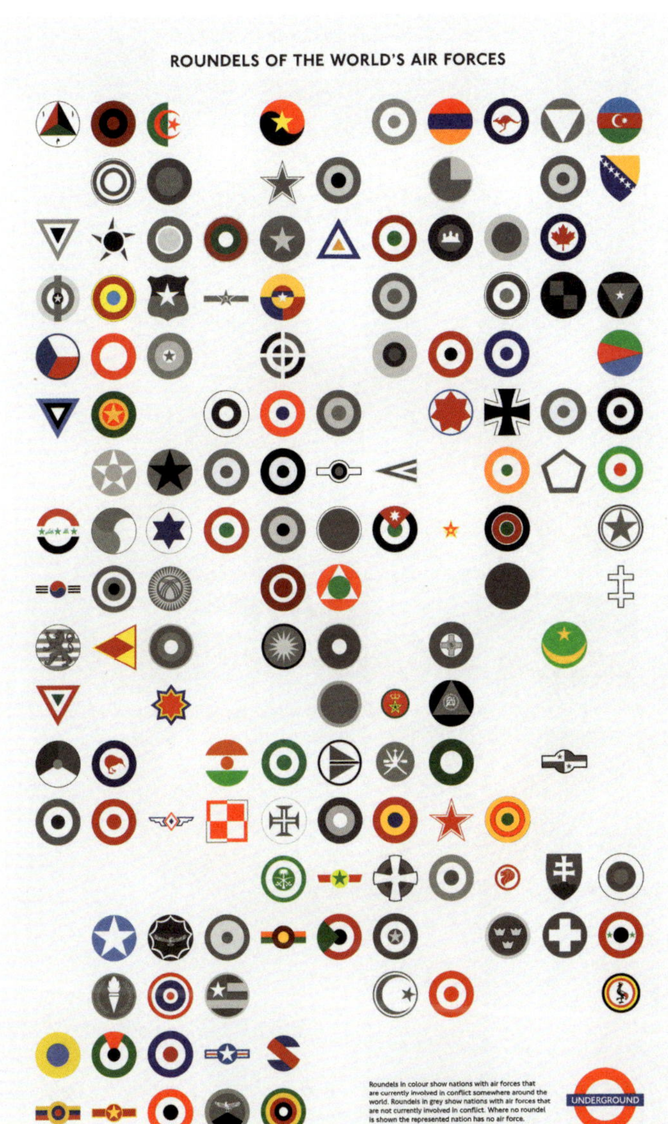

Jamie Shovlin
*Untitled (Roundels of
the World's Air Forces)*

Nations, represented by their air-force roundel, are arranged right to left, top to bottom in alphabetical order. Roundels in colour show nations involved in conflict somewhere around the world. Roundels in grey show nations that are not involved in conflict. Where no roundel is shown, the represented nation has no air force.

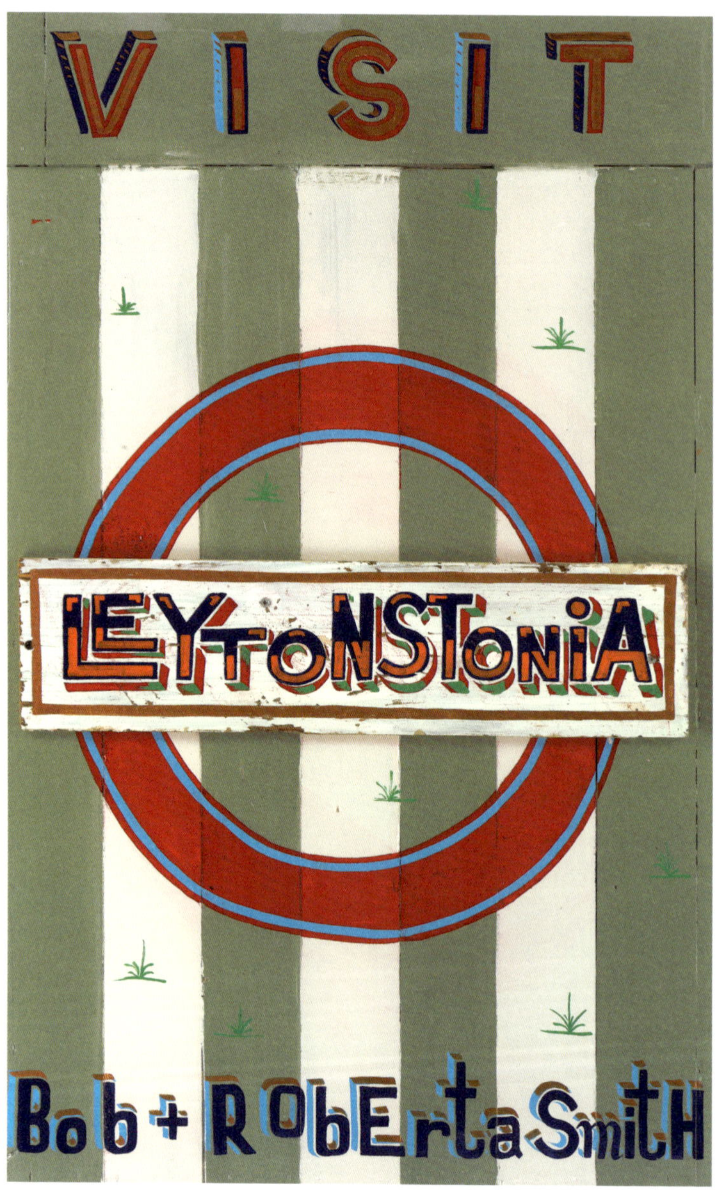

Bob and Roberta Smith
Visit Leytonstonia

When I made this Roundel painting in 2008, I wanted to invite people to travel to the uninspiring suburbs just like Underground posters of the 1940s and 1950s. Now the joke is on me: Leytonstone is full of pubs and cafés packed with film-makers and young people.

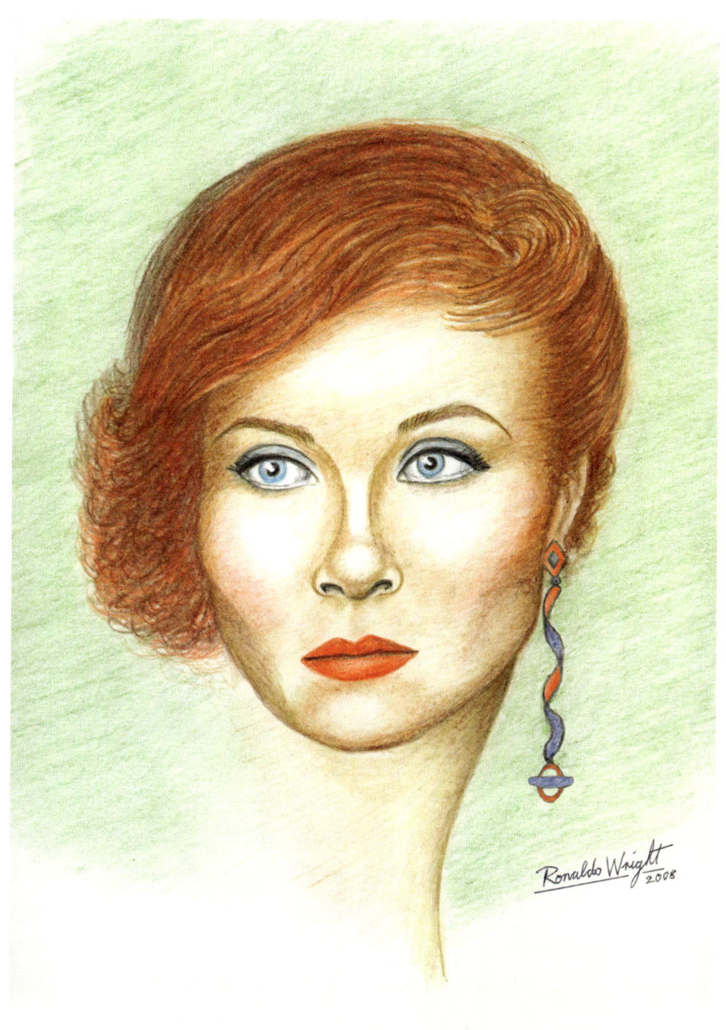

Georgina Starr
*Portrait of Georgina
with a Roundel earring*

This is a portrait by the artist Ronaldo Wright. In the 1950s, he spent his time in London's theatre dressing rooms drawing the stars. The Roundel anniversary coincided with Ronaldo's eightieth birthday, so I invited him to make a portrait incorporating the symbol. I sat happily listening to his tales of travelling around the city and meeting Marlene Dietrich, Vivien Leigh and Mae West.

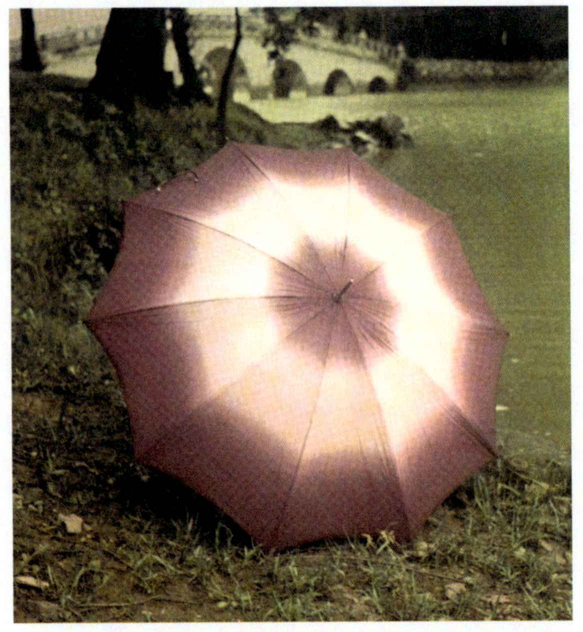

John Stezaker
Lost Image

The image came from a catalogue of Chinese crafts from the period of the Cultural Revolution. It is the first of my 'Lost' images. (Being lost is a precondition to being found). The Roundel shares the combination of circularity and linearity with the umbrella. It seemed the ideal image in which to 'find' the Roundel and to be found in the Underground because of the long association between umbrellas and lost-property offices.

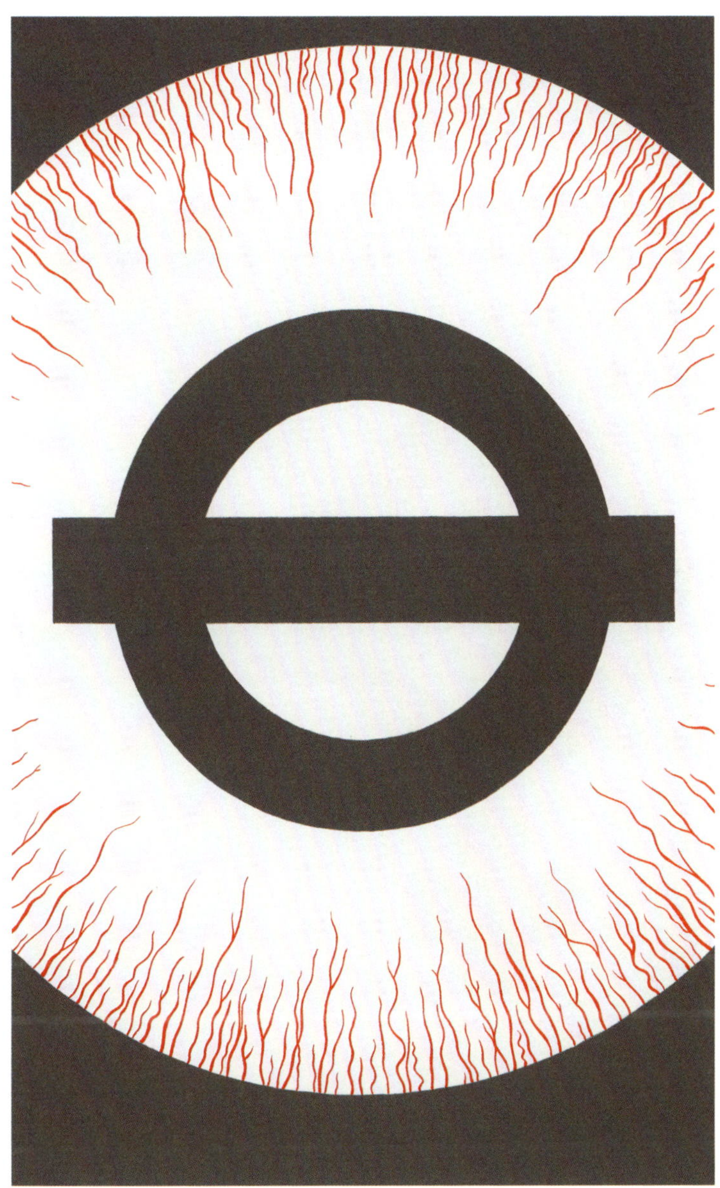

Vincent Tavenne
Untitled

Circles are an ever-recurring motif in my work.
You can see them as:

a zero, a pea, a washer, a button, a marble, a mouse-hole,
a bottle top, an eye, a flower, a slice of sausage, a plate,
a clock, a football, a melon, a wheel, a sign for public
transport, the end of the tunnel, a ferris wheel, the globe,
a planet, the sun, the universe.

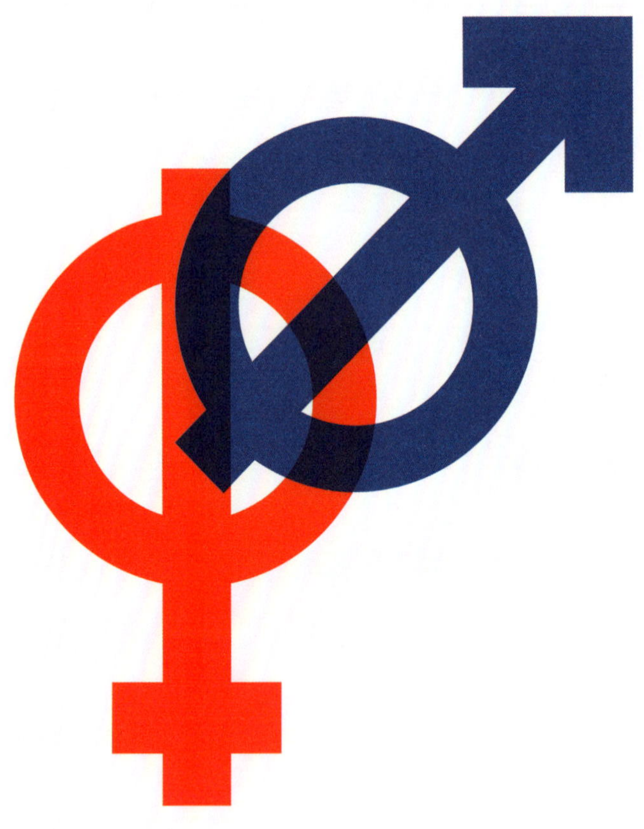

Mark Titchner
All in One, One in All

Ebbs and flows, knots and dissolutions. All in One, One in All. A Roundel for all of us and the space we share, offices.

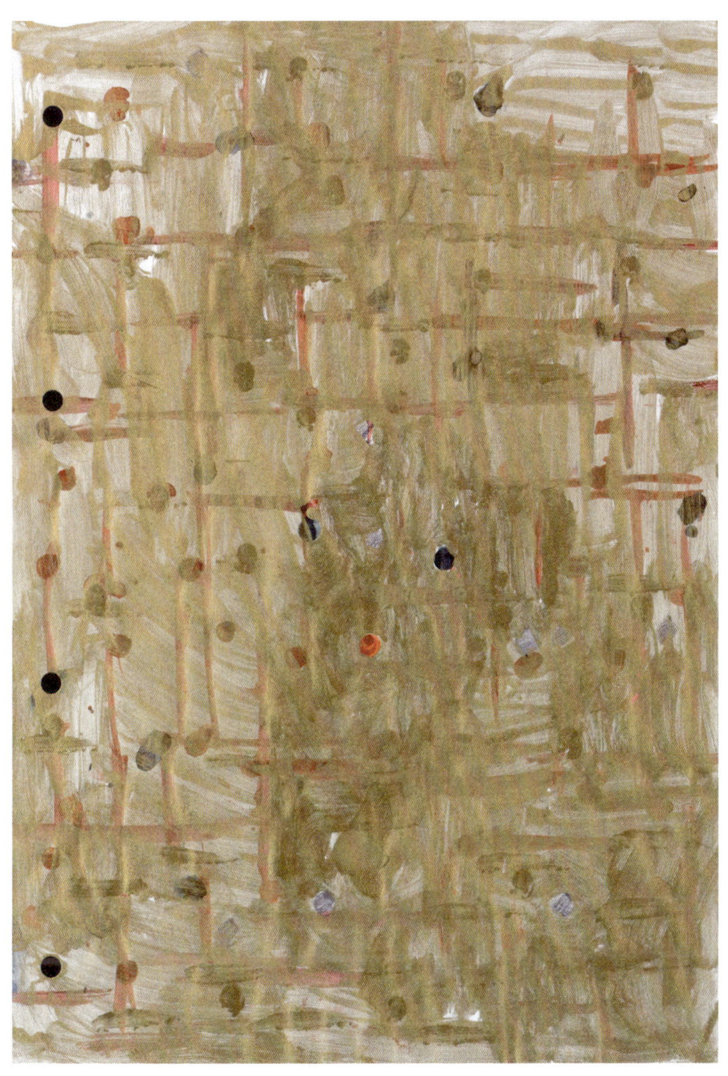

Hayley Tompkins
Inclusion

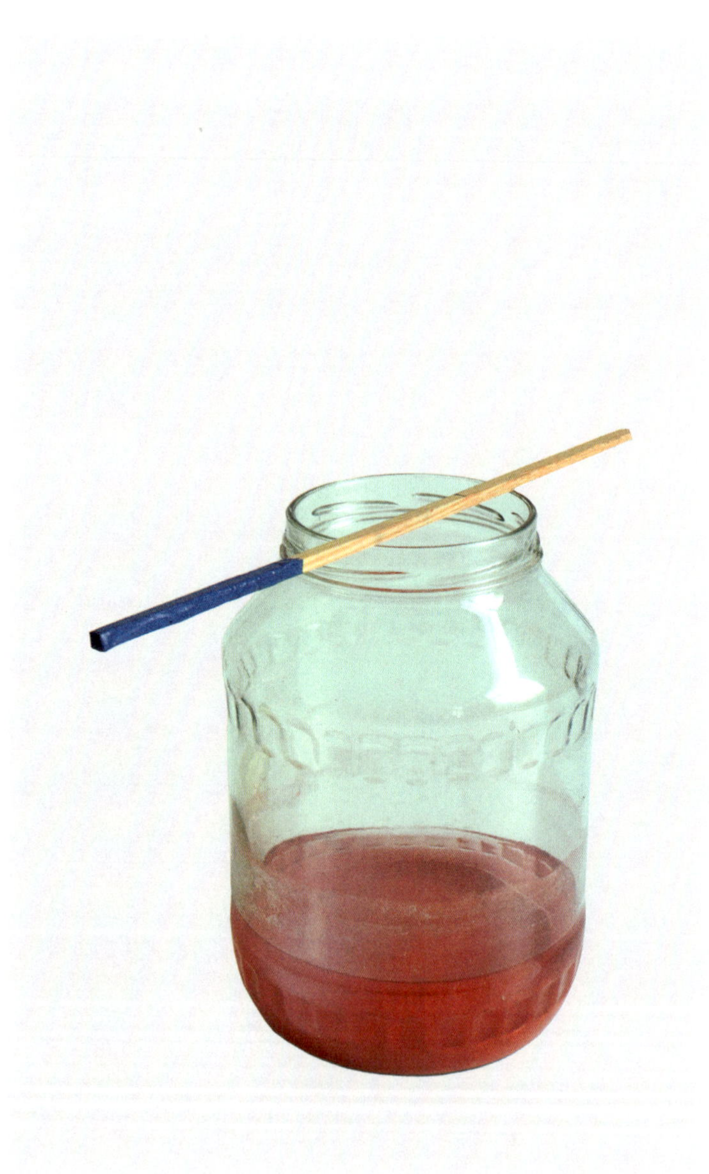

Joëlle Tuerlinckx
Detail d'atelier trouvé — for Art on the Underground

strip of blue colour on a red round volume, a red under a blue. a base. an object object (a wooden stick on / barring the object). the object: a jar of past red (having been there).

110

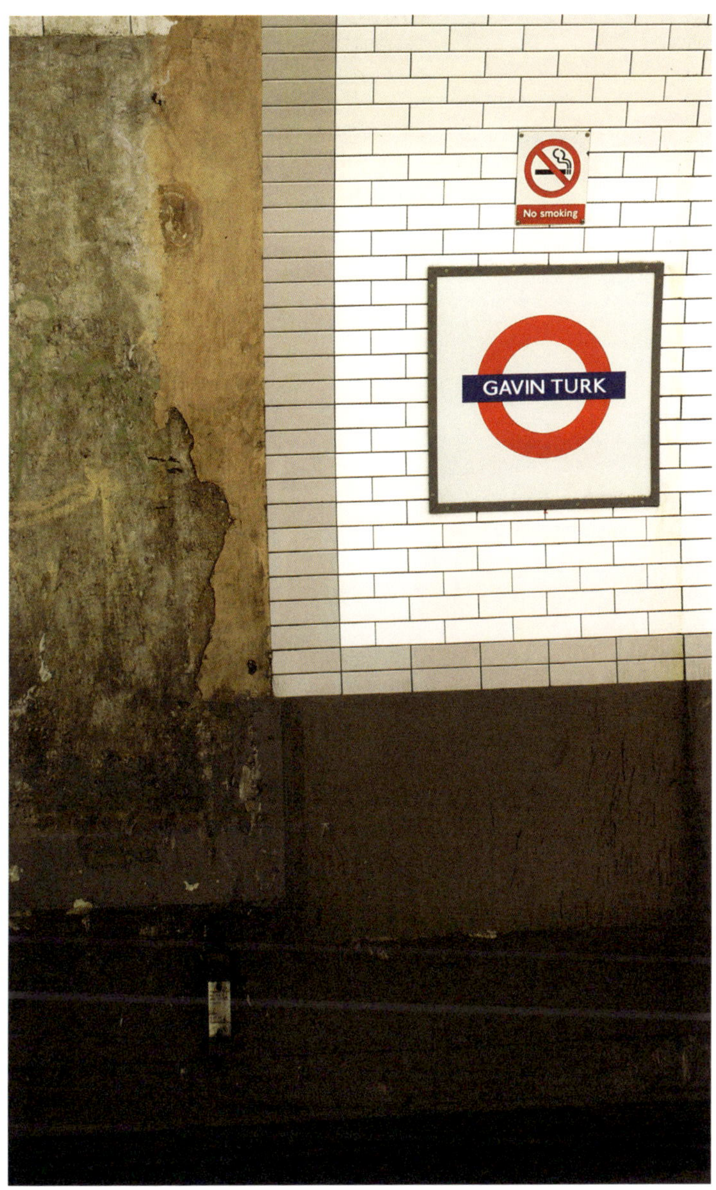

Gavin Turk
Untitled

The Roundel is a cliché, a touristic thing, quintessentially London. It's a space between visitors to the city. It's a crossing out, a 'no entry' sign. Yet it joins everyone up.

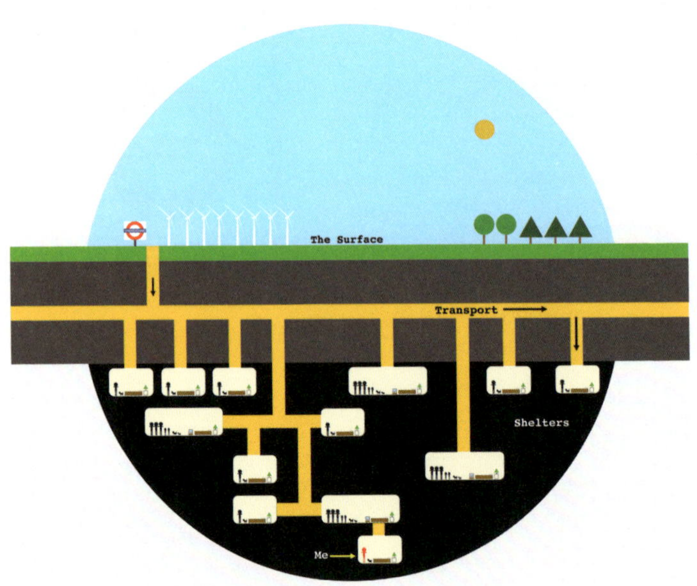

Charlie Tweed

It's time to go below

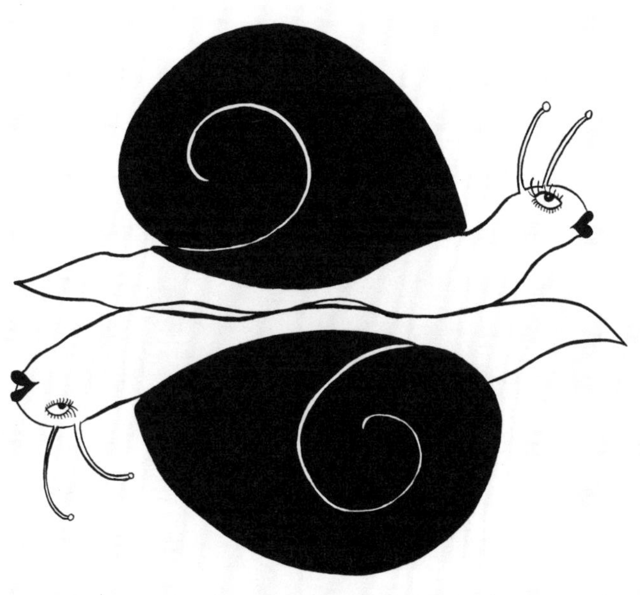

Donald Urquhart
Snail Roundel

London's Underground, although enchanting, at times goes
at the pace of two snails lazily copulating with indifference.
I have endeavoured to suggest this graphically, but endearingly
too as we can't help but forgive this flawed relic and vital aorta.

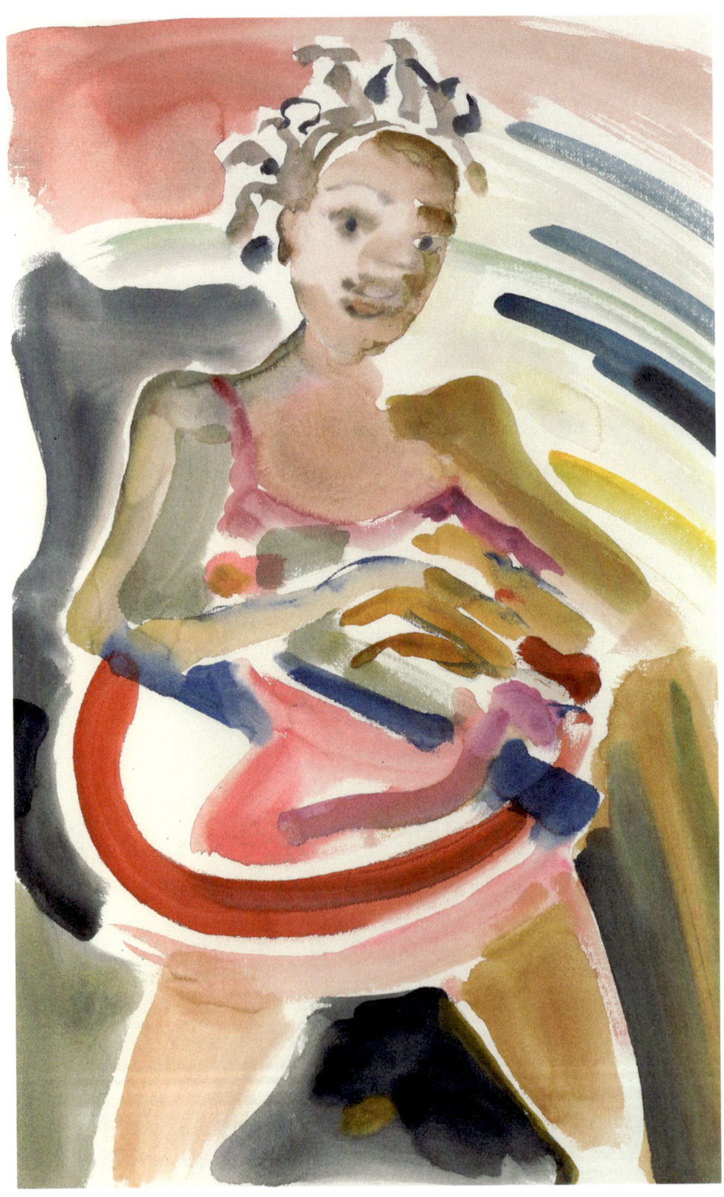

Sophie von Hellermann
One of Seven Sisters

It's an imaginary portrait of a young girl who might get on the Tube to meet friends, enjoying a swift fluid connection in a train finding its way through the tunnels like her body through the ring of the hula hoop.

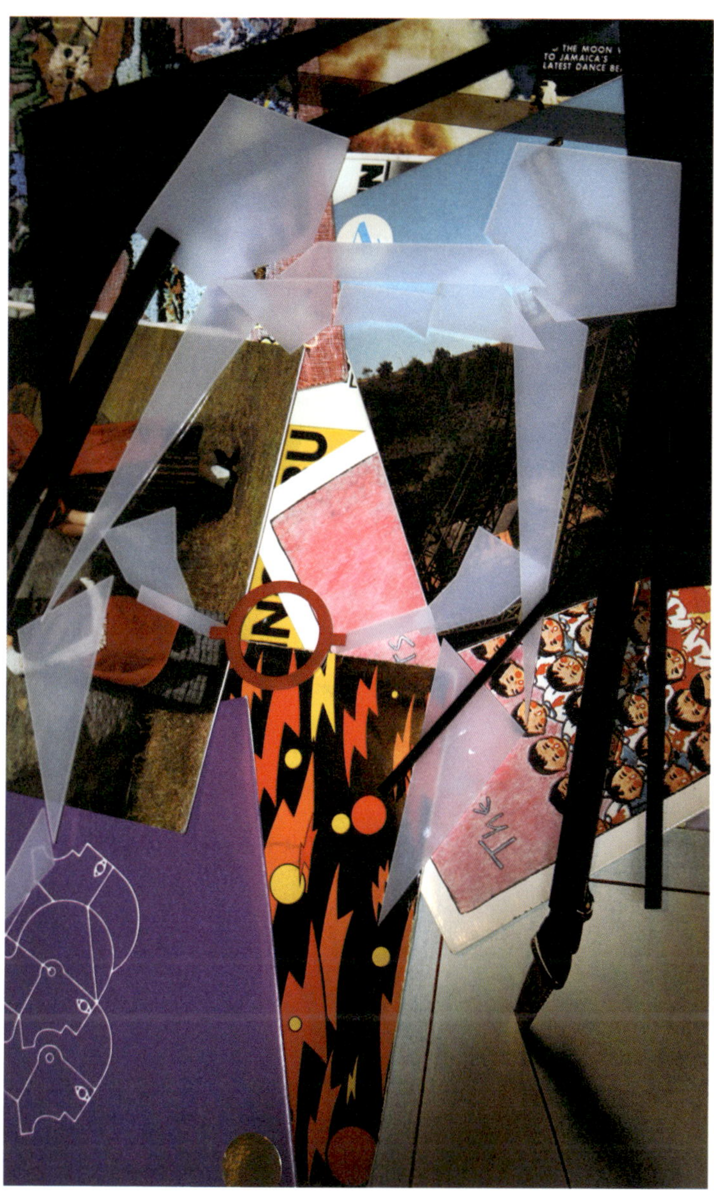

Emily Wardill
NUN

I wanted to make a poster for an imaginary band called
NUN where the nun's mouth would be the Tube sign —
red and glossy. This band, in my mind, are dressed in
naked knitted fat suits.

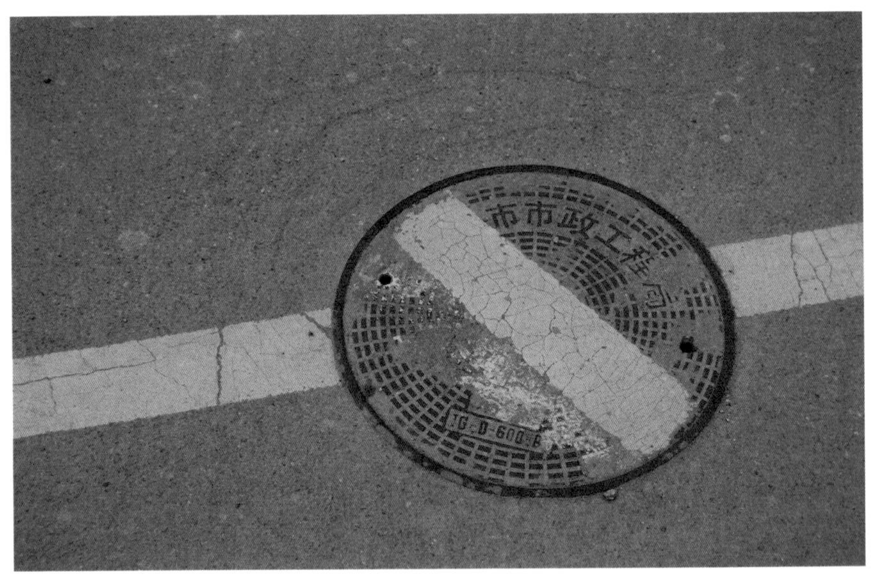

Richard Wentworth
Chinese Whispers
(Underground)

The Underground Roundel struck through with the bold horizontal was a fine way to propose reliability and order.

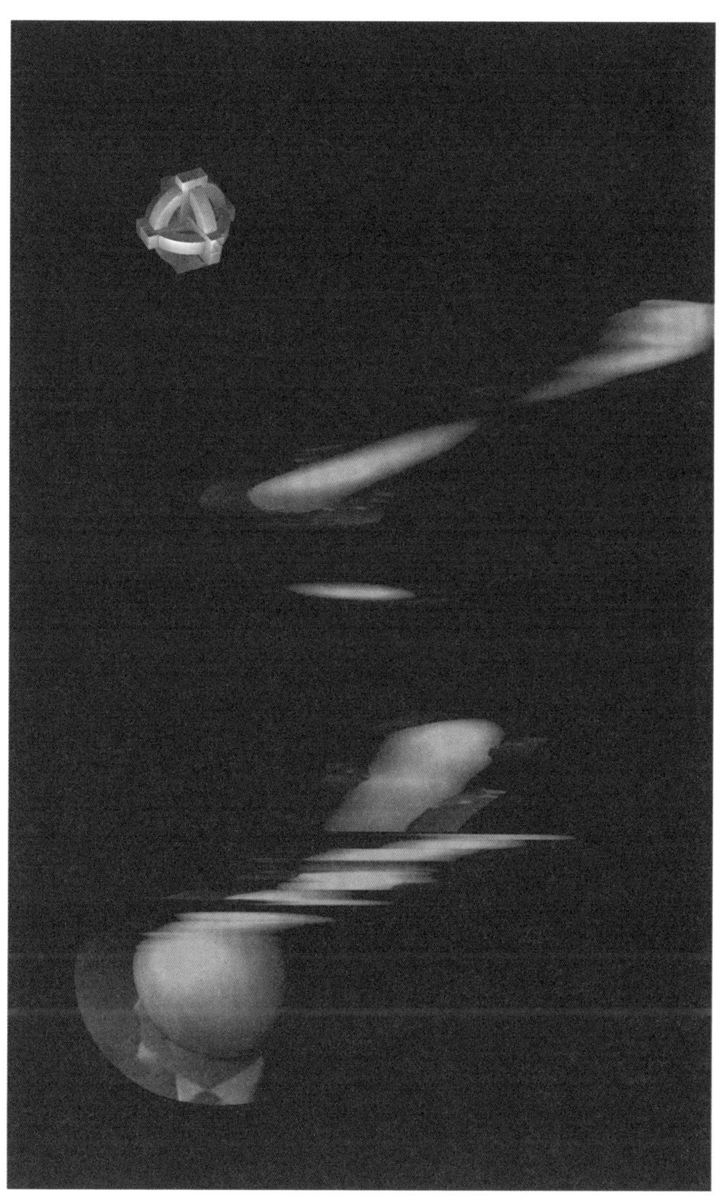

Martin Westwood
Roundel Puzzle

Man Ray's Roundel poster presents a comparative arena of two distinct space–time constructs. Above, an extruding Roundel courses forward with one-dimensional linearity; below, a solar-ringed planet turns along its two-dimensional axis, caught in a continuous returning motion with no beginning, end or escape velocity.

Pae White
Overground

Overground is intended to reference a Tube inversion …
a sudden blast of brilliant daylight in the depth of the
endless darkness.

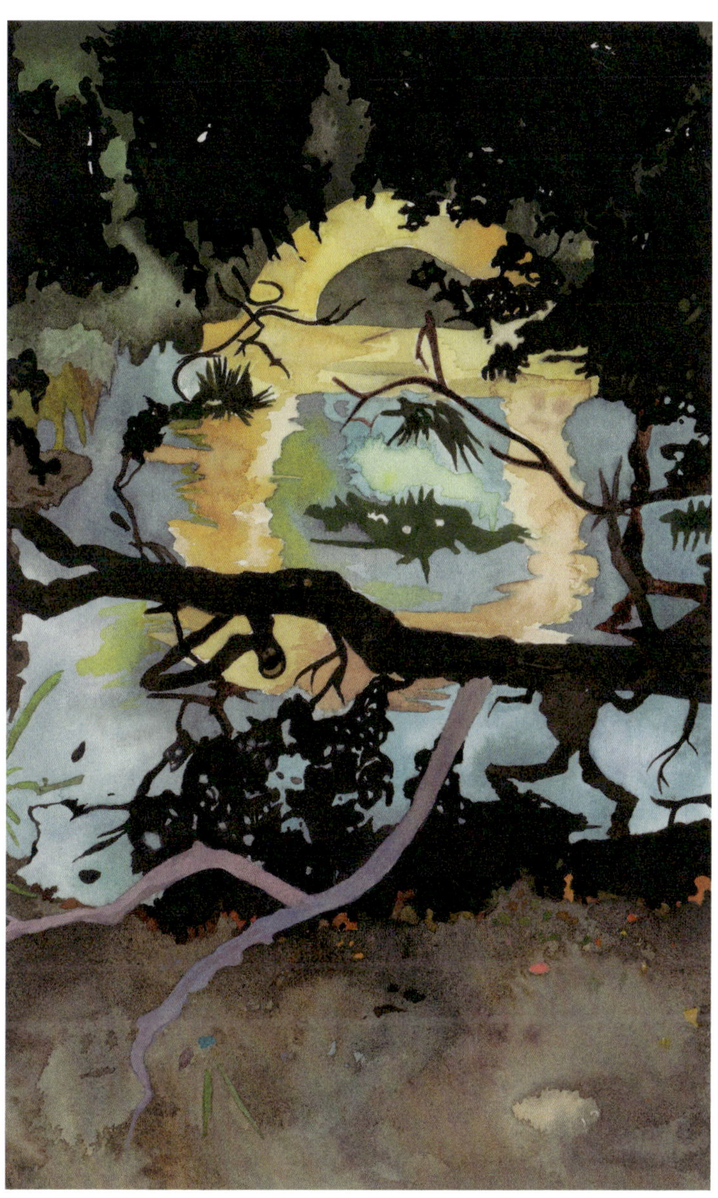

Clare Woods
Hollow Pool

The Roundel for me was the image of escape – leaving the city for those little bits of countryside on the edge of London. But when you arrived, they were never as appealing as they looked in the 1930s Underground posters.

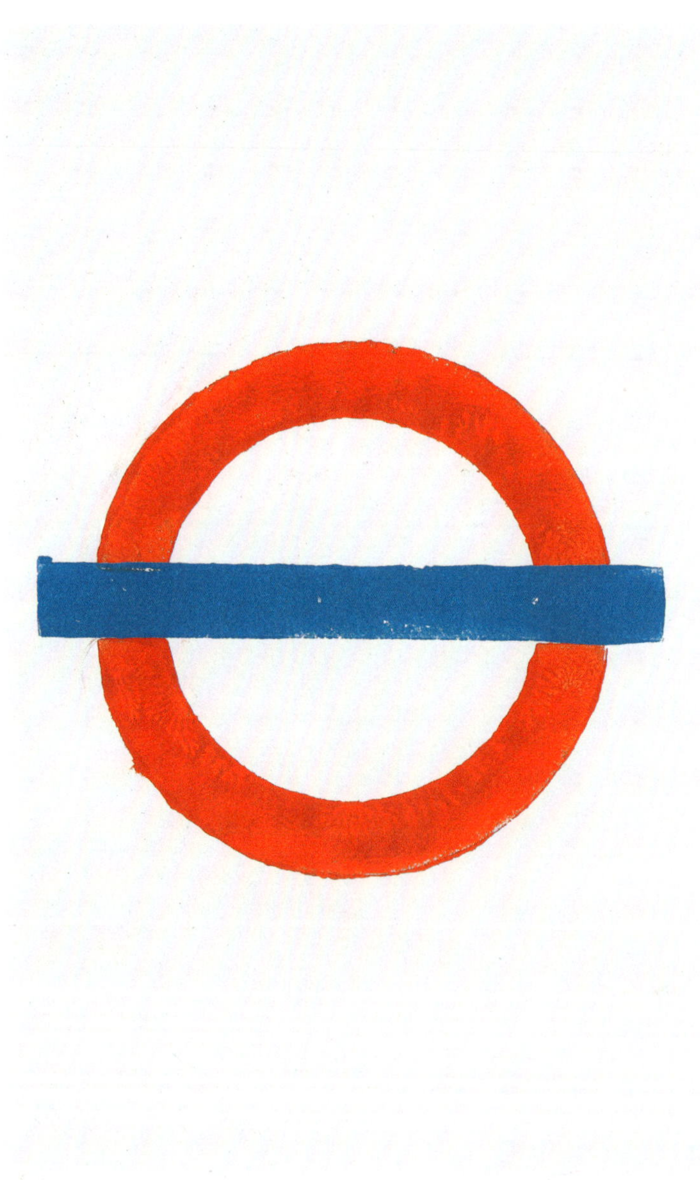

Richard Woods
London Underground Logo

I really like the Edward Johnston Roundel, and I didn't want to muck about with it. I made a simple print block out of plywood, and stamped the copied design using household gloss paint.

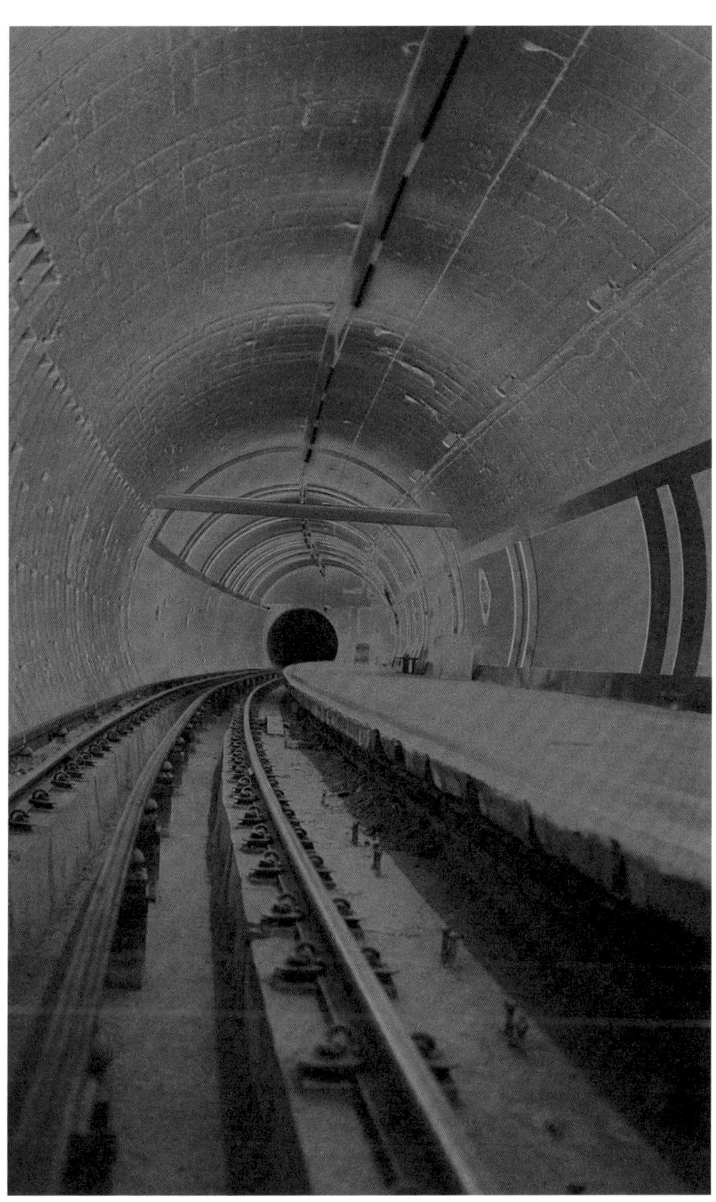

Catherine Yass
Tunnel

Whenever the Tube went through closed stations, I remember
the Roundel hovering in the dark like a ghost as we went past.
I photographed Aldwych station because when it closed,
I felt so sad that this little anomaly of a line had been
rationalized away.

ARTISTIC LICENCE:
A CENTURY OF CREATIVE ROUNDELS

Claire Dobbin

Transport for London's Roundel is one of the most recognized
and imitated logos in the world. While providing a unified corporate
identity for the capital's transport services, it has become a powerful
symbol of the city itself. It has also been a long-standing source of
inspiration to artists and designers. For over a century, Underground
publicity posters have drawn on its distinctive form and inventively
exploited its familiarity with passengers. The artists and works in
this book therefore represent the latest chapter in a long history
of creative adaptation that parallels the story of the Roundel's
use as a company logo.

Although it was not initially commissioned as a brand, the origins
of the Roundel date back to 1908. The 'bar and circle', as it became
known in its earliest form, comprised a solid red enamel disc with
a horizontal blue bar across the centre to bear the names of stations.
This graphic device was introduced to highlight station names on the
walls of platforms, which were awash with commercial advertising
posters, all vying for public attention at every stop. The bar and
circle provided a distinctive and unified form of signage that stood
out from the crowded hoardings.

It was also in 1908 that Frank Pick became responsible for
the publicity of London's underground railways, which were then
operated by separate companies. He began to develop a more
coordinated and effective approach to promoting their services
by commissioning modern graphic posters. The first map to present
all lines as one integrated network was issued free to passengers,
and the distinctive new UNDERGROUND lettering, or logotype as
it is sometimes called, was introduced on signage outside stations.
These changes represented significant steps towards establishing
a coherent identity for the early Underground.

Within four years, the UNDERGROUND logotype had found its
logical home across the centre of the bar and circle. This marked an

important development in the Roundel's evolution into a company logo. The new integrated symbol was used on map covers and publicity material, as well as on signage outside stations.

By 1917, the typographer Edward Johnston, whom Pick had commissioned in 1913 to design a company typeface, had started to rework the proportions of the Roundel to accommodate his new lettering. It was at this point that the solid red disc became a circle, and the symbol was first registered as a trademark. In the 1920s, Johnston introduced exact standards for the reproduction of the Roundel, or 'Bullseye' as he called it. By now, poster artists had been freely and imaginatively using the Roundel in their designs for over a decade. For the company's own publicity purposes, the Underground continued to permit some degree of artistic licence to designers wishing to use adaptations of the Roundel, which resulted in some of the network's most iconic poster designs.

One of the earliest to employ the Roundel in a playful and inventive way was Alfred France. His 1912 design presents an impressive party of mythical gods and goddesses gathered for a game of archery. Their target takes the form of an early Roundel, still retaining the solid red disc of the bar and circle. Hermes, Chronos and Pallas represent three key components of the Underground that posters frequently publicized: speed, punctuality and safety. Eros and Charon stand for pleasure and value for money, while Pan and Pluto represent the countryside and the underworld.

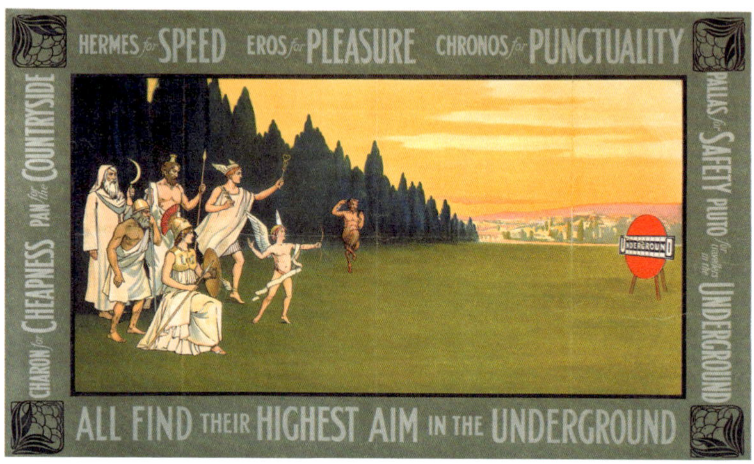

Alfred France *Hermes for Speed, Eros for Pleasure*, 1912

Encouraging leisure travel provided the Underground with an effective way to build up passenger numbers on underused off-peak services. In the 1920s, hundreds of posters promoted evening and weekend leisure attractions that could be reached easily by the Underground. *The Riches of London* was a series of five posters designed by Frederick Charles Herrick in 1927. Each design represents a different sense through which to experience London, with a Roundel incorporated into the central image. By this time, the symbol had become so familiar that only the letters 'U' and 'D' were needed to identify the UNDERGROUND.

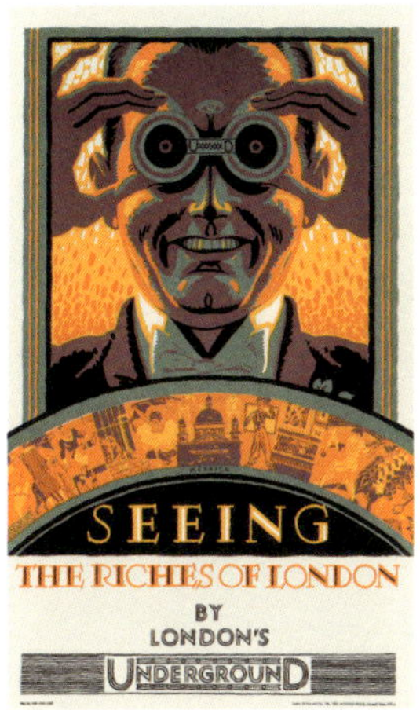

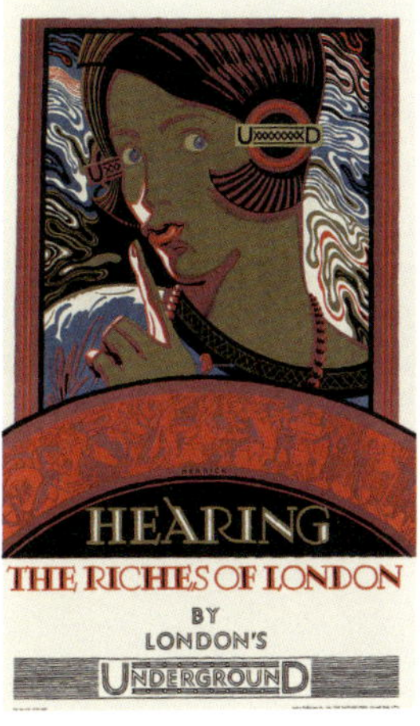

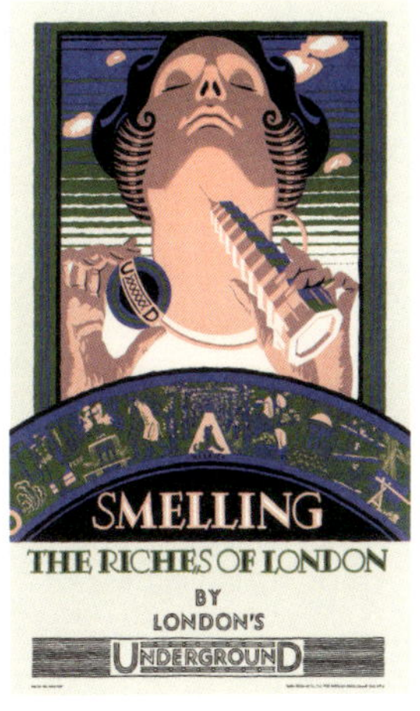

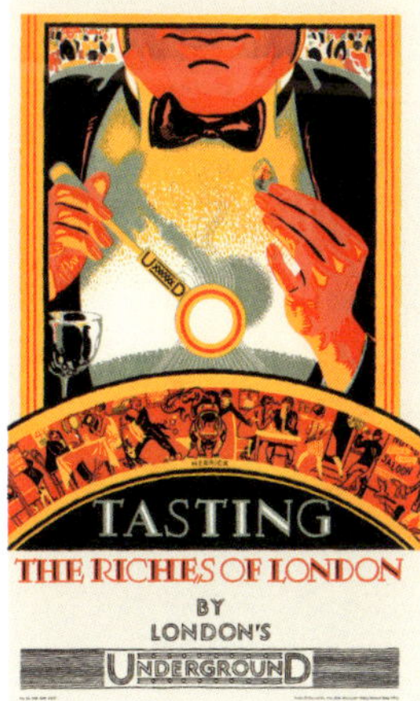

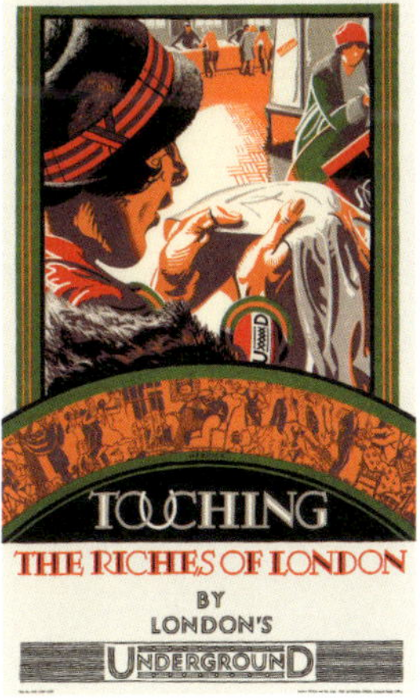

Frederick Charles Herrick *The Riches of London*, 1927

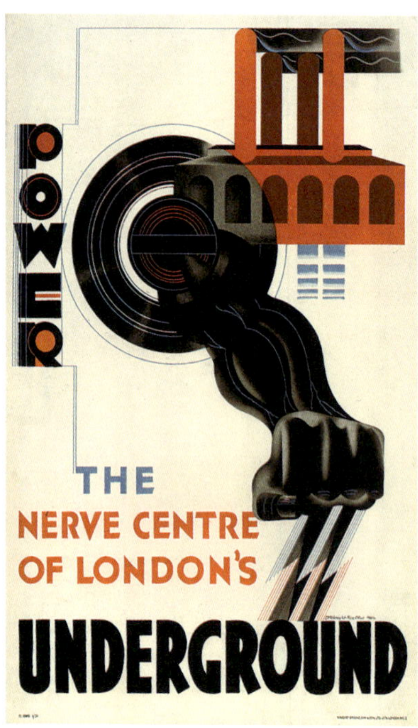

Edward McKnight Kauffer *Power: The nerve centre of London's Underground*, 1931

The prolific commercial artist Edward McKnight Kauffer produced more than one hundred posters for the Underground between 1915 and 1939. His 1931 design *Power: The nerve centre of London's Underground* is one of his best known. It presents man and machine united as the driving forces behind the Underground, with a semi-abstract Roundel at the heart of the image, figuratively the source of the network's strength. As well as underlining the impact electric rail travel was having on urban life in the 1930s, and the technological advancements that London's underground railways had pioneered, the poster reflects Kauffer's understanding of early twentieth-century art. His lettering, for example, which moves away from the use of Johnston's typeface in order to present text as an integral part of the design, suggests an awareness of recent typographical innovations made by the Bauhaus school in Germany. Elements of Futurism, Cubism and Constructivism also find expression in Kauffer's posters, which translate the complicated language of the avant-garde into accessible commercial design.

In the late 1930s, Kauffer briefly shared a studio with the American photographer and Surrealist artist Man Ray, who during a short-term residency in London also received a poster commission from the Underground. His iconic design transformed the Roundel into a planet, mimicking the effect of his trademark use of photograms, or 'rayographs', created by placing objects directly onto light-sensitive paper and then exposing them to light.

Man Ray's design was produced as a pair. Although the image was identical in each, the text at the bottom – 'London Transport – Keeps London Going' – was divided between the two panels. This allowed the posters to be displayed on prime sites such as either side of station entrances, which were always reserved for the Underground's own publicity. Man Ray's design also featured in contemporary press advertisements for the Underground, with additional slogans including '3,800 million passengers a year – you can't get away from it'. In the same way as earlier posters had presented the Roundel as the moon or the sun, Man Ray's design signified the visibility and omnipresence of the symbol in London.

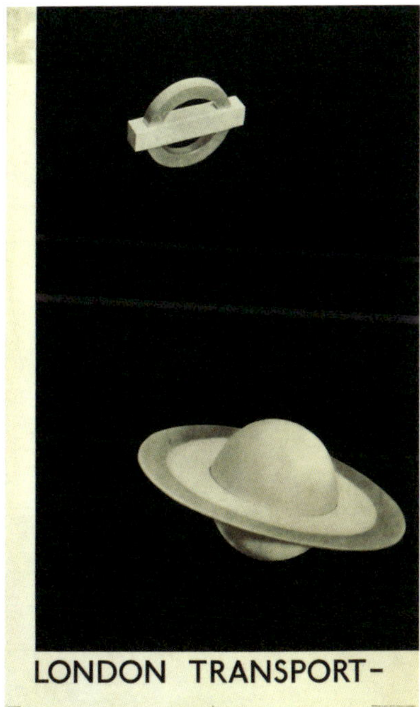

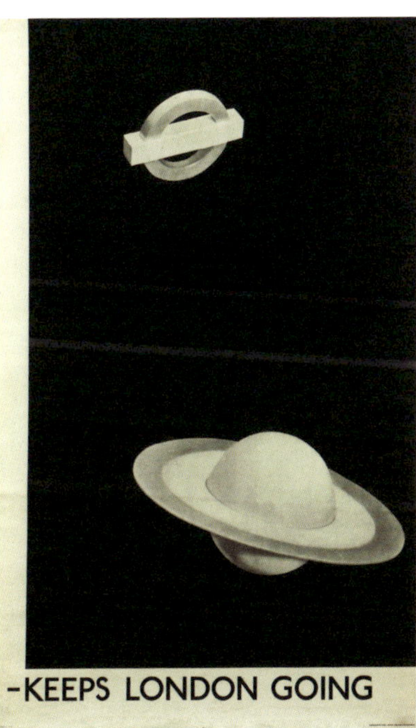

Man Ray *London Transport – Keeps London Going*, 1938

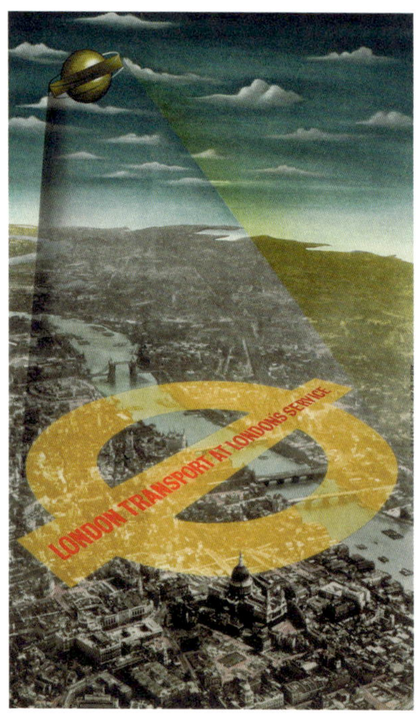

Misha Black and John Barker
London Transport at London's Service, 1947

In 1947, Misha Black and John Barker designed another pair of posters that employed a Roundel in planetary form, this time projecting light and hope onto postwar London. It was one of a series commissioned by London Transport's new publicity officer, Harold Hutchison, which had the title *London Transport at London's Service*. As well as signalling the rebuilding of the transport system after the war, Hutchison recognized the importance of restoring the faith of the public it served. Black and Barker's 'pair poster' featured a series of powerful yet reassuring statistics about public transport services in the capital.

By the mid-1970s, London Transport was facing staff shortages, spiralling costs and falling passenger numbers. A central marketing department was established to deliver more direct, measurable results, and poster commissioning was increasingly contracted out to advertising agencies. When Michael Levey became publicity officer in 1975, the number of posters commissioned directly from artists had reduced to just five or six a year. *London Zoo*, the last of nineteen posters that Abram Games had produced for London Transport since 1937, represents the quality that was maintained in commissions despite the reduced quantity. His design depicts a tiger cleverly constructed out of the components of the Roundel. As well as an effective publicity poster, reproductions of which also sold well in London Transport's shop, the design caught the eye of the eminent art historian E. H. Gombrich. In his 1981 article 'Image and code: scope and limits of conventionalism in pictorial representation', he used the poster to illustrate how images in modern advertisements could convey meaning, by drawing on the audience's conditioned knowledge of established signs and symbols.

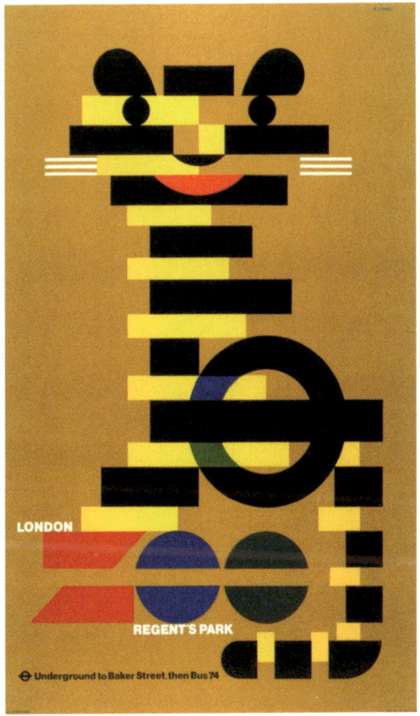

Abram Games *London Zoo*, 1976

By the 1980s the Roundel was recognized as a commercial asset, as well as an integral element of London Transport's corporate identity. In line with an increasingly robust licensing strategy, developed to protect it from unofficial or unauthorized use, the Roundel rarely appeared in posters as anything other than branding. However, a number of commissioning initiatives were introduced in the 1980s and 1990s. *Simply Fashion* by Trickett and Webb was part of a series of such posters that, in addition to promoting leisure travel, were intended to help re-establish direct links with artists and designers. Paying homage to Man Ray's iconic 1938 design, it represents a rare example of the Roundel's creative use during this period.

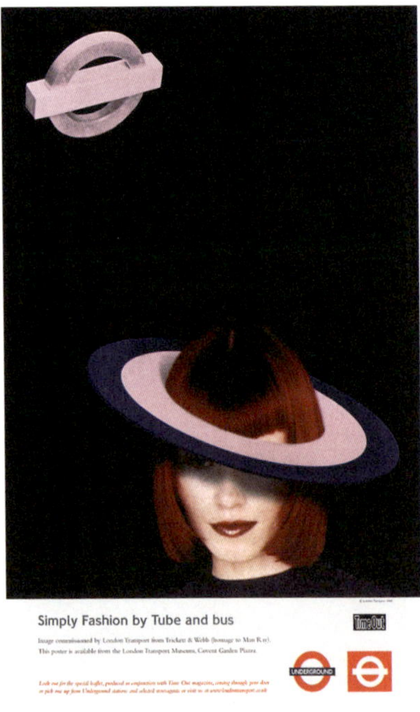

Trickett and Webb *Simply Fashion*, 1999

But now, a century after the first posters to feature creative Roundels appeared, Art on the Underground has returned to the practice by inviting one hundred artists to produce new works drawing inspiration from the Roundel's history as a symbol and as an artistic source. The outstanding range, quality and ingenuity of the designs mark a long overdue commemoration of the creative roundel as an integral strand in the history of Transport for London's iconic logo.

ONE HUNDRED REINVENTIONS OF THE WHEEL

Sally Shaw

Lying in a drawer in one of the archive rooms at the London Transport Museum's depot in west London is one of the few remaining copies of Man Ray's *London Transport – Keeps London Going* (see page 127), commissioned in 1938 by Frank Pick, chief executive officer of the London Passenger Transport Board. The poster is referenced several times in this book, but it is worth noting the continuing influence it has on the contemporary artist. In many respects, the whole Roundel project sprang from this specific work. What better way to celebrate one hundred years of Edward Johnston's famous design than by revisiting the idea behind this famous commission – to invite artists to use this symbol as a means of interpreting our contemporary city?

Pick's commissioning of Man Ray was, at the time, a brave move. To allow such an artist, known for his provocative rayographs and links with the Surrealist movement in Paris, such a degree of artistic licence as to embed the corporate identity within a new art work was generous, and not without risk. Today such an act could be seen as riskier still, considering that the Roundel has become hugely valuable on many levels, an international brand worth millions and with policies and people deployed to ensure its correct and proper use according to Johnston's original guidelines.

Among the many works in the archive, Man Ray's stands out for its striking simplicity, for its ability to communicate the personality of London Underground across the many generations of Londoners and Tube users who have seen it since it was commissioned, for its humour, and for the radical nature of its artistic construction. Who today might be able to make similarly elegant, simple and direct works?

That question became the germ of the project: how do you work with artists in a context as complex as the Tube and create space for artistic exploration while maintaining and enhancing the company identity? How do the myriad limitations and stipulations that come

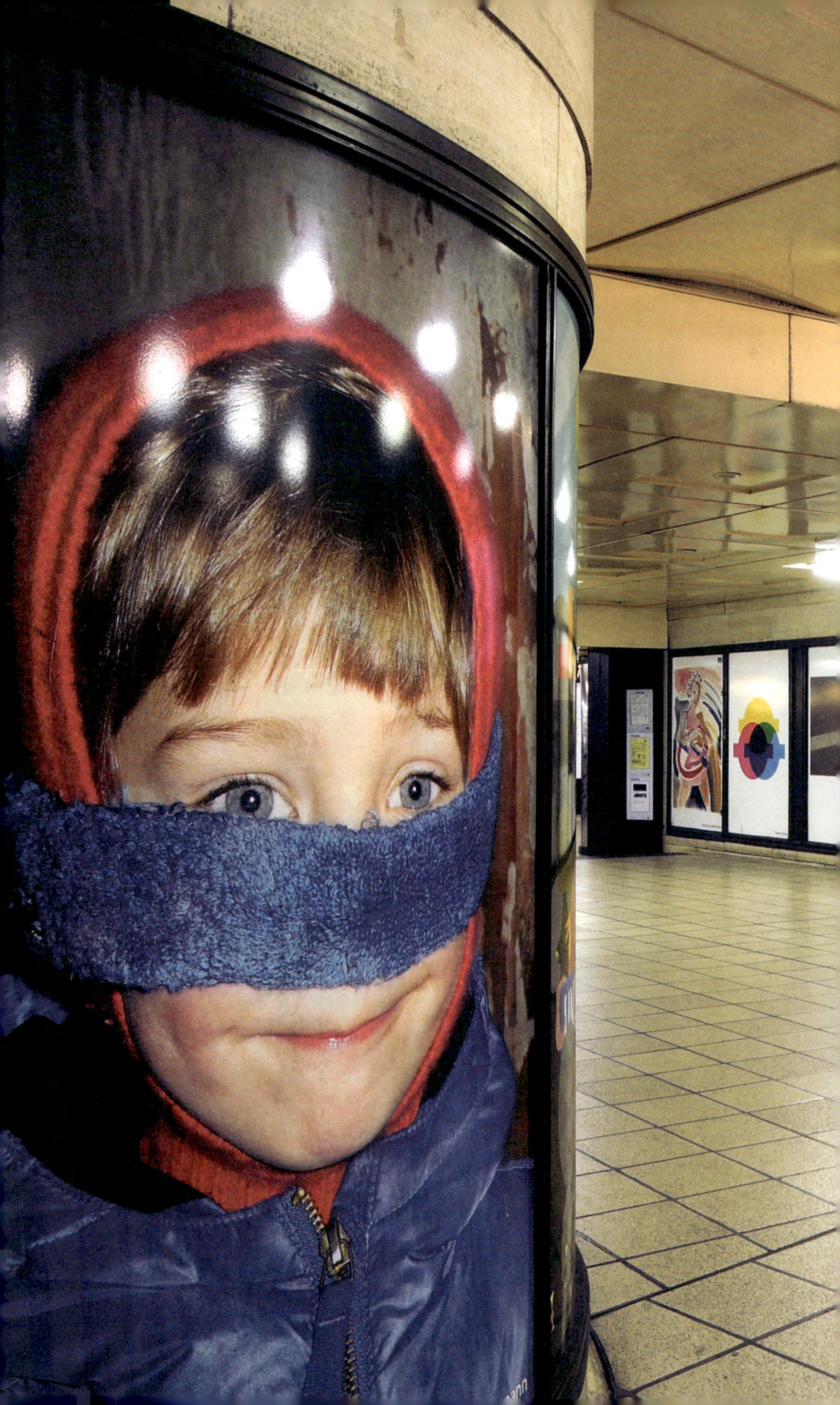

with today's brand guidelines become rules to be played with –
turning the problem into the solution?

The art works I have chosen to look at here represent the range
of approaches taken by the artists we approached. These designs
in particular make me contemplate the Roundel from a fresh
perspective in the same way that Man Ray's poster does. They also
highlight the spectrum of creative practices thriving in London today.
A key aim was not only to construct a collection of works to add
to the extensive catalogue of commissions generated by London
Underground over the past century, but also to attempt a survey of
contemporary art in Britain. But this is just a personal selection: one
of the unforeseen surprises of the project has been to observe other
people's favourites, chosen in response to their own unique interests.

When we were conceiving the project, we had recently
commissioned Jeremy Deller to make a new art work for the cover
of the Tube map. It was clear that Jeremy would be one artist who
would understand the tight corner proposed by this new project
and produce a work that would offer an elegant and humorous
escape route. His contribution, *Graham Hadingham, born 30th
July 1908. London Underground employee – 8th February 1926
until 31st March 1974* (page 42), represents just that. The photograph
shows the eponymous former Tube worker of the title. At the time,
Graham was a hundred years old and was photographed holding
his birthday letter from the Queen. Typical of Deller's work, the
photograph foregrounds the social history of the organization. His
concern was to bring the hidden human stories and faces upon which
the entire network relies to the fore. It is a reminder to both travellers
and staff that there is more to life than increasing its speed. Other
artists too, such as Torsten Lauschmann and Harold Offeh (pages
73 and 88), also made use of photographic depictions of people,
a reflection perhaps of the upsurge in artistic practices that utilize
social circumstances as material for creative production.

Untitled by Doug Fishbone (page 47) is a classic piece of
postmodern appropriation. The work takes the late-fifteenth-century
German Lucas Cranach the Elder's *Venus*, which had been used to
promote an exhibition of that artist's work at the Royal Academy of
Arts in 2008. The original poster had been threatened with removal

Opposite and overleaf: Roundel art works installed at Piccadilly Circus Underground station
Photograph: Thierry Bal

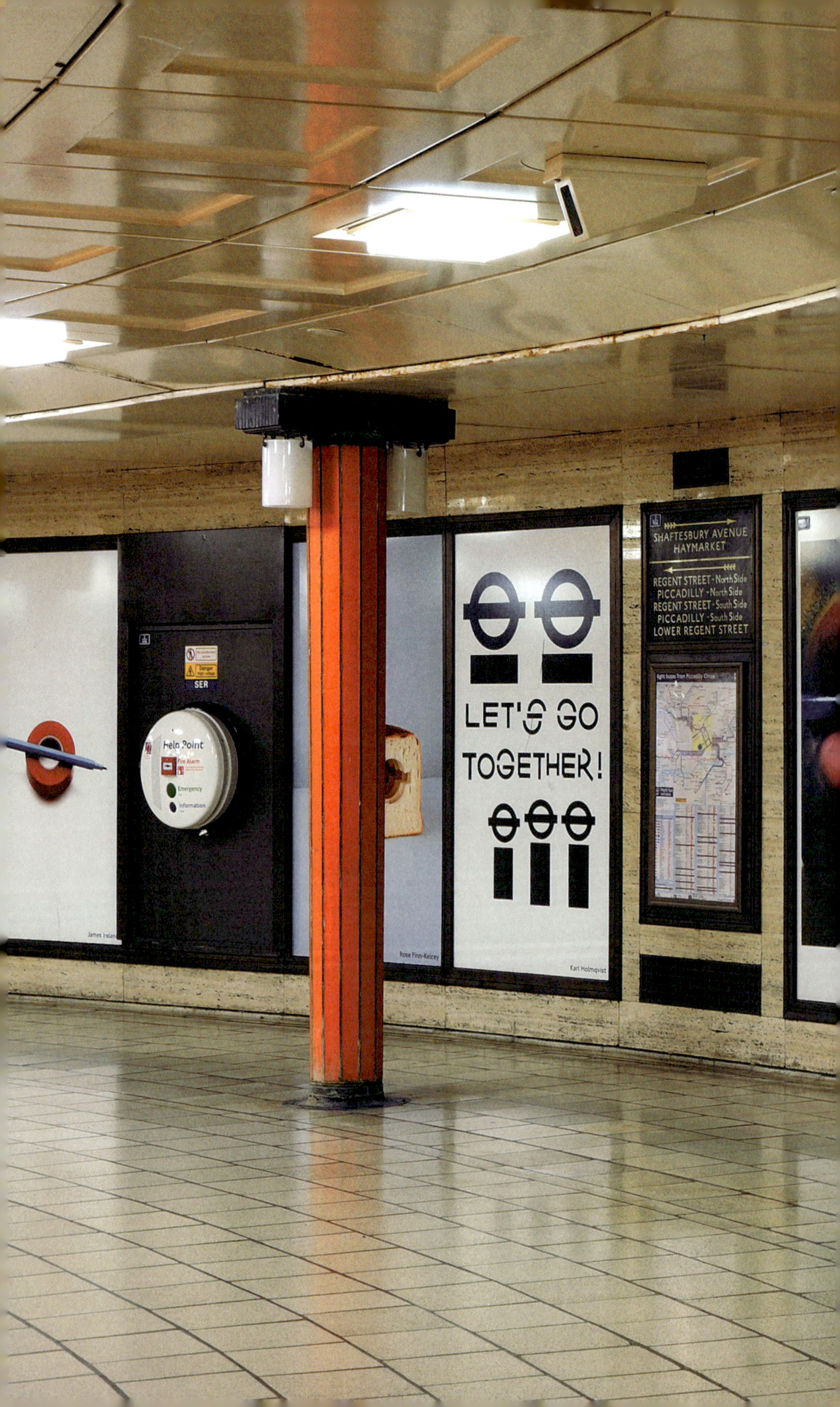
SER
Help Point
Fire Alarm
Emergency
Information
James Ireland
LET'S GO
TOGETHER!
Rose Finn-Kelcey
Karl Holmqvist
SHAFTESBURY AVENUE
HAYMARKET
REGENT STREET - North Side
PICCADILLY - North Side
REGENT STREET - South Side
PICCADILLY - South Side
LOWER REGENT STREET

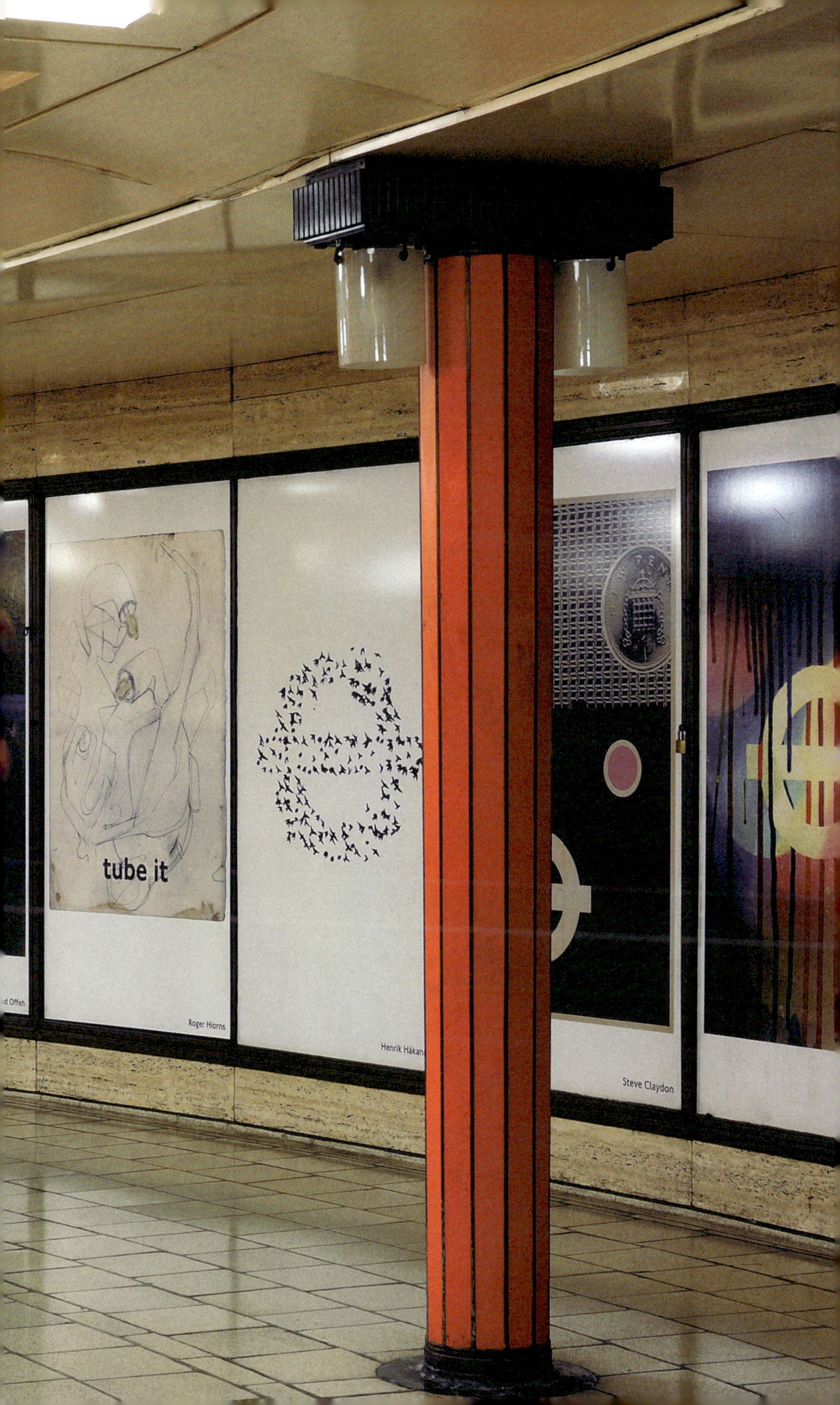
tube it
Roger Hiorns
Henrik Håkans
Steve Claydon

from display on the Tube network – it was considered risqué and potentially contravened London Underground's rules on the depiction of naked human figures – but after some controversy in the press, the threat was lifted. Fishbone's employment of the Roundel as protectors of Venus' modesty allowed the original work to enter the network for a second time. The wry inclusion of the faintly Americanized slogan 'London – we got you covered' links to early wartime posters in which the Tube is presented as a safe haven for travellers, protecting Londoners from all sorts of extremes of wind, rain and foreign invasion. Fishbone, an American living in London, neatly reclaims this territory, pointing towards a hidden contradiction: the suggestion that travellers are shielded from inappropriate messages despite the fact that the Tube is widely understood as an advertiser's dream territory, with the daily passenger commute dissected into pound-rated 'dwell-time' packages sold off for considerable sums.

A jam jar containing slowly evaporating red-tinted water, with a blue-tipped paint stirrer balanced carefully on the top suggests a work in progress. Joëlle Tuerlinckx's *Detail d'atelier trouvé – for Art on the Underground* (page 110) brings into question the continuous remaking, redesigning and refining process that is undertaken in any artist's studio and, in the context of this collection, the momentous growth and progress of the London Underground as it continuously develops under our feet. Tuerlinckx's skill is in her delicate ability to balance objects in relation to one another in a manner that conjures suggestion. For me, this work contains a story about individual human endeavour: the use of very familiar objects and popular clichés from the studio (the paint stick, the jar of thinners) suggests an individual working alone to make a picture of something greater than herself. There are parallels between this and the Tube, a transport system built by many individuals to serve the greater need of the travelling public.

The last work I have selected is Paola Pivi's *Time to Circle* (page 93). A ghostly Roundel floats from the background of hundreds of tiny hand-drawn circles in a scattering of delicately pretty pastel shades. Again, this work suggests a grand perspective constructed from individual elements, but the obvious hand of the artist and prioritization of skill, craftsmanship and draftsmanship is the primary captivator of my interest. I am reminded of Eduardo Paolozzi's

mosaic at Tottenham Court Road station, and the thousands
of hand-crafted ceramic tiles that adorn hundreds of station walls
and that are brushed by a million handbags and coat sleeves everyday.
Pivi's work is also reminiscent of the wonderful early drawings and
sketches that Johnston made in his initial rethinking of the Roundel
and the Johnston typeface: the inherent perfection instilled within
a circle drawn and redrawn over and over again, a practised gesture
that becomes effortless and unnoticeable over time.

This small selection uncovers only a fraction of the works
and responses in the collection as a whole. Looking at all the
contributions one takes a kaleidoscopic peek through the door
of one hundred artists' studios and a glance at the myriad working
methods that constitute art practice today. There are artists who
have constructed works as sculptural forms – Brian Griffiths, James
Ireland (pages 56 and 66), as well as Tuerlinckx. There are those who
have taken the everyday world around them as their inspiration – Alex
Frost and Richard Wentworth, for example (pages 49 and 116). There
are photographers, film-makers and performance artists and painters.
What is striking about the collection is that, while some of these
forms of making are very familiar to us, traditional even, the subject
matter is highly contemporary. What the collection represents
therefore is an animated set of symbols for a modern global city.

Overleaf: Embankment Underground station. Photograph: Thierry Bal

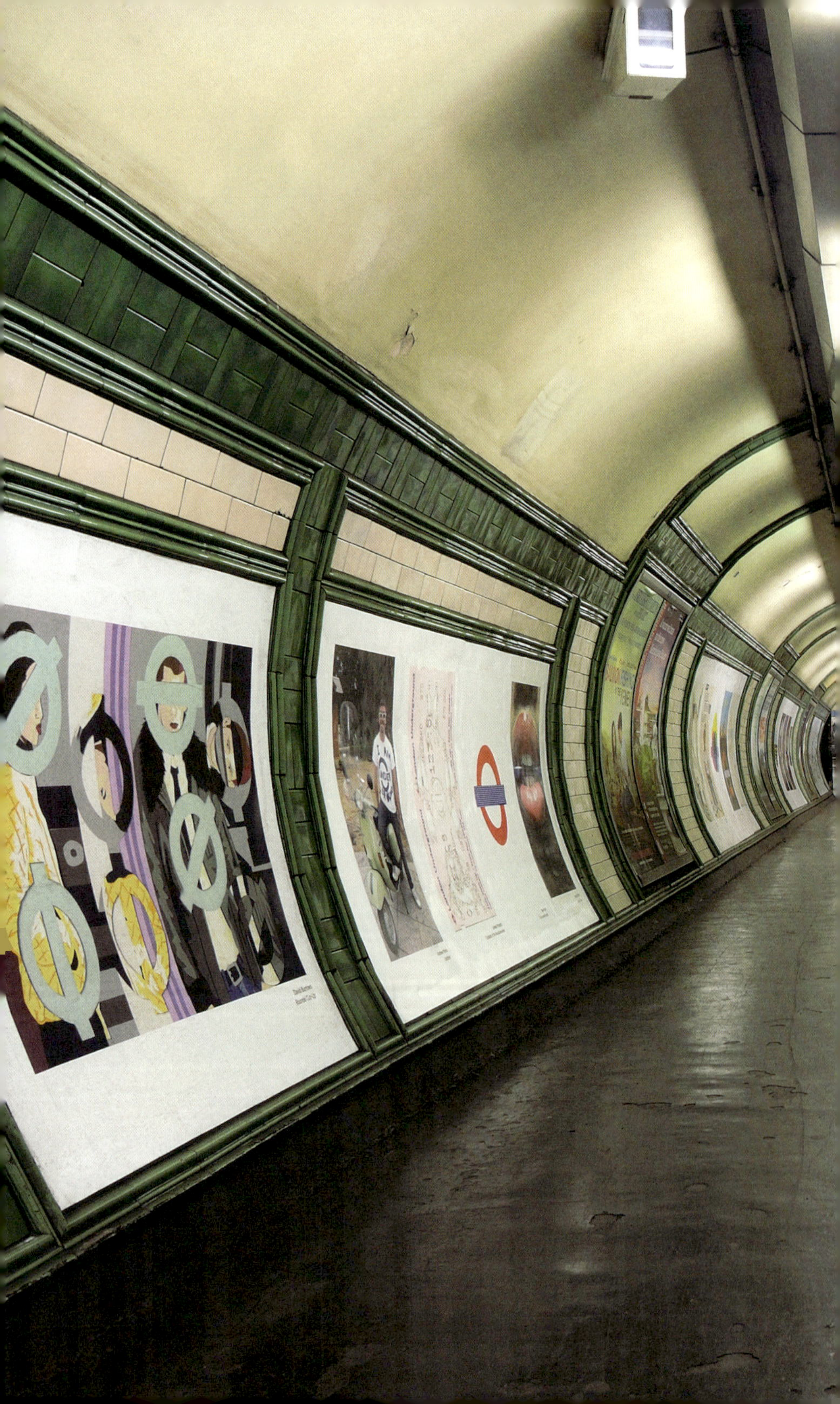

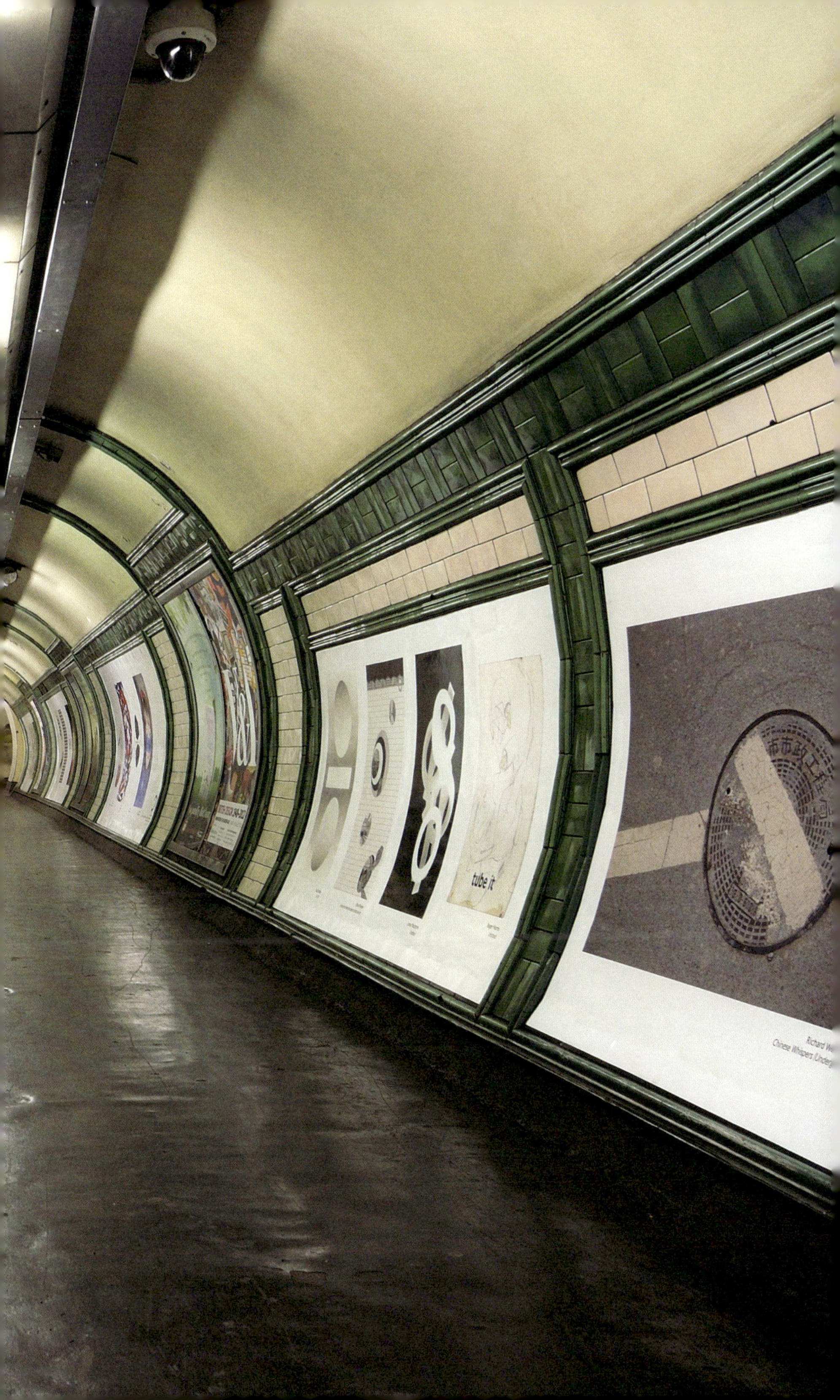

V&A
tube it
Richard W...
Chinese Whispers (Under...

ARTISTS' BIOGRAPHIES

p. 22   **Phillip Allen**
Born 1967, London; lives and works in
London. Recent exhibitions include 'Capital
P', The Approach, London, 2011; '… the
urgent hang around', Bernier/Eliades Gallery,
Athens, 2010; 'Kaleidoscopic Revolver', Total
Museum of Contemporary Art, Seoul, 2009;
'Classified', Tate Britain, 2009, 'M25: Around
London', CCA Andratx, Mallorca, 2008;
'Phillip Allen', Xavier Hufkens, Brussels, 2007;
'Celebrating 20 Years', Kerlin Gallery, Dublin,
2005. Represented by Xavier Hufkens,
Brussels; Kerlin Gallery, Dublin; and
The Approach, London.

p. 23   **Polly Apfelbaum**
Born 1955, Abington, Pennsylvania;
lives and works in New York. Recent
solo exhibitions include 'Planiverse',
Galerie Nächst St Stephan Rosemarie
Schwarzwälder, Vienna, 2012; 'Funkytown
Flatterland', D'Amelio Gallery, New York,
2012; 'Haunted House', Atelier Amden,
Switzerland, 2011; 'Flatland: color revolt',
Hansel and Gretel Picture Garden, New York,
2011; 'Double Nickels on the Dime', Michael
Benevento, Los Angeles, 2011; 'Anything
Can Happen in a Horse Race', Milton Keynes
Gallery, 2009. Represented by Frith Street
Gallery, London; D'Amelio Terras, New York;
and Galerie Nächst St Stephan Rosemarie
Schwarzwälder, Vienna

p. 24   **David Austen**
Born 1960, Harlow; lives and works in
London. Recent exhibitions include 'The
Gorgon's Dream', The Burns Monument,
Edinburgh, with Ingleby Gallery and the
Edinburgh International Film Festival, 2012;
'Papillon', Anthony Reynolds Gallery, London,
2011; 'Smoke Town and End of Love', Modern
Art Gallery Oxford, Oxford, 2010; 'David
Austen and Man Ray', Ingleby Gallery,
Edinburgh, 2008; 'David Austen', Milton
Keynes Gallery, 2007. Represented by
Anthony Reynolds Gallery, London; and
Ingleby Gallery, Edinburgh.

p. 25   **Simon Bedwell**
Born 1963, Croydon; lives and works in
London. Recent exhibitions include 'Asphalt
World', Studio Voltaire, London, 2009;
'The Painter of the Hole', MOT International,
London, 2009; 'The Furnishers', White

Columns, New York, 2007; 'Gents: A Melo-
drama with 2 Acts', Platform, London, 2006.
Represented by MOT International, London.

p. 26   **Vanessa Billy**
Born in 1978, Geneva; lives and works in
London and Zürich. Recent solo exhibitions
include 'Looking for the Pool', Unosolo, Milan,
2011; 'Not Taught', BolteLang, Zürich, 2011;
'Three Times a Day', Kunsthaus Baselland,
Basel, 2011; 'Natural Means Something Like
Vegetables', Christina Wilson, Copenhagen,
2011; 'Who Shapes What', Limoncello,
London, 2010; 'Surfaces For the Mind to
Rest or Sink Into', Photographer's Gallery,
Project Space, London, 2009. Represented by
BolteLang, Zürich; and Limoncello, London.

p. 27   **Sir Peter Blake**
Born 1932, Dartford; lives and works in
London. Recent exhibitions include 'Peter
Blake at 80', Royal Albert Hall, London, 2012;
'Things I Love', Fine Arts Society, London;
'The London Suite', Paul Stolper, London,
2012; 'Homage 10 x 5', Waddington Galleries,
London, 2010. Represented by Waddington
Custot Galleries, London.

p. 28   **David Blandy**
Born 1976, London; lives and works in London
and Brighton. Recent solo exhibitions include
Phoenix Gallery, Brighton, in association with
Lighthouse as part of the Brighton Digital
Festival, 2012; 'David Blandy: Passage of the
Soul', Exeter Phoenix, Exeter, 2012; 'Artistic
Dialogues II: David Blandy and Nilbar Güreş',
Künstlerhaus Stuttgart, 2011; 'Child of the
Atom', Seventeen Gallery, London, 2010.
Recent group exhibitions include 'In the
Woods', Latitude Festival, Suffolk, 2012;
'Thank You For The Music', Kiasma Museum
of Contemporary Art, Helsinki, 2012; 28th
Kassel Documentary Film and Video Festival,
Kassel, 2011; Kunst&Zwalm, public-art
commission, Belgium, 2011. Represented
by Seventeen Gallery, London.

p. 29   **Rut Blees Luxemburg**
Born 1967, Germany; lives and works
in London. Recent exhibitions include
'Lustgarten', Stadtmuseum Simeonstift,
Trier, 2012; 'Dérives et des Rêves',
Château d'Oiron, Deux-Sèvres, 2012;
'New Narrative', Digital Arts Centre,

Taipei, 2011; 'Black Sunrise', Dominique
Fiat, Paris, 2010; 'elles@centrepompidou',
Centre Georges Pompidou, Paris; 'Piccadilly's
Peccadilloes', Heathrow Terminal Four,
Art on the Underground commission,
2007. Represented by Galerie Dominique
Fiat, Paris.

p. 30   **Simon & Tom Bloor**
Both born 1973, Birmingham; live and
work in London and Birmingham. Recent
solo exhibitions include 'Formula for Living',
Art and the Public Realm, Bristol, 2011;
'Happy Habitat Revisited', South London
Gallery, 2011; 'The Fascination of Islands',
Cooper Gallery, Dundee, 2011; 'Hit and
Miss', Modern Art Oxford, 2010; 'As Long
As It Lasts', Eastside Projects, Birmingham,
2009; 'Hey for Lubberland', Ikon,
Birmingham, 2009.

p. 31   **Martin Boyce**
Born in 1967, Glasgow; lives and works in
Glasgow. Recent exhibitions include 'In Praise
of Shadows', Johnen Galerie, Berlin, 2012;
'The Spirit Level', Barbara Gladstone Gallery,
New York, 2012; 'Turner Prize 2011', Baltic
Centre for Contemporary Art, Gateshead,
2011; 'Conceptual Tendencies', Daimler
Contemporary, Berlin, 2011; 'night terrace –
lantern chains – forgotten seas – sky',
The Modern Institute, Glasgow, 2011;
'Through Layers and Leaves (Closer and
Closer)', Massachusetts Institute of
Technology, Cambridge, Massachusetts,
2011;'La Carte d'après Nature', Nouveau
Musée National de Monaco and Matthew
Marks Gallery, New York, 2010–11; 'Winter
Palms', Tanya Bonakdar Gallery, New York,
2010. Represented by The Modern Institute,
Glasgow; Galerie Eva Presenhuber, Zürich;
Tanya Bonakdar Gallery, New York; and
Johnen Galerie, Berlin.

p. 32   **Rachal Bradley**
Born 1979, Blackpool; lives and works
in Glasgow. Recent exhibitions include
'Interiority complex', Cubitt, London, 2012;
'We Love You', Limoncello, London, 2012;
'That is the Dawn', Galerie Gregor Staiger,
Zürich, 2012; 'Bodies Assembling', AutoItalia,
London, 2012; 'EverChangingMoods'
(with Jess Wiesner), AutoItalia South East,
London, 2011; 'Plastic Culture: Legacies

of Pop 1986–2008), Harris Museum
and Art Gallery, Preston, 2009; 'Bad Bat'
performance, Institute of Contemporary
Arts, London, 2009; 'Pop Will Eat Itself',
Piccadilly Circus Underground station,
Art on the Underground commission,
London, 2009.

p. 33   **David Burrows**
Born 1965, London; lives and works
in London. Recent exhibitions include
'Night is also the Sun', IMT Gallery, 2012;
'We are Grammar', Pratt Gallery, New York,
2011; 'Multiverse Expanded', Akershus
Kunstscenter, Lillestrøm, 2011; Tatton Park
Biennial, 2010; 'Event Horizon', Royal Academy
of Arts, London, 2008. Represented by IMT
Gallery, London.

p. 34   **Andrea Büttner**
Born 1972, Stuttgart; lives and works
in the UK and Germany. Recent exhibitions
include Documenta 13, Kassel, 2012;
'Brannon, Büttner, Kierulf, Kierulf, Kilpper',
Bergen Kunsthall, Bergen, 2012; 'The Poverty
of Riches', Whitechapel Gallery, London,
and Collezione Maramotti, Reggio Emilia,
2011; 'Our Colours are the Colours of the
Marketplace', Art Statements, Art Basel
(with Hollybush Gardens, London), 2011;
'There is Always a Cup of Sea to Sail In',
29th Bienal de São Paulo, 2010; 'Andrea
Büttner', Hollybush Gardens, London, 2008;
'On the spot #1 Ð Andrea Büttner', Badischer
Kunstverein, Karlsruhe, 2007. Represented
by Hollybush Gardens, London.

p. 35   **Alice Channer**
Born 1977, Oxford; lives and works in London.
Recent exhibitions include 'Cold Blood', Lisa
Cooley, New York, 2012; 'Out Of Body', South
London Gallery, 2012; The London Open,
Whitechapel Gallery, 2012; 'Open Work',
Drawing Room, London, and Leeds City Art
Gallery, 2012; 'Caroline Achaintre, Sara Barker,
Alice Channer', Eastside Projects, Birmingham,
2012; 'Body-Conscious', The Approach,
London, 2011; 'Other-Directed', BolteLang,
Zürich, 2011; 'Inhale, Exhale', Charles Rennie
Mackintosh Gallery, Glasgow School of Art,
as part of the Glasgow International, 2010;
'Worn-work', The Approach, London, 2009.
Represented by The Approach, London, and
Lisa Cooley, New York.

p. 36   **Declan Clarke**
Born 1974, Ireland; lives and works in Berlin.
Recent exhibitions include 'We'll Be This
Way Until the End of the World', Mother's
Tankstation, Dublin, 2011; 'Der Menschen
Klee', Kunst im Tunnel, Düsseldorf, 2011;
Dublin Contemporary 2011; Whitstable
Biennial, 2010; 'Auto-Kino!', Temporäre
Kunsthalle, Berlin, 2010; 'Loneliness in
West Germany', Goethe-Institut, Dublin,
2009; 'Nothing Human is Alien to Me',
Pierogi, Leipzig, 2008; 'Through the Lens:
New Media Art from Ireland', Beijing Art
Museum of Imperial City, Beijing, 2008;
'10,000 to 50: Contemporary Art from the
Members of Business to Arts', Irish Museum
of Modern Art, Dublin, 2008.

p. 37   **Steven Claydon**
Born 1969, London; lives and works in
London. Recent exhibitions include 'Culpable
Earth', firstsite, Colchester, 2012; 'British
Art Show 7: In the Days of the Comet',
various venues, London, Nottingham,
Glasgow, Plymouth, 2011; 'Ancient Set/
Fictional Pixel', Dublin, 2011; 'Twickenham
Garden', Kimmerich Gallery, New York, 2011;
David Kordansky Gallery, Los Angeles, 2010;
'Newspeak: British Art Now', Part I, Saatchi
Gallery, London, 2010; 'Depression', Marres
Centre of Contemporary Culture, Maastricht,
2009; 'Steven Claydon', International Project
Space, Birmingham, 2008; 'Pale Carnage',
Arnolfini, Bristol, 2007. Represented by
Galerie Dennis Kimmerich, Düsseldorf;
Hotel Gallery, London; and David Kordansky
Gallery, Los Angeles.

p. 38   **Lucy Clout**
Born 1980, Leeds; lives and works in London.
Recent exhibitions include 'Physicalism Or
Near Enough', Limoncello, London, 2011;
'manual non manual manual', International
Project Space, Birmingham, 2010; 'Days',
Transmission, Glasgow, 2010. Represented
by Limoncello, London.

p. 39   **Henry Coleman**
Born 1974, Harpenden; lives and works in
London. Recent exhibitions include 'About
Now: Henry Coleman', Bloomberg SPACE,
London, 2012; '¿Separados al Nacer?',
Salón Nacional de Artistas de Colombia,
Independientemente, Cartagena de Indias,

2011; 'Telón', with Cristina Schiavi, MACRO
Museum of Contemporary Art, Rosario,
2009; 'Los Vinilos', Zoo Art Fair exhibit,
Royal Academy of Arts, London, 2008;
'The Law of Large Numbers', Cell Project
Space, London, 2005; greengrassi, London,
2004. Represented by greengrassi, London.

p. 40   **Joel Croxson**
Born 1978, Bristol; lives and works
in London. Recent exhibitions include
'Ill Communication', Dicksmith Gallery,
London, 2009; 'Salon 2007: New British
Painting and Works on Paper', 319 Portobello
Road, London, 2007; 'MUTINEER',
Atelierhaus Mengerzeile, Berlin, 2007;
'Future Primitive', One in the Other,
London, 2005. Represented by Dicksmith
Gallery, London.

p. 41   **Stuart Cumberland**
Born 1970, Hampshire; lives and works
in London. Recent exhibitions include 'Four
Circle Paintings', The Approach, London, 2011;
'Stuart Cumberland, Comma 10', Bloomberg
SPACE, London, 2009; 'Stuart Cumberland',
Maruani & Noirhomme Gallery, Knokke, 2009;
'What Kind of Painting?', Sprüth Magers
Projekte, Munich, 2008; 'Congratulations',
The Approach, London, 2007; 'The Way We
Work Now: Some Attitudes to Materials and
Making', Camden Arts Centre, London, 2005.
Represented by The Approach, London; and
Maruani & Noirhomme Gallery, Knokke.

p. 42   **Jeremy Deller**
Born 1966, London; lives and works in
London. Recent exhibitions include 'Joy
in People', Hayward Gallery, London; Wiels
Centre for Contemporary Art, Brussels;
Institute of Contemporary Art, Philadelphia;
and Contemporary Art Museum, St Louis,
2012–13; 'Sacrilege', London 2012 Festival,
twenty-five locations across the UK, 2012;
'Jeremy Deller: Manchester Tracks', RISD
Museum, Providence, 2011; 'Jeremy Deller',
Upstairs at The Modern Institute, Glasgow,
2011; 'Local Artist', Void Gallery, Derry, 2010;
'It Is What It Is: Conversations About Iraq',
New Museum, New York, 2009; 'Carte
Blanche à Jeremy Deller', Palais de Tokyo,
Paris, 2008. Represented by Gavin Brown's
Enterprise, New York; Art:Concept, Paris;
and The Modern Institute, Glasgow.

p. 43 **Luke Dowd**
Born 1970, New York; lives and works
in London. Recent exhibitions include
'The constellation comes to life in your
void', Galerie Klaus Benden, Cologne,
2012; 'America Hurts Me Too', Rod Barton,
London, 2011; 'Happy Happy Sad Sad',
Tony Wight Gallery, Chicago, 2009;
'East End Academy', Whitechapel Gallery,
London, 2009. Represented by Galerie
Jacky Strenz, Frankfurt; and Tony Wight
Gallery, Chicago

p. 44 **Sean Edwards**
Born 1980, Cardiff; lives and works in
Abergavenny. Recent solo shows include
'Resting Through', Kunstverein Freiburg,
2012; 'Putting Right', Limoncello, London,
2011; 'The Shape We're In', Zabludowicz
Collection, London, 2011; 'Remaining Only',
Tanya Leighton Gallery, Berlin, 2011; 'Maelfa',
Spike Island, Bristol, 2011; 'No Dust Adheres',
Outpost, Norwich, 2010; 'Quantos Queres',
Galeria Marz, Lisbon, 2010; 'A very, very long
cat', Wallspace Gallery, New York, 2010;
Institute of Contemporary Arts, London,
2008. Represented by Tanya Leighton
Gallery, Berlin; and Limoncello, London.

p. 45 **Chris Evans**
Born 1967, Eastrington, East Yorkshire;
lives and works in London. Recent exhibitions
include 'CLODS, Diplomatic Letters', Juliette
Jongma, Amsterdam, 2012; 'Surplus Authors',
Witte de With, Rotterdam, 2012; 'We Love
You', Limoncello, London, 2012; 'Goofy
Audit', Lüttgenmeijer, Berlin, 2011; 'The
Indirect Exchange of Uncertain Value',
Collective Gallery, Edinburgh, 2011; 'Taipei
Biennial 2010', Taipei Fine Arts Museum;
'I Don't Know If I've Explained Myself',
Mala Galeria, Ljubljana, 2010; 'The Cell That
Doesn't Believe In The Mind That It's Part Of',
Marres, Maastricht, 2010. Represented by
Juliette Jongma, Amsterdam; and
Lüttgenmeijer, Berlin.

p. 46 **Rose Finn-Kelcey**
Born 1945, Northampton; lives and works in
London. Recent exhibitions include 'A Walk
Through the Twentieth Century', Tate Britain,
London, 2012; 'Modern British Sculpture',
Royal Academy of Arts, London, 2011;
'Re.act Feminism #2', Centro Cultural
Montehermoso, Victoria-Gasteiz, 2011;
'Building Bridges', Today Art Museum,
Beijing, 2008; 'Rose Finn-Kelcey', Milton
Keynes Gallery, Milton Keynes, 2006.

p. 47 **Doug Fishbone**
Born 1969, New York; lives and works
in London. Selected solo exhibitions include
Elmina, Tate Britain, London, 2010–11;
Rokeby, London, 2010–11; 'Rude Britannia:
British Comic Art', Tate Britain, London,
2010; Busan Biennale, Busan, 2008;
'Laughing in a Foreign Language', Hayward
Gallery, London, 2008; British Art Show 6,
Newcastle, Bristol, Nottingham and
Manchester, 2006; Gimpel Fils, London,
2006; '30,000 Bananas', Trafalgar Square,
London, 2004.

p. 48 **Alicia Framis**
Born 1967, Barcelona; lives and works
in Amsterdam. Recent exhibitions include
'Daily Future', Kunstzone Rabobank, Utrecht,
2012; Barbara Gross Galerie, Munich, 2012;
'Genealogías feministas en el arte español:
1960–2010', MUSAC, Museo de Arte
Contemporáneo de Castilla y León, 2012;
'Apuntes sobre el cielo', Sala de Exposiciones
de la Diputación de Huesca, Huesca, 2011;
'Imagine Being There', Kunstzone Rabobank,
Utrecht, 2011; 'Aware: Art Fashion Identity
Exhibition', Royal Academy of Arts, GSK
Contemporary, London, 2010; 'Alicia Framis',
Centre d'Art Santa Mònica, Barcelona, 2008.
Represented by Barbara Gross Galerie,
Munich; Annet Gelink Gallery, Amsterdam;
and Galeria Helga de Alvear, Madrid.

p.49 **Alex Frost**
Born 1973, London; lives and works in
Glasgow. Selected solo exhibitions include
'The Old & New Easterhouse Mosaic
(& everything in between)', Platform, Glasgow,
2012; 'Tales of the City', Gallery of Modern
Art (GoMA), Glasgow, 2012; 'Soul Seekers:
Interpreting the Icon', Trinity Museum, New
York, 2012; 'You, Me, Something Else',
GoMA, Glasgow, 2011; 'Industrial Aesthetics',
Hunter College, New York, 2011; 'Works
on Paper & Other Works', Glasgow Project
Room, Glasgow, 2011; 'The Connoisseurs',
Dundee Contemporary Arts, Dundee,
2010; 'Compassion Fatigue', Sorcha Dallas,
Glasgow, 2008; 'BBQ', ArtSway, Sway, 2008.

p. 50 **Franziska Furter**
Born 1972, Zürich; lives and works in Berlin and Basel. Recent exhibitions include 'Gyre', Les Halles, Porrentruy, 2012; 'Reflections from Nature', Songeun artspace, Seoul, 2012; 'Stray Currents', Towner, Eastbourne, 2011; 'Voici un dessin suisse, 1990–2010', Aargauer Kunsthaus, Aarau, 2011; 'Drawn In', Travelling Gallery (touring bus), Scotland, 2011; 'Squall Lines', Palais de Tokyo, les modules, Paris, 2010; 'Nowhere is here', Fruehsorge Contemporary Drawings, Berlin, 2008. Represented by Galerie Lullin+Ferrari, Zürich; and galerie schleicher+lange, Paris/Berlin.

p. 51 **Ryan Gander**
Born 1976, Chester; lives and works in London and Suffolk. Recent solo exhibitions include 'The Fallout of Living', Lisson Gallery, London, 2012; 'Lost in my own recursive narrative', Fondazione Morra Greco, Napoli, 2012; 'An exercise in cultural semaphore', gb agency, Paris, 2012; 'Locked Room Scenario', Artangel commission, London, 2011; 'Really Shiny Things That Don't Mean Anything', Trybuna Honorowa, Plac Defilad, Muzeum Sztuki Nowoczesnej w Warszawie commission, Warsaw, 2011; 'The Happy Prince', Public Art Fund commission, Doris C. Freedman Plaza, Central Park, New York, 2010. Selected group shows include: Documenta 13, Kassel, 2012; 'illumiNATIONS', 54th Venice Biennale, 2011; 'Our Magic Hour', Yokohama Triennale, 2011; 'Intervals: Ryan Gander', Solomon R. Guggenheim Museum, New York, 2011. Represented by Lisson Gallery, London.

p. 52 **Jaime Gili**
Born 1972, Caracas; lives and works in London. Recent exhibitions include 'Newspeak: British Art Now', Part II, Saatchi Gallery, London, 2011; 'The Lakes', Riflemaker, London, 2011; 'Jaime Gili: Afuera', Periférico Caracas/Arte Contemporáneo, Caracas, 2010–11; 'Bill at Pittier', Kunsthalle Winterthur, 2010. Represented by Riflemaker, London.

p. 53 **Alison Gill**
Born 1966, London; lives and works in London. Recent exhibitions include 'Legend Trip', Charlie Dutton Gallery, London, 2012; 'Strange Attractor Salon', Victor Wynd Fine Arts, London, 2010; 'Off the Clock', Mile End Art Pavilion, London and 92Y Tribeca Art Gallery, New York, 2010; 'Brink', Sabine Wachters Fine Arts, Brussels, 2009; 'Space to Draw' Jerwood Space, London, 2008. Represented by Sabine Wachters Fine Arts, Brussels.

p. 54 **Liam Gillick**
Born in 1964, Aylesbury; lives and works in London and New York. Recent major exhibitions include 'One long walk … Two short piers …', Kunst- und Ausstellungshalle der Bundesrepublik Deutschland, Bonn, 2010; German Pavilion, 53rd Venice Biennale, 2009; 'Liam Gillick: Three Perspectives and a Short Scenario', Witte de With, Rotterdam; Kunsthalle Zürich; Kunstverein, Munich; and the Museum of Contemporary Art, Chicago, 2008–10. Represented by Casey Kaplan, New York; Maureen Paley, London; Galerie Eva Presenhuber, Zürich.

p. 55 **Lothar Götz**
Born 1963, Günzburg; lives and works in London. Recent solo exhibitions include 'Lothar Götz: The Line of Beauty', Domobaal, London, 2012; 'Crash', Stufen zur Kunst, Künstlerhaus Hanover, 2012; 'Black', Petra Rinck Galerie, Düsseldorf, 2012; and 'Don't Look Now', Städtische Galerie, Wolfsburg, 2012; 'Wait Until Dark', Chapter, Cardiff, 2012; 'Don't Look Now 1990–2011', Kunsthalle Wilhelmshaven, 2011; 'Don't Look Now 1990–2011', Galerie der Stadt Remscheid, 2011; 'Mulholland Drive', rahncontemporary, Zürich, 2011. Represented by Domobaal, London; rahncontemporary, Zürich; and Petra Rinck Galerie, Düsseldorf.

p. 56 **Brian Griffiths**
Born 1968, Stratford-upon-Avon; lives and works in London. Recent exhibitions include 'The Invisible Show (epilogue)', Galeria Luisa Strina, São Paulo, 2012; 'The Invisible Show', Vilma Gold, London, 2012; 'ON: A Re-imaging of the Blackpool Illuminations by Brian Griffiths', Grundy Art Gallery, Blackpool, 2012; 'In the Darkness of Their Pockets', Grimm Gallery, Amsterdam, 2011; 'Life is a Laugh', Gloucester Road Underground station, Art on the Underground commission, 2007. Represented by Galeria Luisa Strina, São Paulo; Vilma Gold, London; and Grimm Gallery, Amsterdam.

p.57   **Henrik Håkansson**
Born 1968, Helsingborg; lives and works in Varberg and Berlin. Recent exhibitions include 'A Forest Divided', Lunds Konsthall, Lund, 2012; 'The Worldly House', Documenta 13, Kassel, 2012; 'Art Parcours', Art Basel, 2012; 'The End', The Modern Institute, Glasgow, 2011; 'A Tree with Roots', Galleria Franco Noero, Turin, 2010; Mima Sound Space, Middlesbrough, 2009; Henrik Håkansson, Museo Tamayo, Mexico City, 2008. Represented by The Modern Institute, Glasgow; and Galleria Franco Noero, Turin.

p.58   **Thomas Helbig**
Born 1967, Rosenheim; lives and works in Berlin. Recent exhibitions include 'Thomas Helbig', Galerie Guido W. Baudach, Berlin, 2012; 'Form and Fear and Muse', Galerie Diana Stigter, Amsterdam, 2012; 'Quiet Days in Salò', Thomas Brambrilla Contemporary, Bergamo, 2011; 'Use Your Relatives', China Art Objects Gallery, Los Angeles, 2010; 'Thomas Helbig', Jiri Svestka Gallery, Prague, 2010; 'Viper in Bosom', Vilma Gold, London, 2009; 'Stern der Musen', Oldenburger Kunstverein, Oldenburg, 2008; 'Rings of Saturn', Tate Modern, 2006. Represented by Galerie Guido W. Baudach, Berlin; Galerie Rüdiger Schöttle, Munich; and China Art Objects Gallery, Los Angeles.

p.59   **Lothar Hempel**
Born 1966, Cologne; lives and works in Germany. Recent exhibitions include 'The Story of the Old New Girls', Art:Concept, Paris, 2012; 'Opium', La Conservera, Ceuti, 2012; 'Tomorrow', Die Bastel, Cologne, 2012; Herzliya Biennial for Contemporary Art, Herzliya, 2011; 'Suedehead', Anton Kern Gallery, New York, 2011; 'Silberblick/Squint', Stuart Shave/Modern Art, London, 2010; 'Lothar Hempel: ZOO', Sadler's Wells, London, 2010. Represented by Anton Kern Gallery, New York; Stuart Shave/Modern Art, London; Galerie Art:Concept, Paris; and c/o Gerhardsen Gerner, Berlin.

p.60   **Knut Henrik Henriksen**
Born 1970, Oslo; lives and works in Berlin. Recent exhibitions include 'Echoes', Bergen Kunsthall, 2012; 'Villa Savoye redrawn with an Opel Astra 2006', Sommer & Kohl, Berlin, 2012; 'Raw Materials', Museum für Konkrete Kunst, Ingolstadt, 2012; 'ABSTRAKT ////

SKULPTUR', Georg Kolbe Museum, Berlin, 2011; 'A curtain of pearls, like points, defining a line and a plane, hung to define a specific volume', Hollybush Gardens, London, 2011; 'The Go-Betweens and a Black Avalanche', Elastic, Malmö, 2011; 'Rectangle and Square', Kunstmuseum Bern, 2011; 'Space Oddity', CCA Andratx, Mallorca, 2011. Represented by Sommer & Kohl, Berlin; Elastic, Malmö; and Hollybush Gardens, London.

p.61   **Susan Hiller**
Born 1940, Tallahassee; lives and works in London. Recent exhibitions include Documenta 13, Kassel, 2012; 'The Residue of Memory', Aspen Art Museum, 2012; 'Wandering Lines II: From Automatic Drawing to Abstraction', Jane England Gallery, London, 2012; 'From Here to Eternity: Susan Hiller', Tate Britain, London, 2011–12; 'The Provisional Texture of Reality', Kunsthalle Nurnberg, 2011–12; Spazio Culturale Antonio Ratti (ex-Chiesa San Francesco), Como, 2011; 'Susan Hiller: An Ongoing Investigation', Timothy Taylor Gallery, London, 2011; 'The Last Silent Movie', Prefix Institute of Contemporary Art, Toronto, 2011; 'Vorführraum', Kunsthalle Bielefeld, 2011; 'Au loin, une île!', Fondation d'Entreprise Ricard, Paris, 2011; 'The Deconstructive Impulse', Contemporary Arts Museum, Houston, 2011; Moscow Biennale, 2011. Represented by Timothy Taylor Gallery, London.

p.62   **Roger Hiorns**
Born 1975, Birmingham; lives and works in London. Recent solo exhibitions include Marc Foxx, Los Angeles, 2012; 'Wide Open School', Hayward Gallery, London, 2012; Corvi-Mora, London, 2012; 'Common Ground', Public Art Fund, City Hall Park, New York, 2012; 'Out of Control', NEST, The Hague, 2012; 'Courtship of the Peoples', Simon Oldfield, London, 2012; Annet Gelink Gallery, Amsterdam, 2011; 'British Art Show 7: In the Days of the Comet', various venues, London, Nottingham, Glasgow, Plymouth, 2011; 'September 11', MoMA PS1, New York, 2011; Art Institute of Chicago, 2010. Represented by Corvi-Mora, London; and Annet Gelink, Amsterdam.

p.63   **Karl Holmqvist**
Born 1964, Västerås; lives and works in Stockholm and Berlin. Recent exhibitions

include 'The Visit', Bergen Kunsthall, 2012;
'Ecstatic Alphabets/Heaps of Language',
Museum of Modern Art, New York, 2012;
'The Hours of this Watch is Numbered',
Gaga ARTE CONTEMPORANEA,
Mexico City, 2012; 'Education is a Right',
Hollybush Gardens, London, 2011;
'illumiNATIONS', 54th Venice Biennale,
2011; 'The Sun Shines for Everyone',
Kunsthalle Zürich, 2011; 'Spectacle
prescription solo', Fruit and Flower Deli,
Stockholm, 2010; Manifesta 8, Murcia,
2010; 'Je ne travaille jamais', Moderna
Museet, Stockholm, 2010. Represented by
AZPC, New York; Gaga Fine Arts, Mexico
City; Hollybush Gardens, London; and
Galerie Neu, Berlin.

p. 64   Des Hughes
Born 1970, Birmingham; lives and works
in Herefordshire. Recent exhibitions include
'Everything's Inevitable', Manchester Art
Gallery, 2012; 'Thems Please', 76 Chatsworth
Rd, London, 2011; 'Sometimes I wish I
could just disappear', David Risley Gallery,
Copenhagen, 2011; 'Modern British Sculpture',
Gimpel Fils, London, 2011; 'Frame', Frieze Art
Fair, London, 2010; Small Collections Room,
Nottingham Contemporary, 2010; 'Never The
Same River: Possible Futures, Probable Pasts',
Camden Arts Centre, London, 2010; 'Big
Minis: Fetishes of Crisis', CAPC centre d'art
contemporain de Bordeaux, 2010; 'Undone:
Making and Unmaking in Contemporary
Sculpture', Henry Moore Institute, Leeds,
2010; 'Des Hughes', Michael Benevento, Los
Angeles, 2008. Represented by Ancient &
Modern, London.

p. 65   The Hut Project
Formed 2005; based in London: Chris Bird,
born 1971, Birmingham; Ian Evans, born 1982,
Glasgow; Alec Steadman, born 1983, Sidcup.
Recent exhibitions include 'Festivela', Gallery
Vela, London, 2012; 'Assembly', Jerwood
Space, London, 2012; 'Young British Art II',
Dienstgebaeude, Zürich, and Limoncello,
London, 2011–12; 'Giles said …', Limoncello,
London, 2010; 'Machine Gun Corridor',
The Corridor, BolteLang, Zürich, Switzerland,
2010; 'It's Not You, It's Me', BolteLang,
Zürich, 2008; 'Old Kunst', Institute of
Contemporary Arts, London as part of
'Nought to Sixty', 2008.

p. 66   James Ireland
Born 1977, Derby; lives and works in
London. Recent exhibitions include 'Always
Greener: Views from the Contemporary
Countryside', PM Gallery, Ealing, 2012;
'Memory of a Hope', Ceri Hand Gallery,
Liverpool, 2011; 'X Artworks In A Straight
Line (Seeking The Perfect Sphere)', CRISP,
London, 2010; 'Peace and Agriculture in
a Pre-Romantic Ideal Landscape, Without
Sublime Terrors', Haunch of Venison, Berlin,
2008; 'Material Presence: Sculpture and
Installation from the Zabludowicz Collection',
176/Zabludowicz Collection, London, 2008;
Art-O-Rama, Marseille, 2008; 'Joke, Satire,
Irony and Serious Meaning', European
Triennial of Small-Size Sculpture, Gallery
of Murska Sobota, Slovenia, 2007; 'The
Difference Between Truth And Honesty',
f a projects, London, 2007; 'You Mistake
My Horror For Love', Economist Building,
London, 2007; Zoo Art Fair, London, 2006;
'Uncanny Nature', Australian Centre for
Contemporary Art, Melbourne, 2006; 'This
Is A Test', Angel Row Gallery, Nottingham,
2005; 'Scape', Contemporary Art Centre,
Vilnius, 2005.

p. 67   Jim Isermann
Born 1955, Wisconsin; lives and works
in California. Recent exhibitions include
'Jim Isermann: Reunion', Mary Boone
Gallery, New York, 2012; Corvi-Mora, London,
2011; 'Jim Isermann', Art Kabinett, Galerie
Praz-Delavallade, Art Basel Miami Beach,
2011; 'Nouvelles boîtes!', Kunstmuseum
Luzern, 2012; 'Contemplating the Void:
Interventions in the Guggenheim Museum',
Solomon R. Guggenheim Museum, New York,
2010; 'The Artist's Museum', MOCA, Los
Angeles, 2010; 'Plug In #52 – Lily van der
Stokker and Guest: Jim Isermann', Van
Abbemuseum, Eindhoven, 2009; Piccadilly
Line Tube Wrap, Art on the Underground,
London, 2007. Represented by Mary Boone
Gallery, New York; Corvi-Mora, London;
Galerie Praz-Delavallade, Paris; and Richard
Telles Fine Art, Los Angeles.

p. 68   Juneau Projects
Formed 2001, based in Birmingham: Philip
Duckworth, born 1976, Iserlohn; Ben Sadler,
born 1977, Birmingham. Recent exhibitions
include 'The Colour Bright', Site Gallery,

Sheffield, 2012; '3 Megabytes of Hot RAM', Ceri Hand Gallery, London, 2011; 'I am the Warrior', Pumphouse Gallery, London, 2011; 'The Library of Babel/In and Out of Place', Zabludowicz Collection, London, 2010; 'Trappenkamp', Tate Britain, London, 2008; 'Experimenta Folklore', Frankfurter Kunstverein, Frankfurt, 2008. Represented by Ceri Hand Gallery, London.

p. 69   **Alan Kane**
Born 1961, Nottingham; lives and works in London. Recent exhibitions include 'The Unwanted', Zu Gast bei BQ, BQ, Berlin, 2012; 'The Trongate Codex', The Modern Institute and New Jerseyy, Basel, for Glasgow International Festival of Visual Art, 2012; 'Orphan Dishes', Whitechapel Gallery, London, 2011; 'The Asbo Mystery Plays and other Public Works. The Gild the Lily Files' (with Simon Periton), Sadie Coles HQ, London, 2011; 'Rude Britannia: British Comic Art', Tate Britain, London, 2010; 'Life Class/Today's News', Artangel/Jerwood Open commission for Channel 4, London, 2009; 'The Stratford Hoard', Stratford, London, 2008. Represented by Ancient & Modern, London.

p. 70   **Ian Kiaer**
Born 1971, London; lives and works in London. Recent exhibitions include 'Melnikov Project', Aspen Art Museum. 2012; 'Au loin, une île!', Fondation d'Entreprise Ricard, Paris, 2012; 'Utopia Gesamtkunstwerk', Galerie Belvedere, Vienna, 2012; 'Il Baciamano', Fondazione Querini Stampalia, Venice, 2011; 'British Art Show 7: In the Days of the Comet', various venues, London, Nottingham, Glasgow, Plymouth, 2011; 'Endnote, Pink', Kunstverein Munich, 2010. Represented by Alison Jacques Gallery, London; and Tanya Bonakdar Gallery, New York.

p. 71   **Scott King**
Born 1969, East Yorkshire; lives and works in London. Recent exhibitions include Herald St, London, 2012; 'SNAP2012', Art at the Aldeburgh Festival, Aldeburgh, 2012; 'Commercial Break', Venice, 2011; 'Backstage Riders', former Tagesspiegel building, Berlin, 2011; 'Scott King and Richard Serra', Contemporary Art Museum, St Louis, 2011; 'Newspeak: British Art Now', Part I, Saatchi Gallery, London, 2010; 'Scott King:

The Trial Continues', Bortolami, New York. Represented by Bortolami, New York and Herald St, London.

p. 72   **Serena Korda**
Born 1979, London; lives and works in London. Recent exhibitions and performances include 'W.A.M.A: The Work as Movement Archive', Field Art Projects, Bristol, 2012; 'Laid to Rest', Wellcome Collection, London, 2011; 'Spaces for the Imagination', Turner Contemporary, Margate, 2011; 'Decosa Tradition: Stockholm Keifer pin', Camden Arts Centre, London, 2010; 'The Namer of Clouds Lived and Died Here', Tate Britain, London, 2010; ' There's a Strange Wind Blowing', Tintype Gallery, London, 2010. Represented by Tintype, London.

p. 73   **Torsten Lauschmann**
Born 1970, Bad Soden; lives and works in Glasgow. Recent exhibitions include 'Startle Reaction', Dundee Contemporary Arts, 2011–12; 'Alice in Wonderland', Tate Liverpool and touring; Bradford 1 Gallery, Bradford, 2011; Margaret Tait Award, Glasgow Film Festival, 2011; Patchwork Cinema, Collective Gallery, Edinburgh, 2010; Edinburgh International Film Festival commission, 2010; 'Votive', CCA, Glasgow, 2009; 'The Darker Ages', Mary Mary, Glasgow, 2009; 'Running Time: Artist Films in Scotland', Dean Gallery, Edinburgh, 2009; 'Tonite', The Modern Institute, Glasgow, 2009. Represented by Mary Mary, Glasgow.

p. 74   **Delaine Le Bas**
Born 1965, Worthing; lives and works in various locations across the UK and Europe. Recent exhibitions include Gwangju Biennale, Gwangju, 2012; 'Gypsy Revolution', Cable Gallery, Helsinki, 2012; 'Reconsidering Roma: Aspects of Roma and Sinit Life in Contemporary Art', Kunstquartier, Kreuzberg, Berlin, 2011; 'Hexenjagd', Galerie Kai Dikhas, Berlin, 2011; 'The World Turned Upside Down In The Cathedral Of Erotic Misery (After Kurt Schwitters)', Latitude Contemporary Art, Latitude Festival, Suffolk, 2011; 'Paradise Lost', the First Roma Pavilion, 52nd Venice Biennale, 2007. Represented by Galerie Kai Dikhas, Berlin; and Galleria Sonia Rosso, Turin.

p. 75   **Liliane Lijn**
Born 1939, New York; lives and works
in London. Recent exhibitions include
'Ecstatic Alphabets/Heaps of Language',
Museum of Modern Art, New York, 2012;
'Caution Matter', Anglia Ruskin Gallery,
Cambridge, 2012; 'Gallery One, New Vision
Centre, Signals and Indica', Tate Britain,
London, 2012; 'Republic of the Moon/Moon
Futures', FACT, Liverpool, 2011–12; 'Light
Years', Sir John Soane's Museum, London,
2011; 'United Enemies', Henry Moore
Institute, Leeds, 2011. Represented by
Riflemaker, London.

p. 76   **Michael Lin**
Born 1964, Tokyo; lives and works in
Shanghai and Brussels. Recent solo
exhibitions include Rock Bund Art Museum,
Shanghai, 2012; Peabody Essex Museum,
Salem, Massachusetts, 2012; Museum of
Contemporary Art, Vigo, 2011; Towada Art
Center, Towada, 2011; Vancouver Art Gallery,
Vancouver, 2010. Represented by Nogueras
Blanchard, Barcelona; and Eslite Gallery,
Taipei.

p. 77   **Tim Machin**
Born 1978, Sheffield; lives and works in
Hebden Bridge. Recent exhibitions include
'Undone', Henry Moore Institute, Leeds,
2010; 'Tim Machin', Aspex, Portsmouth, 2007;
'NAVIGATOR', The Royal Standard, Liverpool,
2008; 'The Golden Record', Collective Gallery,
Edinburgh, 2008. Represented by Bureau
Gallery, Manchester.

p. 78   **Lorna Macintyre**
Born 1977, Glasgow; lives and works
in Glasgow. Recent exhibitions include
'Midnight Scenes and Other Works', Mary
Mary, Glasgow, 2012; 'A Tree of Night',
Galerie Kamm, Berlin, 2011; 'You, Me,
Something Else', GoMA, Glasgow, 2011;
'Granite and Rainbow', Wiels Centre for
Contemporary Art, Brussels, 2010; 'Form and
Freedom', Kunsthaus Baselland, Basel, 2010;
'Neuglerig?', Kunst- und Ausstellungshalle
der Bundesrepublik Deutschland, Bonn,
2010; 'Better Living With', Museum Ludwig,
Cologne, 2010; 'They Do Things Differently
There', Talbot Rice Gallery, Edinburgh, 2010.
Represented by Galerie Kamm, Berlin; and
Mary Mary, Glasgow.

p. 79   **Andrew Mania**
Born 1974, Bristol; lives and works in Bristol.
Recent exhibitions include 'Portraits', Brera
Art and Design, Milan, 2012; 'Nothing in
the World but Youth', Turner Contemporary,
Margate, 2011; 'Just Photography', Martos
Gallery, New York, 2011; 'Grand National',
Vestfossen Kunstlaboratorium, 2010; 'Comma
09', Bloomberg SPACE, London, 2009.
Represented by Vilma Gold, London; Chez
Valentin, Paris; Diana Stigter, Amsterdam;
Jack Hanley, New York; Francesco Pantaleone
Arte Contemporanea, Palermo.

p. 80   **Marta Marcé**
Born 1972, Barcelona; lives and works
in London and Berlin. Recent exhibitions
include 'Flowing (A Series Trajectory)',
Riflemaker, London, 2011; 'IKI', MasArt Gallery,
Barcelona, 2011; 'Punto.Aparte', Al Borde
Gallery, Maracaibo, 2011; 'IKI', Moriarty
Galeria, Madrid, 2010; 'Reframing', CCA
Andratx, Mallorca, 2009; 'Pinballing',
site-specific installation, Royal Hospital
London, 2009; 'I am throwing the ball',
site-specific installation, British Embassy,
Madrid, 2009. Represented by Riflemaker,
London; and Galeria Moriarty, Madrid.

p. 81   **Paul McDevitt**
Born in 1972, Troon; lives and works in
Berlin. Recent exhibitions include 'About
Stupidity' Petach Tikva Museum of Art,
2012; 'Glamourie', Project Space Leeds,
2012; 'Collaborations and Interventions',
CCA Andratx, Mallorca, 2012; Martin Asbaek
Gallery, Copenhagen, 2012; 'Backstage
Riders', Berlin, 2011; 'Laws and Sausage',
National Museum, Berlin, 2011; 'No
Government No Cry', CIAP Aktuele Kunst,
Hassel, 2011; Stephen Friedman Gallery,
London, 2011; Sommer & Kohl, Berlin, 2010;
APT/Peter Bergman, Stockholm, 2010.
Represented by Sommer & Kohl, Berlin;
Martin Asbaek Gallery, Copenhagen; and
Stephen Friedman Gallery, London.

p. 82   **Peter McDonald**
Born 1973, Tokyo; lives and works in
London. Recent exhibitions include 'Visitor',
21st Century Museum of Contemporary
Art, Kanazawa, 2011; Kate MacGarry, London,
2010; 'Imaginary Realities: Constructed
Worlds in Abstract and Figurative Painting',

Max Wigram Gallery, London, 2008.
Represented by Gallery Side 2, Tokyo;
and Kate MacGarry, London.

p. 83   **Eline McGeorge**
Born 1970, Oslo; lives and works in
London. Recent exhibitions include
'A World of Our Own', Hollybush Gardens,
London, 2012; 62nd International Berlin
Film Festival, 42nd International Forum
of New Cinema, 'Critique and Clinic',
Kunstsaele Berlin, 2012; 'Fine Lines;
A Selection from the National Collection
of Contemporary Drawing', Limerick City
Gallery of Art, 2011; 'When is a human being
a woman', Hollybush Gardens, London,
2011; 'RIGHT RIGHT NOW NOW', Arthur
Boskamp-Stiftung, Hohenlockstedt,
2010; '27 Senses', Chisenhale Gallery,
London, 2010. Represented by
Hollybush Gardens, London.

p. 84   **Paul Morrison**
Born 1966, Liverpool; lives and works
in Sheffield. Recent exhibitions include
'Paul Morrison', Millennium Gallery,
Sheffield, 2012; 'Gold', Belvedere, Vienna,
2012; 'Paul Morrison', Alison Jacques
Gallery, London, 2011; 'Paul Morrison',
Fondazione Volume, Rome, 2011;
'Dark Matters', Whitworth Art Gallery,
Manchester, 2011; 'Nothing is forever',
South London Gallery, 2010; 'Paul Morrison',
Las Vegas Art Museum, 2008; 'Repicturing
the Past/Picturing the Present', Museum of
Modern Art, New York, 2007. Represented
by Alison Jacques Gallery, London; Cheim
& Read, New York and Galerie Bob van
Orsouw, Zürich.

p. 85   **Jack Newling**
Born 1983, Nottingham; lives and
works in London. Recent exhibitions
include 'Then again', SPACE, London, 2011;
'With and without painting', Max Wigram
Gallery, London, 2011; 'Friendships of the
peoples', Simon Oldfield, London, 2011,
'Jerwood Contemporary Painters', Jerwood
Space, London, 2010; Bloomberg New
Contemporaries, Cornerhouse, Manchester
and Rochelle School, London, 2009; 'Pop
Will Eat Itself', Piccadilly Circus Underground
station, Art on the Underground commission,
London, 2009.

p. 86   **Paul Noble**
Born 1963, Northumberland; lives and works
in London. Recent exhibitions include Turner
Prize Exhibition, Tate Britain, London, 2012;
'Welcome to Nobson', Gagosian Gallery,
London, 2011; 'Interloqui', Caterina Tognon
Arte Contemporanea, Venice, 2011; 'Future
Tense: Reshaping the Landscape', Neuberger
Museum of Art, New York, 2008. Represented
by Gagosian Gallery, London.

p. 87   **Nils Norman**
Born 1966, Sevenoaks; lives and works in
London. Norman has participated in various
Biennials worldwide and has developed
commissions for SculptureCenter, Long Island
City, New York; Art on the Underground,
London; Tate Modern, London; Loughborough
University; Creative Time, New York; and
the Centre d'Art Contemporain, Geneva. He
is currently developing two small-scale urban
farming parks in The Hague. He is the author
of three publications: *Thurrock 2015*, a comic
commissioned by the General Public Agency,
London, 2004; *An Architecture of Play:
A Survey of London's Adventure Playgrounds*,
Four Corners, London, 2004; and *The
Contemporary Picturesque*, Book Works,
London, 2000.

p. 88   **Harold Offeh**
Born 1977, Accra; lives and works in London.
Recent exhibitions include 'In Your Face',
SHOWstudio, London, 2012; 'Glamourie',
Project Space Leeds, 2012; 'Garden of
Reason' Ham House and Gardens,
Richmond, Surrey, 2012.

p. 89   **Cornelia Parker**
Born 1956, Cheshire; lives and works in
London. Recent exhibitions include 'Positions',
Eigen+Art, Leipzig, 2012; 'Cornelia Parker',
D'Amelio Terras, New York, 2011; 'Doubtful
Sound', Baltic Centre for Contemporary Art,
Gateshead, 2011; 'The Folkestone Mermaid',
Folkestone Triennial, 2011. Represented by
Galería Carles Taché, Barcelona; Galerie Guy
Bärtschi, Geneva; Frith Street Gallery, London;
and D'Amelio Terras, New York.

p. 90   **Janette Parris**
Born 1963, London; lives and works in London.
Recent exhibitions include 'The Life of the
Mind', New Art Gallery, Walsall, 2011; 'Rude

Britannia: British Comic Art', Tate Britain,
London, 2010; 'The Breakout Tour: Janette
Parris', Angel Row Gallery, Nottingham, 2007;
'Janette Parris', Norwich Gallery, Norwich,
2005; 'Perfectly Placed', South London
Gallery, 2004.

p. 91   **Toby Paterson**
Born 1974, Glasgow; lives and works in
Glasgow. Recent exhibitions include 'Yesterday
Was Already Here', Museo Tamayo, Mexico
City, 2012; 'Quotidian Aspect', Le Grand Café,
Saint-Nazaire, 2012; 'Tales of the City', Gallery
of Modern Art, Glasgow, 2011; 'The Sculpture
Show', Scottish National Gallery of Modern
Art, Edinburgh, 2011; 'Consensus and
Collapse', Fruitmarket Gallery, Edinburgh,
2010; 'Les Lendemains d'hier', MACM,
Montreal, 2010. Represented by The Modern
Institute, Glasgow and Lang + Pult, Zürich.

p. 92   **Paul Peden**
Born in Liverpool; lives and works in London.
Recent exhibitions include 'Folk Art, Art',
Sameheads Gallery, Berlin, 2011; 'Working
Against the System', Gallery North,
Newcastle, and Transition Gallery, London,
2011; 'Paul Peden', The Zetter London,
2008; Summer Show, Royal Academy of
Arts, London, 2007; Paul Peden, Keith Talent
Gallery, London, 2007; 'This Drawing …',
Cynthia Broan Gallery, New York, 2005.

p. 93   **Paola Pivi**
Born 1971, Milan; lives and works in
Anchorage (Alaska). Recent exhibitions
include 'Share, But It's Not Fair', Rockbund
Art Museum, Shanghai, 2012; 'How I Roll',
Public Art Fund, Doris C. Freedman Plaza,
Central Park, New York, 2012; 'Gli artisti
italiani della collezione Acacia', Palazzo
Reale, Milan, 2012; 'Nice Ball', Museo del
Novecento, Milan, 2011; '21st Century:
Art in the First Decade', Queensland Art
Gallery, Brisbane, 2010; '21 x 21: 21 artisti
per il 21° secolo', Fondazione Sandretto Re
Rebaudengo, Turin, 2010. Represented by
Galerie Emmanuel Perrotin, Milan and Paris;
Galerie Michael Neff, Frankfurt am Main;
and Galleria Massimo De Carlo, Milan.

p. 94   **Sam Plagerson**
Born 1978, Plymouth; lives and works
London. Recent exhibitions include 'Tryouts',

Downstairs Gallery, Herefordshire, 2012 ;
'Man, Woman', Simon Oldfield, London,
2012; Bloomberg New Contemporaries,
Cornerhouse, Manchester, and Rochelle School,
London, 2009; 'Pop Will Eat Itself', Piccadilly
Circus Underground station, Art on the
Underground commission, London, 2009;
'Moravia', Cell Project Space, London, 2008;
'Crawford Open 2007: The Sleep of Reason',
Crawford Municipal Art Gallery, Cork, 2007.

p. 95   **Olivia Plender**
Born 1977, London; lives and works in Berlin.
Recent exhibitions include 'Olivia Plender',
MK Gallery, Milton Keynes, 2012; Folkestone
Triennial, 2011; Taipei Biennial, Taipei Fine
Arts Museum, Taipei, 2010; 'Adieu, Aadieu
Apa' (Goodbye Goodbye Father), Gasworks,
London, 2009; 'Altermodern', Tate Triennial,
Tate Britain, London, 2009; 'The Greenroom:
Reconsidering the Documentary and
Contemporary Art', Hessel Museum of Art,
Bard College, New York, 2008; 'Not Quite
How I Remember It', Power Plant, Toronto,
2008; 'The Great Transformation', Frankfurter
Kunstverein, Frankfurt, 2008.

p. 96   **Ruth Proctor**
Born 1980, Scunthorpe; lives and works
in London. Recent solo exhibitions include
'Garden of Reason', Ham House, London,
2012; The London Open, Whitechapel
Gallery, London, 2012; 'En Piste!', Centre
d'art Contemporain de Chamarande, 2011;
'If sameness is in the Centre, the Difference
is on the Periphery', Starkwhite, New Zealand,
2011; 'I'll be your Mirror', Siobhan Davies
Dance Studios, London, 2011; 'Greetings',
Norma Mangione Gallery, 2011; 'Quizas,
Quizas, Quizas', Lugar a Dudas, Cali, 2010.
Represented by Hollybush Gardens, London;
and Norma Mangione Gallery, Turin.

p. 97   **Imran Qureshi**
Born 1972, Hyderabad; lives and works in
Lahore. Recent exhibitions include 'All Our
Relations', 18th Biennale of Sydney, 2012;
'Painting Show', Eastside Projects, Birmingham,
2011; Signature Art Prize Finalists Exhibition,
Singapore Art Museum, 2011; 'Old Intersections:
Make It New', 3rd Thessaloniki Biennale of
Contemporary Art, Greece, 2011; 'Plot of a
Biennale', Sharjah Biennale 10, Sharjah, 2011.
Represented by Corvi-Morva, London.

p. 98 **Damien Roach**
Born 1980, Bromley; lives and works
in London. Recent exhibitions include
'INFRA LION', Arnolfini, Bristol, 2012; 'The
Department of Psychedelic Studies', Wysing
Art Centre, Cambridge, 2011; 'Young London',
V22, London, 2011; 'Self-Similar', Galerie de
Expedite, Amsterdam, 2011; 'Permacultures'
residency, SPACE, London, 2011; 'Shiiin, Jet
Stream, White earphones', David Roberts Art
Foundation, London, 2010; 'Conflicting Tales:
Subjectivity (Quadrilogy, Part 1)', Burger
Collection, Berlin, 2009; 'When the sun goes
down', Le Vestibule, Maison Rouge, Paris,
2008; Neuer Aachener Kunstverein, Aachen,
2007; 'Learn to Read', Tate Modern, London,
2007, 'Quanta (Frieze 005)', Kunst Halle,
St Gallen, 2006; 'The Deepness of Puddles',
Gasworks, London, 2006; Centre of Attention/
Swansong, 'Always a Little Further', Arsenale,
51st Venice Biennale, 2005.

p. 99 **Roland Ross**
Born 1983, London; lives and works in
London. Recent exhibitions include 'Pop
Will Eat Itself', Piccadilly Circus Underground
station, Art on the Underground commission,
London, 2009; '100 Years 100 Artist 100
Works of Art', Art on the Underground,
2008; 'Art Triangle', Münster, 2008.

p. 100 **Giles Round**
Born 1976, London; lives and works in
London. Recent exhibitions include 'The Starry
Rubric Set', Wysing Arts Centre, 2012; '2D-
3D-2D-3D', Camberwell Space, London,
2011; 'April is the cruelest month, breeding',
LIDO, St Leonards-on-Sea, 2011; 'Fifteen',
S1 Artspace, Sheffield, 2010; 'Session_12_
Words+Untitled', Four Boxes Gallery,
Krabbesholm Højskole, Skive, 2010; 'Giles
Round and Mandla Reuter', PELES EMPIRE,
London, 2010; 'The Studio of Giles Round',
Serpentine Gallery, London, 2010; 'The Form
of the Book', SWG3, Glasgow, 2010; 'Living
Structures', S1 Artspace, Sheffield, 2009;
'Strange Days and Nights', 'Nought to Sixty',
Institute of Contemporary Art, London, 2008.

p. 101 **Paul Ryan**
Born 1968, Leicester; lives and works in
London. Recent exhibitions include 'Mirror
Mirror', Roma Pavilion, 54th Venice Biennale,
2011; 'Epstein, Jeremy Deller and Paul Ryan',

The Modern Institute, Glasgow, 2011; 'Manual
Setting', Danielle Arnaud, London, 2011;
'Expansive Mood', The Mansion House, City of
London, as part of Open House, 2011; 'What
the Folk Say', Compton Verney, Warwickshire,
2011; 'The Drawing Incident', Ghent, 2009.

p. 102 **Yinka Shonibare MBE**
Born 1962, London; lives and works in
London. Recent solo exhibitions include
'Globe Head Ballerina', 2012, commissioned
by the Royal Opera House as part of the
London 2012 festival; 'Invasion, Escape:
Aliens do it right!', Anna Schwartz Gallery,
Sydney, 2012; 'Rococo Mania', Designmuseum,
København, 2012; 'Addio del Passato', James
Cohan Gallery, New York, 2012; 'Travelling
Light', Whitechapel Gallery, London, 2011;
Alcalá 31 Centros de Arte, Madrid, 2011;
'Nelson's Ship in a Bottle', Fourth Plinth
Commission, Trafalgar Square, London,
2010; 'Performance/Art', Dallas Center for
the Performing Arts, Dallas, 2010; 'British
Subjects: Identity and Self-Fashioning,
1965-2009', Neuberger Museum of Art,
Purchase, New York, 2009; 'Yinka Shonibare
MBE Prospero's Monsters', James Cohan
Gallery, New York, 2008. Represented by
James Cohan Gallery, New York; Stephen
Friedman Gallery, London; Anna Schwartz
Gallery, Sydney; and Blain|Southern, Berlin.

p. 103 **Jamie Shovlin**
Born 1978, Leicester; lives and works
in London. Recent exhibitions include
'Various Arrangements', Haunch of Venison,
London, 2012; 'Bouvard and Pécuchet's
Compendious Quest for Beauty', David
Roberts Art Foundation, London; 'Thy
Will Be Done', Tullie House, Carlisle, 2011;
'As the World Turns', Anna Schwarz Gallery,
Sydney, Australia, 2011; 'A Film By Jesus
Rinzoli', Horton Gallery, New York, 2011;
'Three (and a Half) Films with Many Shared
Characters', Unosunove, Rome, 2011;
'The Mulberry Tree Press', SE8, London,
2010; 'Hiker Meat', MACRO, Rome, 2010.
Represented by Haunch of Venison, London.

p. 104 **Bob and Roberta Smith**
Born 1963, London; lives and works in London.
Recent exhibitions include 'The Art Party of
the UK', Hales Gallery, London, 2012; 'Who
is Community?', commissioned by Art on the

Underground for Stratford Underground
Station, London, 2012; 'You Should be
in Charge', Work Gallery, London, 2012;
'I have forgotten, was there a past?', Leeds
City Art Gallery, Leeds, 2011; Olympic Poster
commission, LOCOG, 2011; 'Rude Britannia:
British Comic Art', Tate Britain, London, 2010.
Represented by Hales Gallery, London.

p. 105   **Georgina Starr**
Born 1968, Leeds; lives and works in London.
Recent exhibitions include 'The Joyful Mysteries
of Junior', Pinksummer Contemporary Art,
Genoa, 2012; 'THEDA' with Sigune von Osten,
Pier Theatre, Bournemouth, 2011; and 'I am
a Record and I am the Medium', Le Confort
Moderne, Poitiers, 2010.

p. 106   **John Stezaker**
Born 1949, Worcester; lives and works in
London. Recent exhibitions include Tel-Aviv
Museum of Art, 2012; Galerie Gisela Captain,
Cologne, 2012; Deutsche Börse Photography
Prize, Photographers' Gallery, London,
2012; 'Flores; Abismo; Parataxis', La Casa
Encendida, Madrid, 2012; 'John Stezaker',
Whitechapel Gallery, London, 2011;
'Transmitter/Receiver: The Persistence of
Collage', Middlesbrough Institute of Modern
Art, Middlesbrough, 2011; 'Anti-Photography',
Focal Point Gallery, Southend-on-Sea, 2011;
Friedrich Petzel Gallery, New York, 2011;
'John Stezaker: Silkscreens', Capitain Petzel,
Berlin, 2010; 'Lost Images', Kunstverein,
Freiburg, 2010; 'HEAD', The Approach,
London, 2010. Represented by The Approach,
London; Gisela Capitain, Cologne; and
Friedrich Petzel Gallery, New York.

p. 107   **Vincent Tavenne**
Born 1961, Montbéliard; lives and works
in Berlin. Recent exhibitions include 'Étroit,
plat, mince', Galerie Hammelehle und Ahrens,
Cologne, 2012; '30 Künstler / 30 Räume',
Kunsthalle Nürnberg, Neues Museum,
Institut für moderne Kunst und Kunstverein
Nürnberg, 2012; 'Hasenstall', Galerie Giti
Nourbakhsch, Berlin, 2012; 'Déplie-toi!',
Städtische Galerie, Bietigheim-Bissingen,
2011; 'POLARISE-TOI', Saarlandmuseum,
Saarbrücken, 2011; 'Lumière noire', Neue
Kunst aus Frankreich, Staatliche Kunsthalle,
Karlsruhe, 2011. Represented by Galerie
Hammelehle und Ahrens, Cologne.

p. 108   **Mark Titchner**
Born 1973, Luton; lives and works in London.
Recent exhibitions include 'Be True To Your
Oblivion', New Art Gallery, Walsall, 2011;
Vilma Gold, London, 2010; 'The Age of
Happiness', Hellenic American Union, Athens,
2009; 'Run, Black River, Run', Baltic Centre for
Contemporary Art, Gateshead, 2008; 'Plateau
Aurora Borealis', Peres Projects, Berlin, 2008.
Represented by Vilma Gold, London; and
Peres Projects, Berlin.

p. 109   **Hayley Tompkins**
Born 1971, Leighton Buzzard; lives and works
in Glasgow. Recent exhibitions include 'Cairn',
Pittenweem, 2012; 'Currents', Studio Voltaire,
London, 2011; 'A Piece of Eight', The Modern
Institute Glasgow, 2011. Recent group
exhibitions include 'The Imminence of Poetics',
Bienal de São Paulo, 2012; 'Studio 58: Women
Artists in Glasgow Since WWII', Mackintosh
Museum, Glasgow School of Art, 2012;
'Painting Show', Eastside Projects, Birmingham,
2011; 'Watercolour', Tate Britain, London,
2011. Represented by The Modern Institute,
Glasgow; and Andrew Kreps Gallery, New York.

p. 110   **Joëlle Tuerlinckx**
Born 1958, Brussels; lives and works in
Brussels. Recent exhibitions include Wiels
Center for Contemporary Art, Brussels,
and Haus der Kunst, Munich, 2012–13;
Monument dedicated to 'Non Integrated
Arts and Cultures', Halles de Schaerbeek,
Brussels, and Ramallah, 2012; 'La Triangulaire
de Cransac, Musée de la Mémoire – Propriété
Universelle®', Cransac, 2011; 'Geologie einer
Arbeit', Galerie Christian Nagel, Berlin, 2011.
Recent group exhibitions include 'Wanderlust',
Art Sonje Center, Seoul; 'SuperBodies', 3rd
Triennial for Contemporary Art, Fashion and
Design, Z33, Hasselt, 2012; 'Super-Organism',
First CAFAM Biennale, CAFA Art Museum,
Art Museum of China Central Academy of
Fine Arts, Beijing, 2011; 'The Fifth Column/
Die Fünfte Saüle', Secession, Vienna, 2011.
Represented by Galerie Nächst St Stephan
Rosemarie Schwarzwälder, Vienna; and Galerie
Christian Nagel, Berlin/Cologne/Antwerp.

p. 111   **Gavin Turk**
Born 1967 in Guildford; lives and works in
London. Recent exhibitions include 'Gavin
& Turk', Ben Brown Fine Arts, London, 2012;

'London Twelve', City Gallery Prague, 2012;
'Britain Creates 2012: Fashion + Art Collusion',
V&A Museum, London, 2012; 'Before the
World Was Round', Galerie Krinzinger, Vienna,
2011; 'Jack Shit!', Aeroplastics, Brussels,
2011; 'En Face', CAC Malaga and Galerie
Almine Rech, Paris, 2010; 'Jazzz', Sean
Kelly Gallery, New York, 2009; 'Distortion',
Gervasuti Foundation at the 53rd Venice
Biennale, 2009; 'Pop Life', Tate Modern,
London, 2009.

p. 112   Charlie Tweed
Born 1974, lives and works in London.
Recent exhibitions include The London Open,
Whitechapel Gallery, London, 2012; 'Grain'
(performance), Whitechapel Gallery, London,
2012; 'Cultivation Field', The Keep, Reading,
2012; 'Emergency 5', Aspex Gallery,
Portsmouth, 2011; 'Mainstram 2.1', Angus
Hughes, London, 2011; 'Notes 1–3', Alma
Enterprises, London, 2011; 'Videoholica 2011',
Varna, 2011; 'The Box: Season 5', Aberystwyth
Arts Centre, 2011; 'Multichannel: Variable
economies', ArtSway, Sway, 2010; 'Notes
1–3', Spike Island, Bristol, 2010; 'Notes
1–3', Animate Projects, London, 2010;
MAB Film Exercise, Arnolfini, Bristol, 2010;
'MODIFICATIONS 2010', Aarhus Centre for
Contemporary Art, Aarhus, Denmark, 2010.

p. 113   Donald Urquhart
Born 1963, Dumfries; lives and works in
London. Recent exhibitions include 'Big
Jessie', Brunswick Hotel, Glasgow, 2012;
'I Sent My Love A Red, Red Rose', Team
Gallery, New York, 2011; 'Bi', Herald St
and Maureen Paley, London, 2010. Recent
group exhibitions include 'Herald St', Taro
Nasu Gallery, Tokyo, Japan, 2010; 'Tristes
Tropiques', The Barber Shop, Lisbon, 2011.
Represented by Herald St, London; and
Maureen Paley, London.

p. 114   Sophie von Hellermann
Born 1975, Munich; lives and works
in London. Recent exhibitions include
'Watercolour', Tate Britain, London,
2011; Le Printemps de Septembre, Toulouse,
2011; 'Crying For The Sunset', Vilma Gold,
London, 2011; 'The Lucky Hand', Greene
Naftali, New York, 2011; 'Who Shall Survive?',
Almine Rech, Brussels, 2010; 'Sophie
von Hellermann and Josh Smith', MDD

(Museum Dhondt- Dhaenens), Deurle,
2010; 'Library of Babel'/'In and Out of Place',
176/Zabludowicz Collection, London, 2010;
'TAG: From 3 to 45: New London Painting',
Brown, London, 2010. Represented by
Vilma Gold, London.

p. 115   Emily Wardill
Born 1977, Rugby; lives and works in London.
Recent exhibitions include 'x-room', Statens
Museum fur Kunst, Copenhagen, 2012; 'Full
Firearms', Badischer Kunstverein, Karlsruhe,
2012; 'The Hands of a Clock, Even When
Out of Order …', frac Champagne, 2012;
'illumiNATIONS', 54th Venice Biennale,
2011; Future Generation Art Prize, Palazzo
Papadopoli, Venice, 2011; 'British Art Show 7:
In the Days of the Comet', various venues,
London, Nottingham, Glasgow, Plymouth,
2011; 'Windows broken, break, broke
together', De Appel, Amsterdam, 2010;
'Game Keepers without Game', Standard,
Oslo, 2010; The Showroom, London, 2010.
Represented by Standard (Oslo), Oslo;
Jonathan Viner, London; Altman Siegel,
San Francisco; and Carlier | Gebauer, Berlin.

p. 116   Richard Wentworth
Born 1947, Samoa; lives and works in London.
Recent exhibitions include 'The Sculpture
Show', National Galleries of Scotland,
Edinburgh, 2012; 'Sidelines', Museu Farmacia,
Lisbon, 2011; 'Urban Teratologies', École
Spéciale d'Architecture, Paris, 2011; 'Modern
British Sculpture', Royal Academy of Arts,
London, 2011; 'Richard Wentworth', Galerie
Nelson-Freeman, Paris, 2011; 'Three
Guesses', Whitechapel Gallery, London,
2010; 'Fotografia Europea', Photo Festival,
Reggio Emilia, 2010. Represented by Lisson
Gallery, London.

p. 117   Martin Westwood
Born 1969, Sheffield; lives and works in
London. Recent exhibitions include 'Boneus',
The Approach, London, 2012; 'Supermen
made you but only superfluity will release
you', Galerie Fons Welters, Amsterdam, 2012;
'Bold Tendencies 6', Levels 7–10, Peckham
Multi-Storey Car Park, London, 2012;
'Courtship of the Peoples', Simon Oldfield,
London, 2012; 'Capacitor I and II' (with
Oliver Laric), Peles Empire, London, 2012;
'Transmitter/Receiver:

The Persistence of Collage', Middlesbrough
Institute of Modern Art, 2011; 'Der Menschen
Klee', Kunst im Tunnel, Düsseldorf, 2011;
'These Hands Are Models', Stanley Picker
Gallery, London, 2011. Represented by
The Approach, London.

p. 118   **Pae White**
Born 1963, Pasadena; lives and works in
Los Angeles. Recent exhibitions include
'Print/Out: 20 Years in Print', Museum of
Modern Art, New York, 2012; Museum für
Angewandte Kunst, Vienna, 2012; 'SUMMER
XX', Fabric Workshop and Museum,
Philadelphia, 2012; 'Restless Rainbow', Art
Institute of Chicago, 2011; 'Material Mutters',
Site Santa Fe, 2011; 'Spirit and Space',
Collezione Sandretto Re Rebaudengo, Sala
de Arte Santander, Madrid, 2011; Whitney
Biennial, Whitney Museum of American Art,
New York, 2010; 'Fare Mondi/Making Worlds',
53rd Venice Biennale, 2009. Represented by
greengrassi, London; neugerriemschneider,
Berlin; Kaufmann Repetto, Milan; and 1301PE,
Los Angeles.

p. 119   **Clare Woods**
Born 1972, Southampton; lives and works
in Kington, Herefordshire. Recent exhibitions
include 'The Dark Matter', Southampton
City Art Gallery, 2012; permanent large-scale
mural, Olympic Park, London, 2012; Stuart
Shave/Modern Art, London, 2012; 'The
Unquiet Head', The Hepworth, Wakefield,
2011. Represented by Stuart Shave/Modern
Art, London; and Buchmann Galerie, Berlin.

p. 120   **Richard Woods**
Born 1966, Chester; lives and works
in London. Recent exhibitions include
'Nieuwbouw', public commission, Antwerp,
2011; 'Seoul Tudor', private commission,
Seoul, 2011; 'Port Sunlight', Lever House,
Park Avenue, New York, 2009; 'Wrongwoods',
V&A Museum, London, 2009; 'Irony &
Gesture', Kukje Gallery, Seoul, 2008.
Represented by Works | Projects, Bristol.

p. 121   **Catherine Yass**
Born 1963, London; lives and works
in London. Recent exhibitions include
'Lighthouse', Galerie LeLong, New York,
2012; 'Lighthouse', Alison Jacques Gallery,
London, 2012; 'Nuit Blanche', Toronto

International Film Festival, Tiff Lightbox,
Toronto, 2012; 'The World in London',
Photographers' Gallery and Victoria
Park, London, 2012; 'Skyscraper: Art
and Architecture Against Gravity', MOCA,
Chicago, 2012; De La Warr Pavilion,
Bexhill-on-Sea, 2011; 'High Wire', York Art
Gallery, Aesthetica Film Festival, 2011; 'Left
Behind', Phillips Collection, Washington, D.C.,
2011; 'Interventions in the Landscape', Galerie
Lelong, New York, 2011; 'Projections: Works
from The Artangel Collection', Manchester
International Festival, Whitworth Gallery,
Manchester, 2011. Represented by Alison
Jacques Gallery, London.

ACKNOWLEDGMENTS

We would like to thank all the artists who participated in the Roundel project, and also their representatives and galleries, whose support in connection with the project as a whole and this book has been invaluable.

We would also like to thank the contributors, Jonathan Glancey, Claire Dobbin and Sally Shaw, for their texts, and the designers, Fraser Muggeridge studio. We are also very grateful for the support of our colleagues at the London Transport Museum on many aspects of this publication.

The book has grown out of a project initiated in 2008 to coincide with the centenary of the Roundel's creation. We would like to take this opportunity to acknowledge the contribution and support of the many people who have been involved along the way and without whom we would not have achieved such a wonderful result:

Thierry Bal, Charlotte Bonham Carter, Louise Coysh, Sarah Diggins, Alex Drew, Nathan Edmunds, Steve Gumbrell, Claire Hayton, Stuart Humpage, Daisy Hutchinson, Eugenia Ivanissevich, Benedict Johnson, Phoebe Kallin, Emily King, Rebecca King Lassman, Timo Kube, Josephine Martin, Rob Menzer, Jessica Molloy, Tim O'Toole, Bob Pain, Richard Parry, Sylvia Prince, Sarah Purchase, Gian Luca Tonello, Nick Triviais, Niamh Tyman and Carolyn Ware.

MAYOR OF LONDON

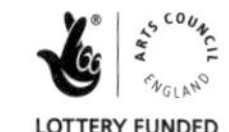

Transport for London 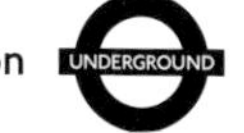

First published in the United Kingdom
in 2012 by Art Books Publishing Ltd

Art Books Publishing Ltd
77 Oriel Road
London E9 5SG
Tel: +44 (0)20 8533 5835
info@artbookspublishing.co.uk
www.artbookspublishing.co.uk

British Library Cataloguing-in-Publication Data
A catalogue record for this book is available
from the British Library

ISBN 978-1-908970-01-5

Project editor Rebecca Bell,
assisted by Snejana Krasteva
Designed by Fraser Muggeridge studio
Printed and bound in Italy by EBS

Distributed outside North America by
Thames & Hudson
181a High Holborn
London WC1V 7QX
United Kingdom
Tel: +44 (0)20 7845 5000
Fax: +44 (0)20 7845 5055
sales@thameshudson.co.uk

Available in North America
through ARTBOOK | D.A.P.
155 Sixth Avenue, 2nd Floor,
New York, N.Y. 10013
www.artbook.com